Leadership in the Open

A New Paradigm in Emergency Management

Leadership in the Open

A New Paradigm in Emergency Management

Adam S. Crowe

CRC Press
Taylor & Francis Group
Boca Raton   London   New York

CRC Press is an imprint of the
Taylor & Francis Group, an **informa** business

CRC Press
Taylor & Francis Group
6000 Broken Sound Parkway NW, Suite 300
Boca Raton, FL 33487-2742

Printed on acid-free paper
Version Date: 20130410

International Standard Book Number-13: 978-1-4665-5823-6 (Hardback)

Library of Congress Cataloging-in-Publication Data

Crowe, Adam S.
  Leadership in the open : a new paradigm in emergency management / Adam S. Crowe.
  pages cm
  Includes bibliographical references and index.
  ISBN 978-1-4665-5823-6 (hardcover : alk. paper)
  1. Emergency management. 2. Leadership. 3. Social media. I. Title.

HV551.2.C763 2013
363.34'80684--dc23   2013013390

Visit the Taylor & Francis Web site at
http://www.taylorandfrancis.com

and the CRC Press Web site at
http://www.crcpress.com

CONTENTS

SECTION I   Changing Expectations

SECTION II   The Effects of Leading through Engaged Social Media: Efficiency, Collaboration, and Magnification

SECTION III Attitude and Engagement

PREFACE

Social media and related emerging technologies are here to stay. With hundreds of millions of followers and users, systems such as Facebook and Twitter are becoming not just commonplace, but intimately and intrinsically connected to all facets of life. This book is not about those systems, per se. It is written to apply the basic principles and purposes available collectively and through the aggregation of information via these social media systems.

Individuals spend an inordinate amount of time utilizing mobile (and fixed) devices to communicate, access maps, write messages (formal and informal), entertain themselves, and, most important, connect with each other and the world. If these uses occur before a disaster, they will most certainly occur after a disaster. The challenge for the emergency management community is that these characteristics of daily use generate expectations of when, where, and how information is exchanged before, during, and after disasters. Although some emergency management organizations have begun to utilize social media, there are few individuals or organizations who have adapted new leadership strategies that fully embrace these changing public prospects such that their communities become more resilient and prepared for the various hazards that they face.

Consequently, this book is intended to be a leadership guide for emergency managers, first-responders, business continuity professionals, and others who want to improve their communities. It is divided into three sections that focus on the fundamentals of social media, the potential effects of its strategic use in disaster management, and the attitude of engagement that is effective for community commitment. Over the 10 chapters, topics such as efficiency, magnification, humility, creativity, ethics, and many more are discussed regarding the tension of changing public expectations and long-standing best practices within the emergency management community.

To accomplish this goal, real-life examples are shared throughout the text that not only reinforce emergency management examples, but also "open the box" to look at examples in the nondisaster world of how the concept is being approached. Likewise, an emergency management leader is profiled at the end of each chapter in the "Leaders in the Open" section.

The leaders, in their own words, describe the focus of the chapter and consider how it is unfolding in their communities. These opinions are their own and do not reflect their employers or affiliates.

These chapters help establish the framework and foundation of how emergency management leadership will change in the future. As a relatively young professional field, emergency management has routinely undergone evolution and change from civil defense to emergency preparedness to an all-hazards approach. It is time to change again. A new paradigm has arrived. Emergency managers must reconsider and re-evaluate best practices and standardized approaches. This will be a difficult process, but this book is intended to be the first step in that direction.

ACKNOWLEDGMENTS

This book would not have been possible without the hundreds of emergency managers and first-responders who have leveraged social media to improve their organizations and communities. By taking the risk, those individuals began to blaze the trail of leadership shown throughout this book. Although social media and emerging technologies continue to be a changing and dynamic field, I am confident that the emergency management community will learn to be flexible and dynamic enough to prepare our communities for response and recovery in the age of social media.

I especially thank those emergency managers who contributed material to this book. They include Alicia Johnson, Patrice Cloutier, Todd Jasper, Jeff Phillips, Sara Estes Cohen, Sarah Waterman, Scott Reuter, Hal Grieb, Ethan Riley, and Bill Boyd. They represent true visionaries in the field of modern emergency management. Their contributions help provide reality and insight to the various components presented within this book.

Lastly, I thank Jennie and Liam for always being there to support and encourage whatever dream I have and to never let me doubt what can get done.

Note: Please forgive material that may seem out of date related to the social media systems. The information contained within this book is as accurate and timely as allowed by the writing, editorial, and publication processes.

1

The Rise of Social Media and Open Government

If public interaction with the government appears antiquated and unintuitive, citizens will not want to engage with the government.

Alan Rosenblatt
Associate Director for Online Advocacy at
The Center For American Progress[1]

LOW TRUST IN GOVERNMENT

Governmental operations of all types are at a crossroads. Social media systems including Facebook, Twitter, and YouTube are facilitating not only the next great communications revolution, but also putting the final nails in the coffin of a cultural rebellion around how government should interact and lead its constituency. Meanwhile, most governmental organizations, including the overwhelming majority of emergency managers across all disciplines, continue to operate their organizations in a tight hierarchical structure that is designed to facilitate actions and decisions for local citizens and the broader constituencies without input or feedback in the process. This schism is expanding at an exponential rate as public expectations change related to when, where, and how government should operate.

Unfortunately, this model is significantly flawed. For instance, in 2010, the Pew Foundation released a study which surmised that Americans' trust in government was at an all-time low. Only 22% of surveyed Americans indicated they could trust government most of the time.[2] This downward trend of trust in government started its slide in early 2002 after the post-9/11 national fervor began to wane. Since that time the public's trust has dropped a drastic 46%.[3] These levels of distrust also mark the lowest levels recorded in national polls since 1973, which was in the middle of the Watergate scandal.

Political corruption, in-fighting, cultural schism, partisan differences, and various other personal and governmental scandals are only some of the components of this dissatisfaction. The general public is changing in a variety of ways. For instance, age and racial diversity are growing throughout the United States of America (see Figure 1.1). Income levels have decreased on average, with a greater number of people reaching poverty or near-poverty levels.[4] In addition, the ages of those in the general population between 45 and 64 and aged 65 and above increased by 32% and 15%, respectively, between the 2000 and 2010 U.S. Census.[5] Additionally, generation Y represents the fastest growing demographic. These changes alter public perceptions and intergenerational and intercultural needs and support mechanisms.

Figure 1.1 Age and racial diversity are affecting public expectations related to government. (From FEMA/Andrea Booher. With permission.)

DEMOGRAPHIC AND TECHNOLOGICAL CHANGES

With the changes in demographics have come changes in the application and uses of technology (see Figure 1.2). Specifically, the general public has adopted social technologies at an astronomical rate. For instance, according to a 2011 Pew Internet study, 65% of all adult Internet users utilized social network sites such as Facebook or LinkedIn. Additionally, this daily usage also grew in all demographics, with a particular focus on the boomer-aged segment of Internet users ages 50 to 64.[6] With the current generation of teenaged individuals, entire generational cohorts will openly and without question utilize social media and text messaging as a primary mechanisms for communication.

Likewise, mobile devices such as tablet computers (e.g., iPads) and smartphones (e.g., iPhones or Android devices) are also on the rise (see Figure 1.3). According to a 2012 Pew Internet study, 46% of all Americans own these types of devices, which is a 10% increase from the year before and more than the 41% of Americans who own traditional cellular devices. This prevalence occurred in every major demographic group including men, women, younger adults, middle-aged adults, urban and rural residents, and all ranges of the economic scale. Adoption of smartphone devices is as high as 60% for college graduates, 18- to 35-year-olds, and those with an income of more than $75,000.[7]

Figure 1.2 Disaster survivors often use mobile devices such as this one to send and receive information. (From FEMA/Liz Roll. With permission.)

Figure 1.3 iPads and other tablet technologies have become powerful tools for information gathering and educational purposes. (From Adam Crowe. With permission.)

Table 1.1 Types of Social Media Systems and Popular Applications

Social Media System	Most Popular Application
Social Networking	Facebook and LinkedIn
Microblogging	Twitter
Blogging	Blogger and WordPress
Video Sharing	YouTube and Vimeo
Photo Sharing	Pinterest, Flickr, and Photobucket
Location-Based Social Networking	FourSquare

Simultaneously, social media systems of all kinds have grown exponentially (See Table 1.1). Facebook, as the leading social network, has more than 955 million users (as of June 2012).[8] Of those users approximately 80% reside outside the United States and Canada. In addition, more than 50% of those users engage in Facebook on a daily basis via traditional websites or mobile technologies.[8] To put this into perspective, one study compared the number of Facebook users to various commonly accepted and understood sizes. For instance, this particular survey noted that the total number of Facebook users was larger than the populations of Japan, Russia, Canada, Indonesia, and the United States of America combined.

Also, Facebook's enormous number of active users is larger than the populations of the United States and Japan combined.[9]

WHAT IS . . . A TWEET?

A tweet is a short message distributed through the Twitter micro-blogging system that is no more than 140 characters. It contains words and characters in traditional formatting as well as stylized, shorthand, and abbreviated styles.

In addition to Facebook, the microblogging service known as Twitter is also a significant social media player. As of 2012, Twitter self-reported more than 140 million active users who generate 340 million tweets a day (or more than one billion every three days). This figure represented a 40% increase from the previous six months. Additionally, the main website for Twitter saw 400 million visitors per month on average with an additional 55 million web hits through their mobile site. This mobile utilization figure is of particular importance considering the growing number of individuals who are beginning to leverage mobile phones and tablet devices for communication and information gathering.

OPENING THE BOX: DIGITAL ADOPTION IN SCHOOLS

Adoption of mobile technologies, social media, and other emerging technologies is not limited to traditional government and emergency management representatives. School districts throughout the United States are beginning to consider how to adapt these technologies to improve the educational experience of their students. These school considerations are based on numerous studies showing an overwhelming growth in the use and comfort of social and mobile technologies in children between the ages of 8 and 18. For instance, nearly 33% of children between the ages of 8 and 10 own their own cell phone and the 13- to 17-year-old age bracket is the fastest growing segment of the smartphone market.[17] Moreover, one study reported that children between the ages of 8 and 18 who owned a smartphone used it daily for 33 minutes of talk and 49 minutes of media consumption.[17] Even 62% of students reported that they were more comfortable with smartphones than laptops for learning opportunities.

The Virginia Department of Education is opening the box and changing how it leads its students and faculty toward improved educational opportunities by using the expectations of its students in conjunction with cost-effective and educationally based technology implementation. Specifically, starting in September 2010, 300 students in four Virginia school divisions were issued Apple iPads in exchange for their history textbooks. These iPads were installed with interactive content, media, and applications aligned with the Commonwealth's standards of learning for history and social sciences.[18] Fifteen classrooms in Arlington, Henry, and Pulaski Counties and Newport News participated in the Virginia Department of Education's "Beyond Textbooks" initiative, which was designed to "explore the potential of wireless technology and digital textbooks to enhance teaching and learning."[18,19] The initiative was funded by a contribution of $150,000 from the Governor's Productivity Investment Fund.[19] The Commonwealth of Virginia partnered with Adobe, Apple, Five Ponds Press, Inkling, MashON, McGraw-Hill, Pearson, and Victory Productions to blend or transition current textbook options to digital formats available on the iPad devices.

In the end, it was strongly evident that students liked the iPad's ability to support individualized learning and that they were comfortable reading from and utilizing the technology available to them. The students and the teachers both felt the iPads increased the students' engagement in the classroom and thus increased their likelihood to comprehend and retain the learned material. Moreover, teachers cited student independence and student collaboration as the two most important advantages to the use of the iPads.[19]

Along with the learning advantages, the conversion to iPads in the classroom made financial sense. According to Commonwealth reporting, Virginia spends more than $70 million per year on textbooks in its classrooms.[18] By converting to digital textbooks available on the iPads, the costs of each textbook dropped by approximately 25% depending on the publisher and particular book.[20] This reduction equated to approximately $20 per book utilized. Many schools also utilized bulk management sync systems that allowed a multitude of devices to be uploaded, managed, or charged simultaneously.

The "Beyond Textbooks" program clearly was only the beginning of academic adoption of emerging technologies. There was significant evidence that embracing the students' comfort levels in technology ultimately improved their learning experience, the enjoyment of the instructor, and the financial bottom line of the school districts in a real and positive way.

SOCIAL MEDIA USE DURING DISASTERS

In addition to the anecdotal evidence about the increasing usage of mobile devices and the corresponding use of social media technologies, it has also become evident that social media are being utilized by citizens during disasters of all sizes throughout the world. Nearly every minor and major emergency as well as large-scale disasters (including some catastrophic events such as the March 2011 earthquake off Honshu island, Japan) are overwhelmingly affected by social technology systems including Facebook, Twitter, and YouTube (see Figure 1.4). Citizens are utilizing these technologies to both send and receive information during

Figure 1.4 During catastrophic events such as the March 2011 earthquake off Honshu island, Japan, citizens are overwhelmingly utilizing social media systems. (From U.S. Coast Guard/Unknown. With permission.)

the emergent events. For instance, during the April 2011 tornado outbreak across the state of Alabama and other parts of the southeastern United States, local citizens utilized Twitter hashtags such as #alneed and #alhave to represent disaster resources that were needed or available, respectively, from local residents, not formalized governmental or nongovernmental operations.

WHAT IS . . . A HASHTAG?

A hashtag is a classification and categorization method utilized in Twitter. Users self-generate any combination of words, letters, numbers, or symbols to represent a certain person, event, location, or opinion that is added to Twitter messages to allow other users to engage in conversations or follow messaging about a particular topic. A pound sign (#) is placed in front of the combination of words. Twitter is then capable of systematically searching for these terms. For instance, Twitter users interested in conversing about the use of social media and emergency management often utilized #SMEM.

The first evidence of this connection between social media and disasters was apparent during the London subway bombings in 2005. Initial government reports indicated large explosions due to utility disruptions. However, local citizens leveraged photographs and self-reporting blogs to show evidence that the explosions were actually not caused by utility disruptions, but rather from multiple bombings in the London subway system and on a bus traveling near one of the stations.[10] Likewise, during the April 2007 shooting on the Virginia Tech campus where 32 students and faculty were killed, social networks such as Facebook collectively confirmed the identities of all the victims hours before any formal notification from university leadership. Although some of the revelation was due to legal and ethical delays[11] (e.g., family notification), it revealed for the first time that social media would force a response pace far beyond traditional mechanisms for disaster management.

Not long after the Virginia Tech shooting, there was a terrorist attack on the financial district of Mumbai, India, in 2008. More than 100 people were killed and another 250 were injured during a concerted attack by a terrorist group who utilized dozens of machine guns and grenade assaults on several resort hotels, a local train station, a Jewish community center, a movie theater, hospital, and several other significant landmarks in the area.[12] The Mumbai event was a significant example of terrorism in the twenty-first century, however, it also marked another benchmark for social media's involvement in disasters. Specifically, the news about the event was first released (or noted) on Twitter and Flickr. As news agencies noted the breaking information in advance of their traditional wire services, many began to embrace and utilize these social media eyewitnesses to move their news coverage forward. It is interesting that one international news agency reported that there were approximately 70 eyewitness reports every five minutes.[13]

For comparison, 2011 marked a significant year for noteworthy emergencies, major disasters, and homeland security events that were widely discussed and shared via Twitter. Specifically, on March 11th of that year, a 9.0 magnitude earthquake struck Japan and a corresponding tsunami caused significant damage to coastal communities. Additionally, this impact led to a meltdown of one of Japan's nuclear plants, creating an event of significant international magnitude and generating 5,530 tweets per second at its peak. Just two months later on May 2nd, U.S. President Barack Obama announced a special forces strike in Pakistan that led to the death of international terrorist Osama Bin Laden. During President Obama's announcement of this event, Twitter had 5,106 tweets per second. Similarly, in August 2011 when the East Coast of the United States was struck by an earthquake near the Washington, DC area, Twitter spiked to a maximum of 5,449 tweets per second.[14] Although these are impressive, the real evidence of Twitter's cultural impact was seen during the 2012 Super Bowl when Twitter spiked to 12,223 tweets per second.[15]

CITIZEN ENGAGEMENT IN TRADITIONAL GOVERNMENT COMMUNICATIONS

This level of public adoption is revolutionary to public organizations. Governmental agencies—including all emergency management disciplines—have long functioned on the premise that local citizens and respective constituents (e.g., traditional media) needed the review and approval of governmental organizations and their appointed and elected leaders to function fully after a disaster. This is the premise commonly seen in community services offered to citizens through one municipal option with little to no input from citizens. Even the concepts of contemporary community town hall events, which date their origins to the foundation of democracy in the seventeenth century, have relatively limited citizen engagement. Although often presented to the public as an open forum, they are usually still heavily controlled by those in charge. Specifically, who gets to speak, for how long, and on what topic is structured by those in charge, who are typically elected or appointed officials. This type of traditional citizen engagement pales in comparison to the freedoms that social media grant citizens.

Likewise, government leaders have been taught modern communication and public information strategies to include concepts of traditional media management through well-framed and faceted statements about the event that are released at timely intervals using structured formats. These messages are often "funnel" structured to allow the most important details to be presented earlier in the message. In addition, these messages, particularly when emergency or disaster related, are empathic in nature, and most often presented in the form of a quote from an elected official or community leader. Unfortunately, there are two significant challenges to this format. First, social media communicate at a pace significantly faster than this customary model of engaging traditional media. Second, because of the organic and often raw format and wording of social media, many in the general public begin to see these types of funneled and empathic messages as disingenuous and insincere. These failures create a lack of trust and thus loss of effectiveness.

WHAT IS . . . A FUNNELED MESSAGE?

A funneled message is a traditional journalistic approach that directs messages to be written from broad to specific in relationship to the topic at hand. Typically the first sentence of the message is a general statement that covers all the relevant information (i.e., the who, what, when, where, and how related to the event). The last few statements in the message might have very specific references or tie-ins to other stories, events, or messages. This structure typically creates a funnel shape for the message, and thus its name.

MANAGEMENT, ADMINISTRATION, AND LEADERSHIP

With the understanding that the use and acceptance of social media have distorted traditional leadership methods, there must be a common understanding of what leadership is within most governmental structures. Because of the highly hierarchical structure present in nearly all governmental agencies, there is a fine distinction between actions that are managerial, administrative, and leading. One is not necessarily exclusive of the others, however, there is a fine distinction that must be established. For instance, management implies the day-to-day oversight of operational considerations and, in the case of emergency management and preparedness, the planning, operations, and logistical considerations that are to be designed for emergencies and disasters. In contrast, public (or government) administration is often focused on long-range considerations of issues that may be financially, politically, or community sensitive and therefore require a more complex understanding of the inner workings of an organization over a period of time.

In the broadest views of management and administration within a public or government structure, there is often very little room for modern leadership qualities to be developed to address public expectations and cultural issues that are rising in importance among those served. That is not to say that organizations do not have leaders (either elected or hierarchical), however, this term is often misleading. Being at the head of an organization simply is a reflection of a physical location within an organization and ignores the intentions or desires of the general body of the people being served. When the opinion of the body of people being led is considered, there is often a far greater energy and drive to achieve not only goals, but objectives that exceed or significantly outpace what would otherwise have been projected (see Figure 1.5).

Contrary to democratic belief and structure, this type of structure is not accomplished in most general political elections. A constituent is given a great deal of power to elect individuals who will be at the top of the particular organization that is (and should be) protected by law. Unfortunately, as local, state, and federal politics have become increasingly expensive and partisan, citizens often elect someone merely as an exercise of their protected freedom and are no more energized or excited than they were by the previously elected official. In these cases and throughout many public organizations, it is extremely difficult to project real success in how that organization

11

Figure 1.5 Leading organizations is different than true leadership. Individual organizational leaders must understand and embrace community-driven expectations. New York Governor Andrew M. Cuomo. (From FEMA/Hans Pennink. With permission.)

is led. Great ideas not only need great leaders to conceptualize and deliver them, but followers to validate and magnify the concept within a given community.

Vulnerable Leaders

Social media are extremely effective because they empower the citizens or the body of followers to engage or deny leaders. This process is often done organically and without the sway of financial burdens often seen in political campaigning. This concept forces leaders to put themselves and their ideas on a very fine, sharp edge as they are exposed to the social media world and thousands of tweets and millions of followers who may consider any concept. Integrally, this high level of personal risk makes leaders open and vulnerable to changing public perception and virtual criticism. Although some ignore the benefit of personal vulnerability, others embrace this concept wholly.

Craig Fugate (@craigatfema) is a prime example of this type of open leadership style. Fugate was appointed the administrator of the Federal

Emergency Management Agency (FEMA) by President Obama in 2009. As a subordinate agency to the U.S. Department of Homeland Security, he could have let FEMA languish away, simply avoiding difficult issues that arose within the field of emergency management. Fugate did the opposite. From early on in his tenure as administrator of FEMA, he began to discuss the issue of how to address the growing concerns about how to deal with what at the time was referred to as special needs or vulnerable needs populations. Since the aftermath of Hurricane Katrina in 2005, local and state emergency managers had struggled with how to address those individuals in their community with special considerations related to mobility, communications, transportation, and cultural integration, just to name a few.

In the end, Fugate (see Figure 1.6) used his own social media presence and the adaptation of social media within FEMA to begin to leverage open, genuine, and honest discourse about tough issues in planning, preparedness, resources, and attention. Most important, he initiated dialogue about how to address the issues. From the beginning, Fugate engaged the constituency to clarify issues and address them directly. This has ultimately been perceived as successful and is a prime example within emergency management on what

Figure 1.6 Administrator Fugate delivers an address on the impact of social media at the American Red Cross seminar. (From FEMA/Bill Koplitz. With permission.)

successful leadership will look like in the future as public institutes continue to learn to embrace social media in all forms and from all directions.

SOCIAL MEDIA: CONNECTIVITY AND CONVERSATION

To understand Administrator Fugate's success in addressing issues related to functional and access needs of vulnerable populations, it is important to understand social media. Some of the most popular social media systems have already been established earlier in this chapter, but the foundations of social media are greater than the systems that reflect them. Specifically, this consideration must go beyond Facebook, Twitter, Pinterest, and YouTube and focus on the principles and practices that make social media an efficient and effective tool that has grown exponentially in the past several years.

At the most fundamental level, social media are natural connections between people. They leverage technology to facilitate conversations, partnerships, and collaboration among colleagues, coworkers, friends, family, and sometimes strangers. In the past, this level of connectedness would have been geographically limited to shared office spaces, household poker games, church pews, water coolers, or barstools. It was at these types of locations where people exchanged ideas, both constructive and ridiculous, and established relationships. Technology has simply filled the connectivity gap created by dispersed populations who no longer share a common geography but still maintain relationships, such as family, colleagues, or other organic relationships (e.g., ex-college roommates). Although the technology does not permit the same level of personal connectivity that would be present face to face, it is clear that more and more people are comfortable with technology and the connectivity that it affords. In addition, social media systems allow for asynchronous (and sometimes synchronous) communication between two individuals which would provide the same level of connectedness as e-mail and phone, respectively.

At its root, this connectedness facilitates conversations. In parallel with traditional conversations, they can be person to person, organization to organization, or person to organization on any topic that is of interest to the respective parties. This process is no different from any other conversation. However, social media do allow conversations to be engaged in such a fashion that the topic or parties involved can shift at an exponential rate. For instance, a Twitter conversation about local disaster recovery

Figure 1.7 Public perceptions about notorious events such as the Deepwater Horizon oil spill can be significantly shaped by social media systems. (From U.S. Coast Guard/Unknown. With permission.)

might quickly shift to the effectiveness of FEMA at community recovery and then again on to disasters such as Hurricane Katrina or the Deepwater Horizon oil spill that continue to have notoriety (see Figure 1.7). These shifting topics can add and drop participants as their interest and engagement ebbs and flows.

SOCIAL MEDIA: COST EFFECTIVE AND TIMELY

Although the strong connectivity and corresponding conversational structure of social media are fundamental, it is also important to consider the high cost effectiveness of social media. Specifically, all true social media systems maintain full services for free to any user interested in their functionality. This includes individuals or organizations leveraging the capabilities of social media to further their messaging. As financial accountability becomes increasingly important (see Chapter 2) to governmental organizations (especially during economic recessions and depressions), the real and potential benefit of social media systems is nearly immeasurable, as the only expenses associated with social media are indirect costs from personnel management and engagement.

FUNDAMENTAL COMPONENTS OF SOCIAL MEDIA
1. Connectivity
2. Conversations
3. Cost effectiveness
4. Instantaneity
5. Transparency
6. Community
7. Self-control/determination
8. Self-correction
9. Techno-altruism/advocacy

In addition to the connectivity and cost effectiveness of social media, it is also critical to understand the speed and pace that is fundamental to support these concepts. Unlike e-mail or traditional postal services, conversations (and eventually collaboration) via social media systems are nearly instantaneous. When a question is asked, a response is expected immediately just as during a traditional conversation. Social media conversations act and respond in a give and take fashion with similar positive and negative visceral reactions that people have when they are face to face or on a telephone. For instance, if someone engages in a conversation and the other party does not respond for several hours or days, there is a perception that there is minimal desire to be engaged in that conversation. Consequently, the conversation typically ends with a strongly negative perception. This issue of timely participation in social media conversations is particularly important to government agents and emergency managers. First, if they are going to be successful in the social media realm, governmental and nongovernmental volunteer agencies must be engaged in those conversations in the timely and instantaneous fashion they would use as individuals. In some ways, organizations risk significant damage to their social media reputation if they are unwilling or unable to engage at the expected pace of exchange.

Additionally, the challenge of the instantaneous nature of social media conversations is compounded by the fact that these conversations happen simultaneously within a given system such as Facebook or Twitter. The resulting effect is similar to the challenges of a one-on-one conversation in a crowded and noisy room. The intended conversation can sometimes be missed or confused with other conversations and messages.

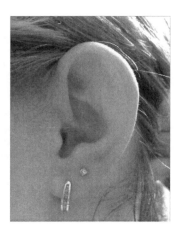

Figure 1.8 Much like the human ear, leveraging the correct social media tools can help emergency management leaders decide between important and irrelevant information. (From Adam Crowe. With permission.)

However, much like the human ear's ability for auditory discrimination, it is possible to decipher this information in constructive and productive ways (see Figure 1.8). Consequently, it is critical to understand this characteristic to ensure that all tools are leveraged to manage the information and stay engaged in an appropriate and timely manner. When organizations understand this fundamental concept of social media before they engage in systems such as Facebook and Twitter, it will help minimize the white noise and distraction often cited as deterrents to implementing social media.

WHAT IS . . . AUDITORY DISCRIMINATION?

Auditory discrimination is the process by which the human ear differentiates between sounds. It is important to language mastery as words must be recognized as independent and unique combinations of sounds. It is also particularly important in crowded rooms as there is a combination of noise or "white noise" that would otherwise be confusing and irrelevant.[21] It is this same discrimination that must occur in social media because of the multitude of conversations that occur simultaneously in a given system.

SOCIAL MEDIA: TRANSPARENCY
AND SELF-CORRECTION

An additional fundamental component of social media is the need for transparency and openness. Because social media systems are available to anyone, it is very difficult to hide information or limit its access to the social media realm. Consequently, there is a central concept in social media to be open and honest with all intentions. This creates a transparent view of a user's or organization's true intentions and helps establish a level of trust within the social media system that would be similar to traditional relationships that are strengthened with honesty and respect. For example, in 2011 New York Representative Anthony Weiner was accused of utilizing Twitter to engage in conversations with various women. This activity included sexually suggestive pictures of a man. Initially, Weiner publically stated that his Twitter account had been hacked and the distributed picture was a "prank". Unfortunately for Weiner, social media users he had engaged with (or who otherwise saw some of his messages) immediately fired back claiming falsehoods. Unfortunately the delay and lack of openness caused additional public and media scrutiny over the next several weeks before Weiner resigned in disgrace (see Figure 1.9).[22]

Figure 1.9 Former U.S. Congressman Anthony Weiner's own struggles strongly indicate the power of social media and the inability to cover up lies, misjudgments, and potentially unethical acts. (From U.S. Congress/Unknown. With permission.)

As Representative Weiner's example shows, social media are also driven by self-control and self-determination. Because messaging is inherently public and conversational, anything shared or distributed is directly attributed to the user or organization attached to the account. As such, the determination to create a certain image or programming is wholly under the control of the user. This control also extends to corrective actions within social media as well. For instance, if a traditional print newspaper makes a mistake in a daily or weekly publication, any correction will not be shared with the readership until the next edition and will most likely be located and phrased based on editorial discretion. If it is a politically charged issue that runs counter to the editorial leaning of the media outlet, the mentioned error may simply be corrected in a small or "buried" way. On the other hand, social media allow the affected user also to have a voice and platform equal to the media outlet. Corrections, defense, and updated versions can be released immediately rather than later via multiple channels.

This individual self-correction also leads to systematic self-correction within social media. For instance, many emergency managers are concerned that misinformation, rumors, and malicious activity will run rampant on social media systems such as Twitter after a disaster. This level of concern is mostly erroneous. When an individual or organization understands the fundamental components of social media established here, the collection of the users within a given system will help correct any intentionally malicious information that is being distributed. The caveat to this systematic self-regulation is that it cannot regulate what is not known. For instance, early on during a disaster or emergency, it is very difficult to have a clear picture of what is accurate and what is merely rumor or conjecture. Consequently, it is difficult for social media systems including Twitter to maintain their fundamental self-correction mechanism during these situations. However, the final fundamental consideration of social media helps address this limitation of self-correction.

SOCIAL MEDIA: ALTRUISM AND ADVOCACY

Social media users are strongly altruistic as a side effect of the inherent community built on the transparency and conversational interactions that occur with regularity via social media. Consequently, this techno-altruism creates a strong desire to help spread information via social media systems that is ultimately helpful to the virtual and physical communities to which the user belongs. For instance, during the tornado outbreaks in April 2011 that affected multiple Southern states and killed more than 300 people, Twitter users in Alabama quickly adopted the hashtags #alhave and #alneed to start organically identifying survivor needs and available resources, respectively.[10] These hashtags were unsolicited by local emergency management representatives. They were simply an outgrowth of this fundamental concept of social media. As this techno-altruism tends to naturally gather and collect timely and accurate information (as that is the most beneficial to the community), it inherently ostracizes inaccurate, incorrect, or even potentially malicious information as discussed earlier. Consequently, this is an easy method for emergency management leaders to utilize the collective knowledge of the group to clarify accuracy at any given time.

This altruistic nature of social media is also closely related to advocacy. As each individual user or organization is empowered to say anything at any given moment, social media platforms quickly become platforms to promote and encourage certain actions or involvement in particular functions. This inherent platform of advocacy is important to both the individual user and the potential governmental organizations trying to engage in social media. From the governmental perspective, it allows for a great opportunity to leverage the social media tools to promote education or awareness regarding certain issues. Organizations such as FEMA, CDC, and DHS leverage these capabilities during emphasis periods such as National Preparedness Month or Hurricane Preparedness Week. On the other hand, this potential for advocacy is also a strong tool for individual users as well when they feel there has been a disservice or an injustice performed against them (often by a governmental agency). This can be particularly difficult for governmental organizations—particularly emergency managers—when they are not already engaged in social media in proper and effective ways.

TRADITIONAL LEADERSHIP MODELS

In contrast to the transparent and open structure inherent in social media, traditional emergency management models of administration and leadership are strongly based on hierarchical structures that are heavily influenced by paramilitary components borrowed from military and first-responder best practices. For example, President George W. Bush issued Homeland Security Presidential Directive 5 (HSPD-5) in 2003 to help establish a national preparedness and response structure that would facilitate a common operating picture for all responding jurisdictions and agencies involved in formalized emergency response. This system was later formalized into the National Incident Management System (NIMS).

As its most basic level, NIMS divides operational considerations into five components: preparedness, communications and information management, resource management, command and management, and ongoing maintenance. The command and management component is then further divided into the incident command system (ICS), multiagency coordination systems (MACS), and public information.[24] Although ostensibly flexible, these command and management components are flexible only within a limited range. For instance, the ICS structure subdivides or expands operations to ensure a supervisor maintains three to seven response entities (e.g., span of control). Likewise, all decisions (including information dissemination) must be reviewed and approved, with ultimate responsibility falling to the incident commander or EOC manager in charge of the overall operation.

WHAT IS . . . NIMS?

According to FEMA, "The National Incident Management System (NIMS) provides a systematic, proactive approach to guide departments and agencies at all levels of government, nongovernmental organizations, and the private sector to work seamlessly to prevent, protect against, respond to, recover from, and mitigate the effects of incidents, regardless of cause, size, location, or complexity, in order to reduce the loss of life and property and harm to the environment."[23]

These structures are based on more than 40 years of best practice within emergency response and help minimize conflicts that have arisen both within a response agency and in coordination with other groups. For example, during the response to the September 11, 2001, terrorist attacks, there were significant communications challenges between response agencies as there was no central body to ensure coordination between them. As such, NIMS helps establish uniform and consistent communications channels and protocols to reduce, if not eliminate, these kinds of issues (see Figure 1.10). The challenge for NIMS (and its corresponding components) is that it is incompatible with many of the fundamentals of social media mentioned above.

Figure 1.10 Command and control are significant foundations of traditional leadership with emergency and disaster management. (From FEMA/Robert Rose. With permission.)

For instance, because social media are conversationally based and expect nearly instantaneous response to online engagement (see Chapter 3), it is difficult to fathom how a command and control structure dependent on review and approval of messages and activities could move at a pace sufficient to not alienate social media users. In addition, formalized public information activity has long been structured around the distribution of media releases and press conferences. Unfortunately, much as with the decision-making process already mentioned, this moves far too slowly to adequately engage social media systems and is structured to serve traditional media only.

Likewise, the flexibility present in ICS is truthfully limited in comparison to the flexibility possible through the open and transparent systems available in social media. As evidence, emergent and effective social media advocacy groups are now routinely spawned during short-term and long-term recovery. For example, the organic online group Toomers for Tuscaloosa grew in response to the 60 tornados of April 2011 that affected the state of Alabama. What started as a small and loosely organized group quickly grew via Facebook and Twitter to more than 80,000 followers because of a growing desire to help and a perceived lack of response to some communities within the state. This group (as well as others like it) were not recognized by state emergency management, FEMA, or traditional voluntary disaster organizations. It did not fit the model and certainly did not operate under unified operations under a NIMS and ICS model, but created positive results throughout Alabama.

This conflict between social media and NIMS is not a new challenge to emergency managers or their response partners. Rather, emergency management leaders throughout the United States have long been trying to find ways to resolve this conflict or consider changes to some of the NIMS structure to facilitate the use of social media. One area where emergency management and homeland security leaders have begun to see convergence in these areas is the use of social media as an intelligence-gathering tool. Social media are routinely monitored during large events (e.g., football games, large conventions, etc.) for security and awareness reasons. The U.S. Federal Bureau of Investigation (FBI) has also begun research into how it can better mine social media systems for large-scale homeland security monitoring and prevention.[25] In 2012, the American Red Cross even announced a partnership with Dell to establish the first digital operations center that was specifically created to leverage social media for greater incident awareness.[26] There is an intelligence component specifically built into the NIMS structure, however, it is unclear where responsibility for social media should be assigned. Likewise, the concept of a digital operations center and how it integrates within traditional command structures such as an incident command post or emergency operations center (EOC) are far outside what is currently accepted as standard within NIMS. Clearly exceptions are being made, but this invalidates some of the structure and configuration of NIMS.

MIND-SET CHALLENGES

In addition to the response-structure challenges mentioned above, the demographic makeup of the emergency management community is also challenging to the integration of social media. For example, one report released by the International Association of Emergency Managers found that the mean age of a local emergency manager was between 46 and 51 years old and overwhelmingly (greater than 75%) male.[27] Although the report identified a notable shift in the type of person interested in emergency management after the September 11th terrorist attacks, the report defined the emergency manager "stereotype" to include a lack of formalized college education, middle to late middle-aged, second or third career, emergency-services oriented, lack of experience with jurisdictional diversity, and very bureaucratic, just to name a few.[27]

Unfortunately, this stereotype of emergency managers often reflects additional challenges that can hinder integration of emerging technologies such as social media. For instance, rather than the conversation-centric style of social media that inherently creates a social community equal to one another without any pre-existing obedience to office, title, or position, the opposite exists in many traditional emergency management offices, which are strongly based on military or paramilitary models of structure and experience where title and position are critical to understanding the values and flexibility (or lack thereof) within an organization. Likewise, long-standing engagement in one community can also lead to emotional attachments to the status quo.[28] This comfort with the current structure is extraordinarily limiting given the willingness of the general public to utilize social media quickly to receive and distribute information. Overall, these traditional emergency mangers are often affected by additional faulty assumptions such as positive illusions (e.g., ignoring challenges), egocentric attitudes, discounting the future, and a lack of personal experience.

INEFFECTIVE ASSUMPTIONS OFTEN NOTED IN TRADITIONAL EMERGENCY MANAGERS[29]
1. Positive illusions
2. Egocentric manner
3. Discounting the future
4. Maintaining the status quo
5. Lack of personal experience

The other significant challenge to traditional emergency management is the appropriate level of emergency preparedness and planning. Finding the right balance is critical to ensure the organization appears genuine in its attempts to prepare the community, but does not push so much that the realistic outcome is exceeded. Seth Godin provides an example for this challenge.[31] Specifically, he speaks about the perspective of an emergency manager's drive to achieve the unachievable. In the emergency manager's case that often centers on the concept of a community becoming completely prepared for emergencies and disasters, that is, to have every plan written perfectly, every responder know his or her role and responsibilities completely, and to have every citizen be engaged and fully prepared. These are asymptotic concepts according to Godin. They can be achieved with increasing efficiency and incremental resources, but will never be fully completed. At some point, emergency managers must decide on an acceptable level of readiness. Without this acceptance, the asymptotic approach is ultimately seen in the public and in social media as not genuine (or unrealistic) and potentially not cost effective. Both assumptions by the social media community would undermine positive relationships via social media systems such as Twitter, Facebook, and YouTube.

WHAT IS . . . AN ASYMPTOTE?

An asymptote is a geometric principle that describes a line that gets closer and closer to another line (or object) without ever actually touching it. From a business or marketing perspective, it relates to the continued financial investment in a product that has diminishing returns on the investment. For instance, if a company produced 10,000 widgets for $100, 100,000 widgets for $10,000 or one million widgets for $500,000, it would be clear that at some point the added value of producing more product loses its financial justification.

THE RISE OF OPEN GOVERNMENT

Although the emergency management community has only recently begun to engage in modifications to address these flourishing social technology expectations of the general public, there has been a growing umbrella movement called open government (OpenGov) or government 2.0 (gov2.0). Although this movement has a variety of nuanced components, fundamentally it is based on the concept of greater transparency of government with the intention of allowing citizen (and constituency) engagement in all processes of government to improve efficiency, accountability, and effectiveness of government operations.

This concept has quickly risen from the fringe of governmental operations to an area of emphasis for many state and federal agencies including the White House. Specifically, the Memorandum on Transparency and Open Government was the first executive order signed by President Barack Obama when he took office in 2009 (Figure 1.11).[32] This executive order led to the establishment of the U.S. National Action Plan in 2011.

Figure 1.11 President Barack Obama issued the Memorandum on Transparency and Open Government in 2009 to begin a focus attempted at the federal level to improve openness within government. (From White House/Unknown. With permission.)

This plan called for an open government initiative that promoted accountability and improved performance through the "harnessed" new technologies and public engagement. The plan specifically states that "Knowledge is widely dispersed in society and public officials benefit from having access to that dispersed knowledge and hence [leads] to collective expertise and wisdom."[32]

This push to increase open government is not limited to the federal government. Several major local jurisdictions including Seattle and San Francisco have open government initiatives including access to government data and programming.[34,35] From the emergency management perspective, the most interesting government 2.0 initiative is in Manor, Texas. The city of Manor created ManorLabs to engage cities in an open and technocentric way regarding local issues affecting the community.[33] Likewise, the city of Manor deployed quick response (QR) codes throughout the community to provide links and updates to citizens regarding projects and significant components of localized infrastructure.[10] The codes were also incorporated into emergency management components within the community to aid in the openness and transparency available to all residents.

This open government movement is often driven by leveraging the social media tools and the emerging technology that has become ubiquitous in its use by the general public. Governmental organizations, including the vast majority of emergency management organizations, have had to create Facebook and Twitter sites to begin engaging in these conversations. This integration is not always effective, as organizations are unwilling to engage in social media fully or base the sites on the fundamental principles discussed earlier in this chapter. Objectives typically revolve around liability concerns, time for personnel management, and record retention to name a few. However, even for other cities such as New York that engage in social media in broad and effective ways, there is still the challenge of the "constant referendum" according to city leadership.[36] For example, New York City struggles to manage the techno-advocacy component that was established earlier as a fundamental component of social media. Citizens and engaged social media users find their issue important and have a voice through the technology that cannot be easily silenced. In fact, it can often compound complex issues for municipalities such as New York that are already dealing with operational components as well as traditional media management issues.

A NEW PARADIGM OF LEADERSHIP

Although challenging, it is clear that governmental organizations and emergency management professionals can no longer simply ignore social media. The overwhelming use of social technologies by citizens and groups of constituents is forcing a change in the paradigm of how emergency management organizations and other governmental bodies approach communication and engagement with their communities. The emergency management industry, and to a lesser degree the homeland security industry, are based on very traditional paradigms of leadership and future change. There is a far greater comfort in looking at the past for inspiration and the basis of leadership choices rather than to engage with constituents and look to public expectations and future technology changes for visionary choices. Although the traditional paradigm still has a potential role in some managerial and emergency response operational decisions, the long-term leadership components of emergency management must embrace a new paradigm to ensure that future emergency management activities are efficiently integrated into local communities.

This chapter and the rest of this book are dedicated to establishing the framework for this new paradigm of leadership. Specifically, this book divides this new leadership model into three major sections by considering the revolutionary change driven by social media and emerging technologies, methodologies of engagement to ensure success, and a review of the styles of approach necessary to engage the online community in effective and efficient ways. The first section expounds on how transparency (Chapter 2) and the instantaneous behavior of social communities (Chapter 3) are revolutionary changes in how emergency management leaders must address the style and structure of their approach. Additionally, there is a strong consideration as to how an entrepreneurial approach will help engage communities in cost-effective and efficient ways (Chapter 4). The second section of the book focuses on how leveraging social media tools in methodical ways can help improve efficiency (Chapter 5), magnification (Chapter 6), and collaboration (Chapter 7) within a given community. These components are particularly important during emergencies and disasters for underresourced and poorly funded emergency preparedness organizations. The last section of this book focuses on how emergency management organizations adopting this new leadership paradigm should maintain high levels of humility (Chapter 8), creativity (Chapter 9), and ethical principles (Chapter 10) to ensure they are highly trusted by the social media component of their community. This section also focuses on the need for specific consideration of public relations and creativity in relationship to emergency management practices. These nine components establish the groundwork of what this new paradigm in emergency management will look like, and more specifically, what leadership in the open looks like to social media systems and communities at large.

LEADERS IN THE OPEN: ALICIA JOHNSON

Alicia D. Johnson is the Resilience and Recovery Manager for the City of San Francisco Department of Emergency Management and previously served the Salt Lake City Urban Area Initiative. She holds both a Bachelor of Arts and Masters of Public Administration from the University of Colorado. Her major interests include building economically strong and culturally competent communities. She discusses how open government is affecting emergency management in the following essay written for this book. She can be found on Twitter @UrbanAreaAlicia.

The Cultural Change of Open Government

Alicia Johnson

Open Government, Gov 2.0, or Participatory Government—call it what you will—the concept is often thrown around as a cure-all for modern government woes. But it isn't, pure and simple. Modern civil society expects an open, responsive, and accountable government as part of the nature of democracy. The acceleration of such traits is at the core of the open government movement. During a disaster, the voice of civil society grows louder. Being open, responsive, and accountable has become an expectation for all levels of government. During a disaster, communities want to know the details of the response and perhaps more important, the recovery, and they will do everything in their power to find out. Meeting this expectation builds reciprocal trust far more than traditional public relations practices. Implementing open government strategies can begin to increase community support and interest in emergency preparedness, which directly leads to a more connected and resilient community.

The traditional government relationship is often viewed as consumer driven; taxpayers consume government-delivered services. The open government concept is different. It rekindles the bi-directional relationship between citizen and government. Open government equates with public participation and open information exchange between organization and citizen. Open government is not a one-way street full of government types pushing information out to consumers. It is, instead, a relationship designed to exchange information with citizens. It's often accomplished, in part, through the use of open data principles (allowing access to data that would otherwise be available from more restricted means; i.e., a Freedom of Information Act request). By further opening information, government begins a trusted dialogue with the communities we serve. Building trust is the ultimate goal of the open government movement.

The fields of disaster response and emergency management have spent a great deal of time, effort and dollars teaching people the importance of preparedness and resilience. Campaigns such as Ready. Gov's Are You Ready and the now nationwide ShakeOut initiative, designed to teach people to Drop, Cover, and Hold On during an earthquake, use public information, public relations, and advertising to reach out and teach residents. On the whole, these opportunities are successful, but often produce a degree of indifference among residents. Every public servant has encountered the pointed statement, "I don't trust the government, all they do is . . ." The crux of this indifference isn't the preparedness message itself; it's the fundamental distrust of the entity as a whole. Aiming to become more open, responsive, and accountable, adhering to the very nature of democracy is a strong opportunity to restore a measure of interest.

Stay or go? That choice, disaster science tells us, is often made because a relationship of trust encouraged the decision. Whether asked to shelter in place or evacuate, most residents call a neighbor or family member, or reference a trusted source of information, such as a news station or social media channel before following through. Government entities want to become a trusted source, but we can't utilizing the means we've engaged thus far. The command to obey no longer works, and frankly, has not worked for many years.

So what does it take to become a trusted entity? By sharing what we know ahead of time and preparing our public to respond in the best way possible, we gradually build trust. For decades, the relationship between citizen and government has been evolving. Disaster management must accept and embrace that relationship. In this modern era of hazards, government will not be able to save the day. Our acknowledgement of risks, the encouragement of citizen responsibility, and being honest about response capabilities is vital to implementing open government in emergency management. Explicit discussions of the hazards that affect the area and what the likely and worst-case impacts could be will go a long way to cultivate trust. It's vital that we accept this reality and begin building an informed and responsible community prepared to respond with resilience. In an emergency, trust is the responder's ultimate collateral.

The implementation of open government, be it the cultural change within an organization to more effectively educate the public about risks or the technical mechanisms necessary to open data to citizens, is not simple. Despite the complexity, or perhaps because of it, the impact of the work can be significant. As expectations for participation in government increase the pressure for emergency management entities to become even more open, responsive, and accountable will only grow, being unable to meet those expectations during a disaster could, in fact, be devastating for a community. As hazards increase and become more complex, the notion of an individual or community being saved by an outside force is no longer applicable. Government, at all branches, must be realistic about the hazards and the behaviors necessary to bounce back from a disaster. An open conversation regarding hazards, impacts, and expectations must be had, as traditional mechanisms are no longer enough to solidify resilient community behaviors. Certainly, open government will not solve the ills of civic society or build a disaster-free community, but it will increase the conversation, participation, and responsibility of both citizen and government. That interaction will build a stronger, more resilient community.

ENDNOTES

1. Walker, Mary Bernhart. (2011) "Alan Rosenblatt: Citizen expectations require a cultural shift on the part of government." Fierce Government Blog. http://www.fiercegovernment.com/story/rosenblatt-citizen-expectations-require-cultural-shift-part-government/2011-05-13. Accessed on February 2, 2012.
2. Halloran, Liz. (2010) "Pew Poll: Trust in Government at Near-Historic Low." NPR. http://www.npr.org/templates/story/story.php?storyId=126047343. Accessed February 2, 2012.
3. Jones, Jeffrey M. (2008) "Trust Remains Low in Government." Gallup Polls. http://www.gallup.com/poll/110458/trust-government-remains-low.aspx. Accessed March 19, 2012.
4. "Income, Poverty, and Health Insurance Coverage in the United States: 2010." (2011) U.S. Census Bureau. News Release – September 13, 2011. http://www.census.gov/newsroom/releases/archives/income_wealth/cb11-157.html. Accessed March 19, 2012.
5. "Age and Sex Composition: 2010." (2011) U.S. Census Bureau. http://www.census.gov/prod/cen2010/briefs/c2010br-03.pdf. Accessed March 19, 2012.
6. Madden, Mary and Zickuhr, Kathryn. (2011) "65% of Online Adults Use Social Networking Sites." Pew Internet. http://pewinternet.org/Reports/2011/Social-Networking-Sites.aspx. Accessed March 19, 2012.
7. Smith, Aaron. (2012) "Nearly Half of Americans Are Smartphone Users." Pew Internet. http://www.pewinternet.org/Reports/2012/Smartphone-Update-2012.aspx. Accessed March 23, 2012.
8. "Facebook Fact Sheet." Facebook Newsroom. http://newsroom.fb.com/content/default.aspx?NewsAreaId=22. Accessed March 23, 2012.
9. "Facebook's Gignormous Size Put into Context (Chart)." (2011) Pingdom. http://royal.pingdom.com/2011/04/07/facebook-user-base-in-context/. Accessed March 24, 2012.

10. Crowe, Adam. (2012) *Disasters 2.0: The Application of Social Media on Modern Emergency Management*. Boca Raton, FL: CRC Press.
11. Lipka, Sarah. (2010) Education department rules that Virginia Tech violated the law in response to 2007 shootings. *The Chronicle of Higher Education*. http://chronicle.com/article/Education-Dept-Rules-That/125676/ Accessed March 25, 2012.
12. Sengupta, Somini. (2008) At least 100 dead in Indian terror attack. *New York Times*. http://www.nytimes.com/2008/11/27/world/asia/27mumbai.html?pagewanted=all. Accessed March 25, 2012.
13. Mackay, Deborah. (2011) "Social Media and the New Wave of Journalism." TheNextWeb. http://thenextweb.com/socialmedia/2011/07/27/social-media-and-the-new-wave-of-journalism/. Accessed March 25, 2012.
14. "Year in Review: Tweets Per Second." (2012) Twitter. http://yearinreview.twitter.com/en/tps.html. Accessed March 26, 2012.
15. Beckham, Jeff. (2012) "Giants' Win Draws 12, 233 Tweets Per Second." *Wired*. http://www.wired.com/playbook/2012/02/super-bowl-twitter-record/. Accessed March 26, 2012.
16. "What Is Your Definition of Leadership?" 10 Questions about Leadership. Kansas University Medical Center. http://wichita.kumc.edu/fcm/documents/Ten%20questions%20about%20Leadership.pdf. Accessed March 26, 2012.
17. "Blackboard Mobile for K-12." Blackboard mobile. Washington, DC.
18. Pyle, Charles. (2010) "Students in Four School Divisions Trade Textbooks for iPads." Virginia Department of Education Press Release. September 29, 2010. http://www.doe.virginia.gov/news/news_releases/2010/sep29/shtml. Accessed March 27, 2012.
19. "Beyond Textbooks: Year One Report." (2011) Virginia Department of Education Report. http://www.doe.virginia.gov/support/technology/technology_initiatives/learning_without_boundaries/beyond_textbooks/year_one_beyond_textbooks_report.pdf. Accessed March 27, 2012.
20. "Beyond Textbooks: The Learning Return on Investment." (2011) Virginia Department of Education Report.
21. "What Is Auditory Perception?" (n.d.) WiseGeeks. http://www.wisegeek.com/what-is-auditory-perception.htm. Accessed March 28, 2012.
22. Cuomo, Chris. (2011) Rep. Anthony Weiner: "The picture was of me and I sent it." *ABCNews*. http://abcnews.go.com/Politics/rep-anthony-weiner-picture/story?id=13774605#.T3M-thEgexs. Accessed March 28, 2012.
23. "About the National Incident Management System (NIMS)." (n.d.) FEMA Training. http://www.fema.gov/emergency/nims/AboutNIMS.shtm. Accessed March 29, 2012.
24. "NIMS Resource Center." (n.d.) FEMA Training. http://www.fema.gov/emergency/nims/. Accessed March 29, 2012.

25. Koenig, Brian. (2012) FBI pursues social media surveillance to gather information. *New American.* http://thenewamerican.com/tech-mainmenu-30/computers/10853-fbi-pursues-social-media-surveillance-to-gather-intelligence. Accessed March 29, 2012.

26. "The American Red Cross and Dell Launch First of Its Kind Social Media Digital Operations Center for Humanitarian Relief." (n.d.) American Red Cross Release. http://www.redcross.org/portal/site/en/menuitem.94aae3 35470e233f6cf911df43181aa0/?vgnextoid=1cc17852264e5310VgnVCM10000 089f0870aRCRD. Accessed March 29, 2012.

27. Cwiak, Carol, Kline, Cathy, and Karlgaard, Tammy. (n.d.) "Emergency Management Demographics: What We Can Learn from a Comparative Analysis of IAEM Respondents and Rural Emergency Managers." IAEM Study. http://www.google.com/url?sa=t&rct=j&q=&esrc=s&source=web&cd=4&ved=0CEIQFjAD&url=http%3A%2F%2Ftraining.fema.gov%2FEMIWeb%2Fedu%2Fsurveys%2FSurvey%2520-%2520CwiakCarol%2520-%2520%2520EM%2520Demographics-What%2520Can%2520We%2520Learn.doc&ei=42N0T73LNIfy0gHkyeH_Ag&usg=AFQjCNFRFlC1vXppURAt3uTNyK9Jjlzqv Q&sig2=iKhWVvdk21sF33DILp5yRQ. Accessed March 29, 2012.

28. Godin, Seth. (2006) *Small Is the New Big: And 183 Other Riffs, Rants, and Remarkable Business Ideas.* New York: Portfolio Hardcover.

29. Bazerman, Max H. and Watkins, Michael D. (2008) *Predictable Surprises: The Disasters You Should Have Seen Coming and How to Prevent Them.* Boston: Harvard Business School Press.

30. Godin, Seth. (2005) "Clean Firetrucks." Seth Godin's Blog. http://sethgodin. typepad.com/seths_blog/2005/12/clean_firetruck.html. Accessed March 29, 2012.

31. Godin, Seth. (2010) *Linchpin: Are You Indispensable?* New York: Portfolio Hardcover.

32. "Open Government Partnership: National Action Plans for the United States of America." (2011) White House Report. http://www.whitehouse.gov/sites/default/files/us_national_action_plan_final_2.pdf. Accessed March 30, 2012.

33. Gonzalez, Suzannah. (2010) 23-Year-old techie puts Manor on the map. *The Statesman.* http://www.statesman.com/news/texas/23-year-old-techie-puts-manor-on-map-160878.html. Accessed March 30, 2012.

34. "Data.Seattle.Gov." (2010) City of Seattle. https://data.seattle.gov/. Accessed March 30, 2012.

35. "San Francisco Data." (n.d.) City of San Francisco. https://data.sfgov.org/. Accessed March 30, 2012.

36. Grynbaum, Michael M. (2012) Mayor warns of the pitfalls of social media. *New York Times.* http://www.nytimes.com/2012/03/22/nyregion/bloomberg-says-social-media-can-hurt-governing.html?_r=3. Accessed March 30, 2012.

Section I
Changing Expectations

If you play by those rules, you will almost certainly lose... the alternative is both obvious and scary: Change the rules.

Seth Godin[1]

The opening chapter of this book set the perspective for emergency management and disaster responders regarding changing public perceptions and expectations about the use of social media during emergencies and disasters. This included a consideration of changing demographics and altered levels of trust in government. Likewise, there was a careful consideration of the difference between management, administration, and leadership with a particular focus on the need for a new paradigm of approach to address these changing public standards.

Consequently, Section I will continue this consideration by addressing transparency (Chapter 2), instantaneous information exchange (Chapter 3), and the need for entrepreneurial emergency managers (Chapter 4). These three functions lay the conceptual foundation for what these new public expectations mean for emergency managers throughout the world. This will include difficult issues such as reduced secrecy, digital altruism, transactional values, and embracing failure.

These next three chapters will also identify why these new characteristics thus far have been difficult to integrate within the field of emergency management. This will include individual, organizational, and industrial hurdles that must be overcome to change the leadership paradigm and fully apply social media and emerging technologies within emergency management and disaster response.

ENDNOTE

1. Godin, Seth. (2006) *Small Is the New Big: and 183 Other Riffs, Rants, and Remarkable Business Ideas.* New York: Portfolio Hardcover, p. 200.

2
Transparency

When we talk about transparency in government, we mean that citizens must be able to "see through" its workings, to know exactly what goes on when public officials transact public business. Government that is not transparent is more prone to corruption and undue influence because there is no public oversight of decision making.

Judy Nadler and Miriam Schulman[1]

INTRODUCTION

As discussed in Chapter 1, transparency is one of the radical changes necessitated by the growing adaptation of social technologies and the corresponding alterations in public expectations related to governmental interaction. This increased use of social media is particularly present in emergencies and disasters where citizens throughout the world have begun to take information exchange upon themselves during disaster preparedness, response, and recovery when governmental organizations and emergency management agencies fail to engage fully in social systems such as Facebook and Twitter.

This move toward transparency is most often expressed via an organization's engagement in traditional open government initiatives. For example, during his first week in office, President Barack Obama distributed a memo to his executive agencies encouraging them to "create an unprecedented level of openness in government . . . to ensure the public

Figure 2.1 President Obama working with OMB Director Peter Orszag in January 2009 on a new dedicated policy for government transparency. (From Pete Souza/White House. With permission.)

trust and establish a system of transparency, public participation and collaboration . . . [which] will strengthen our democracy and promote efficient and effective government" (see Figure 2.1).[2] Likewise, in a separate memo, the Obama administration stressed that "Transparency and the rule of law will be the touchstones of this presidency."[3] Although far from completely implemented, this top-down approach is a significant step forward for the U.S. federal government.

President Obama's initiative became the Open Government Directive under the supervision of various federal governmental agencies. During this period, President Obama nominated economist Peter Orszag as the director of the Office of Management and Budget (OMB). Part of Orszag's assignment was to oversee the Open Government Directive and provide a structure to improve the various methodologies deployed by the diverse executive agencies. Consequently, in a December 2009 memorandum, Orszag stated that executive agencies were required to do four things: publish governmental information online, improve the quality of government information, create and institutionalize a culture of open government, and create an enabling policy framework for open government.[4] This memo included a specific directive to have a strategic action plan for transparency that "(1) Inventories agency high-value information currently available for download; (2) fosters the public's use of this information to increase public knowledge and promote public scrutiny of agency services; and (3) identifies high-value information not yet available and establishes a reasonable timeline for publication online in open formats with specific target dates."[4] It is with this framework that the U.S. government moved into a more concerted attempt at transparency.

OPEN GOVERNMENT DIRECTIVE REQUIREMENTS[4]
1. Publish governmental information online
2. Improve quality of government information
3. Create and institutionalize a culture of open government
4. Create an enabling policy framework for open government

As this initiative was only recently implemented and required a significant push by the administration to get universal adoption, it is not unexpected that state and local governments have not yet adopted the same level of openness and corresponding transparency. This chapter helps identify definitions and strategies for implementation so that leaders—particularly in emergency management—can successfully and efficiently create transparent organizations and communities. Understanding this revolutionary expectation, and how to address it, will help communities embrace public requirements driven by the use and integration of social media technologies.

DEFINITION OF TRANSPARENCY

Before understanding the importance of transparency in effective emergency management leadership, a clear definition must be established. Unfortunately, as with many components of the new leadership paradigm being discussed within this book, there is not yet a commonly agreed upon industry definition, especially as it relates to emergency and disaster response and coordination. For instance, in *Tactical Transparency* the authors note that transparency should be defined (or perhaps structured around) the degree to which an organization shares its leaders, employees, values, culture, business results, and business strategies with its constituents.[5] This framework is not to suggest complete disclosure of this component, as this would put businesses, organizations, and governmental entities at some industrial, legal, or competitive risk. Rather, organizations of all types must balance the level at which each of the suggested components can be engaged by the constituents (both traditional and unorthodox) at any given time.

WHAT ARE ... CONSTITUENTS?

Constituents are those individuals, organizations, or sectors that are served by an appointed or governmental organization. This term is often associated with citizens, but should more broadly be applied to citizens, community organizations, traditional media, and businesses within the given area. This includes the online representation of these same entities. Keeping constituents engaged is often politically prudent and operationally beneficial.

Noted marketer and leadership maven Seth Godin describes this process as translucence. He stresses that the general public does not want to be, nor is it imperative for organizations and their leaders to be, transparent, where nothing is hidden from view. Instead he proposes that when items and organizations are translucent and allow a limited amount of view they are more fully illuminated as to their purpose, effectiveness, and role within the broader community.[6] It can be presumed that this illumination and magnification occur because constituents are not distracted by the minutiae and overly technical detail that can sometimes be present when organizations are completely open about all components.

WHAT IS ... THE FIRE HOSE EFFECT?

The fire hose effect is an analogy often used to express an overwhelming amount of information or data at a rate at which it is impossible to take measurable pieces. In the context of open leadership, the fire hose effect can occur when an organization attempts to be completely open, revealing all data or information related to a given topic.

Transparency is not an overwhelming stream of data and information. Ironically, this type of release of information can create a "fire hose"

Figure 2.2 Screenshot of City of Seattle's Open Data website. (From Adam Crowe. With permission.)

effect where information can be so open that it is overwhelming to the average citizen. For example, this can easily occur when organizations and governmental groups open their budgetary process to public review and feedback. Although budgets and governmental expenditures at all levels can be some of the most politically sensitive (especially in tight economic times), releasing all data is often equally overwhelming and frustrating to a citizen seeking engagement. For example, the city of Seattle proudly maintains an open data stream with a particular focus on public feedback on budgetary considerations. (See Figure 2.2.) However, there are 277 separate budgetary funds with unique and corresponding departments, codes, names, purposes, and proposed funding levels.[7] For the average user, this kind of transparency would simply be overwhelming.

TYPES OF TRANSPARENCY

There are primarily two forms of transparency: governance and financial. These models of transparency are intended to break down the functions of government to ensure the general public has access to the operational and budgetary decisions and considerations that are critical to their form of government. These two types of transparency are present at local, state, and federal levels and sometimes are even present in regional collectives of governmental agencies (particularly when grants are involved).

The primary focus of governance transparency is to empower and engage citizens and partnering constituents such as private entities, jurisdictional neighbors, and other levels of government. This engagement most often occurs through specific allowances for openness and the integration of new technologies into the process. This openness is not simply the availability of information, but rather an intentionality and purpose built around the sharing of information to eliminate the perception of governmental mistrust and to allow citizens to influence and engage in the process more actively. Likewise, the utilization of emerging technologies is intended not only to create a medium for this engagement, but to help augment and magnify the experience.

Governance transparency should help eliminate or minimize the influence and impact of special interest and advocacy groups that often have great sway with elected and governmental leaders. These groups will not be eliminated from communication or contact with governmental leadership. But when transparency is applied by the government agencies, these decisions and processes related to them are often more quickly and clearly seen by citizens and brought to the attention of both mainstream and social media outlets in an attempt to self-correct the actual or appearance of governmental abuse, or to magnify the positive decisions and implications of a given community (see Figure 2.3).

Figure 2.3 Elected officials must stand shoulder to shoulder with emergency responders before, during, and after a disaster to manage the event effectively. (From FEMA/Jacinta Quesada. With permission.)

WHAT IS . . . GOVERNANCE TRANSPARENCY?

Governance transparency is a type of open government philosophy that allows citizens and special constituents (e.g., traditional media) to engage in governmental processes before, during, and after they are implemented. This engagement allows for far greater citizen empowerment and trustworthiness between the government and those who are represented.

Governance transparency helps address legal requirements such as freedom of information and sunshine laws that have been commonplace at all levels of government for decades. These laws were adopted at local, state, and federal levels in an attempt to better engage citizens in governmental processes, but not necessarily decisions. In the case of freedom of information laws (e.g., federal Freedom of Information Act, FOIA), citizens and other constituencies, including the traditional media, were given the legal right to request any piece of governmental data or information that was not excluded within the law (e.g., information related to law enforcement investigations). However, this information is only available after government has utilized it for decisions or policy making. Likewise, sunshine laws mandated the right for the general public and special constituents to have the right to attend certain public gatherings such as city council meetings or special commission gatherings. Although these too have some limitations, they also are designed for watchdog activities rather than active citizen engagement. When governmental organizations are actively applying open government philosophy and allowing for transparency before, during, and after the process, citizens and constituents are far more engaged in the political and governmental process and can influence processes before they occur.

WHAT IS . . . FINANCIAL TRANSPARENCY?

Financial transparency is an open government philosophy that directs governmental organizations at all levels of government to empower citizens to be engaged in budgetary and financial decisions before, during, and after any formal resolutions are made regarding the issue. An example of financial transparency is the www.USASpending.gov website operated by the White House.

In addition to governance transparency, there is also financial transparency. In some ways this is a subset of governance transparency, but it deserves special consideration given the high level of importance and the strong desire for fiscal accountability. Financial transparency directly relates to the governmental choices that empower citizens to contribute to and influence financial choices before, during, and after formal governmental approval. This includes traditional budgets, but is most often seen in more compartmentalized financial considerations such as special projects, tax rate considerations, loans, and grants. At the federal level, examples of financial transparency include Recovery.gov and USASpending.gov. Likewise, states such as Texas have developed repositories of local organizations engaged in open and transparent budgetary processes.[8] Many local cities, counties, and municipalities throughout the United States have adopted such strategies, with the most notable being Seattle's budget simulator mentioned earlier in the chapter.[7]

OPENING THE BOX: THE TRANSPARENT COFFEE BEAN

In "Wired to Care: How Companies Prosper When They Create Widespread Empathy," noted author Dev Patnaik talks about the history of coffee beans. As with many topics covered by Patnaik, coffee seems to be a benign object, but in the end is one of the most important beverages in the world. According to this report, Americans consume more than 400 million cups of coffee per day or more than 146 billion cups per year, which makes the United States the leading consumer of coffee in the world. Additionally, this represents 75% of the caffeine consumed in the United States.[9] To support this strong desire for coffee, beans are grown in special regions throughout the world that can support the environmental and climatic conditions necessary to grow and harvest the little black coffee beans. (Please see Figure 2.4.)

Although manufacturing coffee is fundamentally a simple and cheap process, all coffee beans are not equal in the eyes of producers and consumers. The two most common types of coffee beans are Arabica and Robusta. Both types of coffee beans make good coffee, but Arabica beans are often considered preferable to Robusta beans because of their flavorful and complex signature structure. This is compared to the Robusta bean, which is typically more bitter and has less body. Both types of beans are grown in tropical climates and often are grown side by side in certain countries including Brazil and India. However, the most significant difference between the types of beans is the growth time and hardiness of the crops during nonideal growing seasons. Specifically, Robusta beans can grow to maturity in roughly half the time of the Arabica beans and are far more sustainable during dry and wet seasons. This creates a price difference for producers who ultimately sell the Arabica beans for a higher rate than the Robusta beans.[10]

These differences between coffee beans are ultimately insignificant when this information is common knowledge. Unfortunately, that has not always been the case. Patnaik shares in his essay that in 1953, after a hard frost significantly affected Arabica production and increased consumer prices by nearly double, Maxwell House started blending Arabica and Robusta beans together in their standard mixture. Although previously it had only been Arabica beans, consumers were indifferent to the small production changes, but Maxwell House continued to face challenges in their Arabica production and realized that there also was a proportional increase between profits and increases in Robusta content. Up until this point, American coffee companies had resisted incorporating Robusta beans into their mixes.

To ensure customers did not notice a flavor change due to the incorporation of Robusta beans, Maxwell House conducted sensory tests and confirmed that minor additions were unnoticed by consumers. Because of the ability to keep costs down with no apparent loss of quality, many of the remaining American coffee companies followed suit to ensure they could stay economically feasible. Because of continued high demand for coffee and repeated problems with Arabica bean production, minor incorporations of Robusta continued annually until 1964 when coffee sales declined for the first time in the history of the United States. Manufacturers determined that older coffee drinkers continued to drink coffee, having grown accustomed to the Robusta flavor, whereas younger generations were not embracing coffee due to its now bitter flavor profile. In contrast, more contemporary coffee drinkers now drink as much or more coffee and regularly pay more money for blends or brews that are predominately made from Arabica beans.

Figure 2.4   Coffee is very important before, during, and after disasters as a tool to spread disaster-related information and the importance of transparency. (From FEMA/Annette Foglino. With permission.)

EROSION OF PUBLIC TRUST

It is critical to understand that transparency is ultimately driven by the changing public expectation that was discussed in Chapter 1. Citizens and constituency groups such as the traditional media are keenly aware of how closed government operations or large businesses are often rife with potential abuse and mismanagement. In many ways, there is one watershed historical moment that has driven the general public toward suspicion rather than inherent trust. This event was the Watergate scandal in the 1970s during Richard Nixon's presidency. This event must be considered in greater detail in order to understand the rising distrust of citizens that left citizens unequipped to access information before the advent of social media technologies.

In many ways, prior to the revelation of the Watergate scandal the American public trusted their leaders and put their full faith in the power and strength of their government. In the aftermath of the Great Depression and later the baby boom of post-World War II America, citizens were eager to continue the growth and success of the country and government (see Figure 2.5). Unfortunately, the beginnings of the Cold War and national struggles such as the McCarthy trials began to erode public confidence, but not without the hope that ultimately the country

Figure 2.5 Optimism during World War II was high with citizens embracing the need for self-sacrifice for the greater good, especially through the purchase of war bonds such as this one. (From Library and Archives Canada/Alfred Joseph Casson. With permission.)

would remain strong. President John F. Kennedy was the last president to serve in this time of optimism and hope (see Figure 2.6). This level of positivity was summarized by Kennedy, who stated that "the energy, the faith, the devotion which we bring to this endeavor will light our country and all who serve it, and the glow from that fire will truly light the world."[13] Public polls taken from 1958 to 1964 showed that more than 75% of Americans maintained a high level of confidence in their government, particularly the federal government.[13]

Then, on June 18, 1972, the *Washington Post* ran a story which reported that a team of burglars had been arrested inside the offices of the Democratic National Committee in the Watergate complex in Washington, DC.[14] Over the next few weeks additional connections were made between Nixon's re-election campaign and the individuals who had been arrested. Over the next two years, additional links were made with clear and consistent evidence that Nixon administration officials engaged in decisions

Figure 2.6 President John F. Kennedy was the last American president to serve in a time of heightened public trust in government. (From National Park Service/ Unknown. With permission.)

to undermine the election process (via the break-in) and repeatedly covered up information about the investigation or attempted to hinder the release of information.[15] Ultimately, the scandal uncovered connections to President Nixon himself, or to his implied knowledge, and led to his resignation on August 8, 1974. His final words as president clearly acknowledged the growing public distrust: "By taking this action, I hope that I will have hastened the start of the process of healing which is so desperately needed in America. . . . I deeply regret any injuries that may have been done in the course of the events that led to this decision" (see Figure 2.7).[16]

In comparison to the public surveys from a decade earlier, by the time of Nixon's resignation in 1974 only 36% of Americans stated that they still trusted government.[13] Since that time, the level of public trust has never vastly improved, with additional public trust challenges from the economic recession of the late 1970s, the Iran Contra affair, the shutdown of the American government in 1996, and the Clinton impeachment just to name a few. Only major domestic events such as the September 11, 2001 terrorist attacks have briefly improved the public's faith in government. Unfortunately, upticks like this were quickly eroded by political dissension and public disagreement over the governmental commitments to the "War on Terror" in both Iraq and Afghanistan. In short, "Watergate turned an erosion of public confidence into a collapse" that has not yet been overcome.[13]

Figure 2.7 President Nixon's connection to the Watergate scandal and his ultimate resignation from office serves as the watershed event for the lack of public trust in government. (From White House/Unknown. With permission.)

REASONING FOR PUBLIC EXPECTATIONS OF TRANSPARENCY

Transparency is not a method of operation adopted by government organizations based on normal justification. Although debatable by some technology leaders, transparency is not inherently cheaper or more efficient, which are often standards for typical public administration functionality. Additionally, transparency is not some new vogue leadership style being pushed by leadership gurus for businesses and governmental organizations. On the contrary, transparency is an offshoot of citizen empowerment and awareness that has forced governments to have greater accountability to their citizens and constituents.

This empowerment started with the introduction and astronomical growth of social media systems. By most accounts, the first social media platform was Friendster, which was introduced in 2002 as a social network. By 2004, Facebook was introduced with only limited access to the general public (initially it was only available to colleges). By 2006 and 2007, Twitter and Tumblr were introduced as the first microblogs (or limited blogs), respectively.[17] In less than a decade, these sites as well as hundreds like them added users and networks resulting in more than 955 million Facebook (June 2012) users and more than 140 million active Twitter accounts.[18,19] These various types of social media systems have become ubiquitous on personal computers, as well as mobile devices such as smartphones and tablets, and therefore strongly influence when, where, and how people receive information, whether emergent or simply mundane. This is particularly true of information during emergencies and disasters.

Specifically, in 2011, the American Red Cross completed a citizen survey to ascertain public expectations for the use of social media. This survey determined than 24% of the general public and 31% of the online population would use social media systems such as Facebook and Twitter to let friends and family know they were safe during an emergency or disaster. Likewise nearly 80% of the general population and nearly 70% of online respondents believed that emergency response organizations (e.g., the Federal Emergency Management Agency) should regularly monitor social media sites in order to respond promptly to emergencies and disasters. In addition, nearly 40% of those surveyed who stated they would request help through social media would expect assistance in less than one hour.[20]

This increased use of social media and the corresponding changes in public perception are related to two sociological concepts: social presence and media richness. Social presence is defined as the influence of intimacy and immediacy of a particular communications medium.[21] The intimacy of a medium is an evaluation based on the balance of interpersonal and mediated connectivity between individuals. Likewise, the immediacy of communication is defined as the balance between asynchronous and synchronous behaviors. These two components create a spectrum of social presence that is lower for mediated and asynchronous behaviors and higher for interpersonal and synchronous communications.[21] In other words, social presence is a measurement of how engaged two communicating parties may be, based on the style and medium in use. For example, the intimacy between two communicating entities is far greater when interpersonal opportunities exist. Likewise, so is communication that is synchronized where questions have immediately corresponding responses. Therefore, the higher the social presence, the greater the influence each communication partner has on the other.

WHAT IS . . . SOCIAL PRESENCE?

According to noted researcher Patrick Lowenthal, social presence is defined as "the degree of salience (i.e., quality or state of being there) between two communicators using a communication medium."[22] Or in more simplified terms, social presence is the value of the communication being had between two different groups. Social media have high social presence and therefore empower citizens to engage more deeply in these systems.

The theory of media richness is a closely related communications concept to social presence. This theory is based on the assumption that the goal of any communications system is the resolution of ambiguity and uncertainty regarding the topic in question.[21] In other words, things are not written without a purpose (e.g., persuasion or education). Consequently, different media types have different levels of media richness and therefore capability to resolve the opacity related to certain information. This theory also supports the concept that information changes based on circumstances and time, and therefore a medium's richness also relates to its ability to adapt to these changes. Researchers have determined that media richness has four characteristics: language variety, multiplicity of cues, personalization, and rapid feedback.[23]

WHAT IS . . . MEDIA RICHNESS?

Media richness is a communication theory built on the concept that each type of communication medium has a unique capability to address situational and time-based ambiguity. It is comprised of four components: language variety, multiplicity of cues, personalization, and rapid feedback. These components address the ability of the system to convey natural language in a way that is more than just numeric values, personalization of the message, and response in real-time.[23] Social media have a high level of media richness because they contain a high level of each of the characteristics.

Social media maintain a high level of both social presence and media richness. Specifically, social media maintain a high level of intimacy and immediacy with regard to their communications capability. The immediacy of social media is further discussed in Chapter 3 (instantaneous); the intimacy of social media is extremely effective. Users of systems such as Facebook get a high level of familiarity not only with close friends who they routinely have synchronized interaction with, but also with fringe connections that are located throughout the world and include the representation of business, organizations, governmental entities, and advocacy groups. This intimate connectivity is delivered through text, photos, videos, and web links that can create a depth of understanding about a person, event, activity, or location previously only available in second-hand asynchronous communications.

Likewise, social media also maintain a high level of media richness. Because of the aforementioned ability to present information in multiple formats and styles they maintain a high level of flexibility for appropriate application to a given event or scenario. The requirement for language variety is met in multiple ways through the formats (e.g., photos, video, and texts) and coding (e.g., Twitter hashtags) as well. In addition, social media are wholly customized to the individual communication consumer. Likewise, the transparent and instantaneous nature of social media not only contributes to the social presence but to the media richness because conversations can happen in a synchronized or asynchronized pattern.

Social presence and media richness are extraordinarily effective during emergencies and disasters. Citizens in both the affected area and those individuals concerned about those in the affected area are equally likely to utilize social media to send, share, and disseminate information. Because of this process, disaster-related information moves very quickly during disasters. Even though social media systems are inherently self-correcting,[24] it is not always possible during the early stages of an emergency or disaster. However, surprisingly quickly, standards of accuracy will soon arise. As such, transparency is one of the only tools available to emergency managers to help manage the rapid spread of information during an emergency or disaster.

TRANSPARENCY LEADS TO INCREASED TRUST

Formal governmental and nongovernmental response to emergencies and disasters is built on trust. When the general public has a high level of trust in the emergency response process, response and recovery efforts are more efficiently and effectively run as the general public responds in a cooperative fashion and often in greater compliance with operational considerations. Likewise, when trust is not present, it can alter the public trust far beyond the period of time necessary for response and recovery. For example, following the 2011 Japan earthquake and tsunami, the world waited nervously to hear how damaged the Fukushima Daiichi nuclear power plant was. Tokyo Electric Power Company (TEPCO), the plant operator, announced on national Japanese television that the accident was under control and no radiation had been released. Meanwhile traditional media and social media outlets ran stories on individuals in nearby communities holding up Geiger counters showing radiation that was beyond the measurable scale in that area.[25] Because of the clearly misleading statements of the national utility, many cultural experts noted a profound shift in the trust younger Japanese citizens placed in government and formal response organizations.

Trust is specifically measured as perceived competency, benevolence, and honesty between the two parties. Each of these characteristics creates foundational components of trust. However, no matter how competent, benevolent, or honest an emergency response organization is when responding to a disaster, public trust is only as high as the public's perception of these character traits. Public perception is influenced by a variety of characteristics, including humility, ethics, and creativity, which are discussed in the last section of this book; however, one key element necessary before these can be considered is for organizations to be transparent. According to one researcher, "The relationships between transparency and trust is influenced partly by the perceived credibility of the message . . . [and] people well informed about the process are included to base their judgment of perceived competence."[26] Perception is often reality; it is important to maintain transparency to help present a version of an event that is not modified by the medium used or any pre-existing bias from the presenter.

COMPLIANCE WITH OPEN GOVERNMENT LAWS

If transparency is critical for governmental and nongovernmental organizations to ensure trust as well as open and honest engagement with their constituency, it is important to identify what tools and methodologies can be deployed to leverage the benefits of transparency. Understanding the methodologies is a critical first step for emergency management and response leaders to begin addressing public expectations regarding disaster management.

The first practical approach to improve transparency in emergency management leadership is as a tool to address freedom of information and open record laws that exist at federal, state, and local levels. Examples of these laws include the Clery Act for Higher Education, Emergency Planning and Community Right-to-Know Acts, Sunshine laws, Hurricane Katrina Recovery Act, Freedom of Information Acts, and many others (see Figure 2.8). In each case, laws have been established to help facilitate public interaction in the governmental process and provide some accountability (see Figure 2.9). However, with the exception of open meeting laws, these regulations are only initiated after the event, activity, or situation

Figure 2.8   Laws such as the Community Right-to-Know Act were passed in an attempt to increase transparency related to disaster preparedness and response. (FEMA/Marvin Nauman. With permission.)

has occurred when correction or punishment is needed. This retroactive process is often irritating to citizens and constituents because the account-ability is limited to only after-the-fact review and consideration. This limi-tation can be additionally frustrating and ultimately cause more oversight and upheaval to the governmental operations.

Perhaps the most notable example of this process was the public outcry after Hurricane Katrina affected much of the southeastern United States in 2005. In the aftermath of its impact, it was clear that emergency response to Hurricane Katrina showed evidence of failure at every level of government. Blame and ridicule were shared and dispensed by governmental agencies and the various constituencies and continue to be discussed and studied by academic professionals and the traditional media outlets nearly a decade later. As late as 2012, five New Orleans law enforcement officers were finally sentenced for their involvement in shooting unarmed citizens in the aftermath of Hurricane Katrina. Only in the retroactive analysis of the emergency response (particularly relat-ing to safety and security) was it evident that the New Orleans Police Department was influenced by some internal corruption and poor management.

However, if governmental leaders adopt transparent policies, pro-cedures, and, perhaps most important, open attitudes, the constituency

Figure 2.9 Major events such as Hurricane Katrina often drive legislation meant to promote transparency related to preparedness, response, and recovery. (From NASA/Unknown. With permission.)

can engage in the process before, during, and after an event. Because citizens are engaged earlier in the process, there is a public sense of ownership that is far greater than the retroactive engagement discussed previously. Consequently, any sense of success or failure is shared and therefore results in less extreme accountability due to the fact that the review and engagement are spread across the entire spectrum of activity and throughout the community. Transparency certainly cannot fully eliminate the possibilities of fraud or mismanagement in a government organization, but it can help reduce mismanagement, fraud, and abuse. In addition, maintaining strong transparency will help comply with open government laws in a more efficient and effective process.

METHODOLOGY OF TRANSPARENCY: REDUCTION OF SECRECY

In addition to compliance with open government laws, when leaders adopt a strong philosophy of transparency there is a significant reduction in governmental secrecy. For instance, prior to the terrorist attacks of September 11, 2001, the majority of the general public had never heard of Osama Bin Laden or Al Qaeda. The federal government—particularly the various intelligence agencies—was the only part of the American community who had any knowledge or experience with these new enemies of the American way. In addition, there was significant organizational and disciplinary conflict between first responder groups such as law enforcement and fire departments that led to so-called "turf wars" and an intentional lack of sharing related to incident or intelligence. Consequently, in the aftermath of this event both the 9/11 Commission and the Congressional Joint Inquiry into 9/11 recommended reforms related to transparency that would ultimately lead to a reduction in unnecessary secrets (see Figure 2.10).[28]

However, there are clearly situations where information needs to be protected for reasons of homeland security, law enforcement investigations, and certain disaster situations. These suggestions for increased transparency are simply attempting to reduce or eliminate the information that

Figure 2.10 The terrorist attacks on September 11, 2001, led to wholesale changes in how information was shared between governmental agencies. (From New York Fire Department (NYFD)/SFC Thomas R. Roberts. With permission.)

is held back based on organizational or managerial discretion. A prime example of positive transparency that does not adversely affect investigations or other security issues is the Clery Act (Jeanne Clery Disclosure of Campus Security Policy and Campus Crime Statistics Act). The Clery Act is a federal mandate that requires higher education institutions that participate in federal student financial aid programs (which is nearly all schools) to disclose real-time and collective information about crimes on their campuses.[29] This law was originally passed in 1986, but was amended in 2008 to clarify issues that arose after the 2007 shootings on the Virginia Tech campus. The Clery Act requires the publication of annual security reports, submission of crime statistics to the U.S. Department of Education, and issuance of timely campus alerts.[29] This final component of timely campus alerts has been the most challenging, as some higher education institutions in the past have been slow to release this kind of information for fear of a public perception that their campuses are unsafe and therefore less likely to be attended.

When leaders apply a finer review of organizational processes with a stronger philosophy of transparency, it is evident that there will be a balancing of issues between those than can be openly shared through an active campaign of transparency and those that must be limited for legal or investigative reasons. However, when the right balance is struck between these issues, the broader constituency will feel that the governmental response agency is not being secretive even though there are issues that will remain removed from the view of the general public. It is this paradox that is the most challenging to understand for most emergency management and response leaderships. However, strong leadership in a transparent paradigm will begin to address these issues with the general public.

CREATING SPACE THROUGH TRANSPARENCY

In addition to the reduction of secrecy and compliance with open government laws, an emergency management professional employing this new paradigm of leadership can also create space within his or her community for advocacy, education, and discussion. Because transparency is critical to this activity, it allows for the governmental agent and the constituency to come together in an area of mutual trust and respect. Much as with the reduction of secrecy mentioned above, utilizing transparent methodologies creates this space that is figuratively equivalent to a demilitarized zone between two conflicting agencies.

Figure 2.11 House of Representatives Majority Leader Eric Cantor initiated a transparency-driven campaign called the "Citizen Co-Sponsor Project" to drive citizen engagement. (From U.S. Congress/Unknown. With permission.)

One type of this figurative space focuses on advocacy for certain sociological or political issues. For example, in 2012, House of Representatives Majority Leader Eric Cantor initiated the "Citizen Co-Sponsor Project" (see Figure 2.11).[30] This initiative allowed citizens to publicly state support for proposed legislation by "co-sponsoring" the initiative. Not only does this simply engage the constituency at large, it also empowers the citizens directly by granting (conceptually) the same power as the elected officials who represent them and have long been seen as untrustworthy (as mentioned earlier). This is a wildly transparent activity that is an excellent example of leveraging transparent methodologies to move an organization forward.

This type of utilization of conceptualized open spaces through transparency is relatively new and not common in emergency management. Many emergency management agencies have long wanted to engage citizens in planning and preparedness processes, but have struggled to do this effectively. Emergency managers throughout the world have held public gatherings in civic centers to announce certain programming or ask for engagement and review. However, without the political polarity associated with politicians and other governmental leaders embroiled in controversy, emergency managers struggle to generate the public interest necessary for true and widespread public engagement in the process.

WHAT IS . . . A TWITTER TOWN HALL?

A Twitter town hall is a concept originally started by the U.S. White House as a social media engagement strategy for the president of the United States to hear from and engage with the general population. Some local or nonprofit emergency management organizations have modified this effort to provide similar engagement with the local constituency during public events such as monthly testing of alerting technologies or community exercises (see Figure 2.12).

However, some emergency management organizations are beginning to explore transparency to create a more engaged general public and facilitate better public advocacy and education. For instance, the Federal Emergency Management Agency (FEMA) initiated the Think Tank in late 2011 as a recognition that "The best solutions to the challenges we face are generated by the people and the communities who are closest to those challenges."[31] The FEMA Think Tank concept brings emergency managers and passionate citizens from all levels, disciplines, and communities to discuss challenges and issues that are affecting the field. Much like the "Citizen Co-Sponsor Project" this type of transparency helps reduce perceived barriers between the local practitioners and the federal government. Likewise, some local emergency management offices have dabbled in "Twitter Town Halls" or some other

Figure 2.12 President Barack Obama has led many online engagement sessions in an attempt to support a more transparent government leadership core. (From White House/Unknown. With permission.)

Figure 2.13 Traditional town hall meetings have become less and less significant in communities as more individuals move toward social systems such as Twitter and Facebook. (From FEMA/Tim Burkitt. With permission.)

similar concept to help create open forums or conceptual spaces to allow citizens to engage in discussions about real issues in their community to which they may or may not previously have had access.[32] (See Figure 2.13.) In reality, the actual level of access is much less significant than the perceived level of access, which is critical for emergency managers trying to adopt this new leadership paradigm. This process of greater efficiency and collaboration is discussed later in Chapters 5 and 7, respectively.

SPECIFIC STEPS TO TRANSPARENCY

The state of Utah has repeatedly been acknowledged as a truly forward-leaning governmental agency when it comes to transparency. Because of the inherent sense of transparency and the desire to continue to see its implementation across all governmental entities including emergency preparedness and response, students at the University of Utah in observation of their state's transparent policies presented five specific strategic steps that can be implemented by governmental organizations. Some of these steps are more applicable to governmentwide organizations rather than a specific emergency management program, but several can be specifically deployed before, during, and after emergencies or disasters to ensure transparency and engagement throughout the process.

For example, all documentation that is not considered protected for homeland security, investigative, or other proprietary reason should be shared and available to the general public. This includes meeting notes, minutes, agendas, attendee lists, and so on. This is an extraordinary shift for most emergency management and public safety officials who default to closed rather than open. On the contrary, the public should be given the opportunity to be engaged in the process at any step that would not contradict the protection or preservation of an investigation or response process. Obviously, there are significant challenges to changing this component of the paradigm, including the time commitment necessary to maintain this support before disasters, but the ability to maintain the technological support to share may be difficult during active response or short-term recovery.

Although challenging, this level of commitment to openness and transparency is not unprecedented. For example, within two weeks of the devastating F5 tornado that destroyed most of Greensburg, Kansas, the local government administration created a blog to document and share information about the recovery process.[34] Although the term "transparency" was as much in its infancy as social media were when this event occurred in 2007, the blog was initiated because the leadership knew the local citizens' engagement and understanding of the recovery process were vital to rebuilding their community efficiently (see Figure 2.14).

Figure 2.14 An early example of citizen engagement with social media systems during emergencies and disasters was after the EF-5 tornado that affected Greensburg, Kansas, in 2007. (From FEMA/Greg Henshall. With permission.)

On the other hand, large-scale events such as the 2010 Haiti earthquake that significantly affected already vulnerable infrastructure were supplemented by virtual volunteers who leveraged social systems to transmit (and often translate) real-time and accurate information about what was occurring during response and recovery efforts.[17] Although challenging, transparency must be present to facilitate effective engagement.

SPECIFIC STEPS FOR STRATEGIC TRANSPARENCY

1. Organizations should establish a dedicated open government web page that provides a searchable repository for all public information that is accessible by three clicks or less.
2. Online information needs to be collected, generated, and maintained in a digital form and made available through the open government website in a timely way.
3. All electronic communications made with government-supplied equipment, including e-mails and instant messages, should be considered public records.
4. Senior government administrators should post their schedules publicly, maintain open settings on social media sites, and commit to a culture of transparency.
5. Governmental bodies should make all public meetings as open as possible by posting agendas and meeting materials in advance, streaming live meeting audio or video, posting recordings within 48 hours, and allowing remote participation.[33]

In conclusion it is important for emergency managers and other related government entities to embrace transparency as public expectations shift toward a higher real or perceived level of engagement on all aspects that can be reasonably shared. Maintaining a strong commitment to transparency before a disaster will ultimately lead to greater public acceptance and flexibility during and after disasters or other major conflicts and crises that may occur. There will be significant public flexibility and significant buy-in from the public when they have been granted equal and open access to the workings of the governmental agents that are representing or protecting them. This process can ultimately be facilitated in a variety of ways but in the end, is based on policies and procedures established for governance, engagement with constituents and stakeholders, and reporting on all activities to ensure nothing remains (or appears to remain) hidden.

LEADERS IN THE OPEN: PATRICE CLOUTIER

Mr. Cloutier is a former broadcaster and reporter who became a government communicator in 1997 after leaving the Canadian Broadcasting Corporation. He has specialized in emergency information and crisis communications with a particular focus on emergency management and business continuity. His specialties include crisis communications, emergency information planning and delivery, strategic communications planning, speech writing, and social media. His writings can be found at his Crisis Comms Command Post blog (http://crisiscommscp.blogspot.com/). In the following essay written for this book, Mr. Cloutier addresses the need for transparency in government leadership.

Transformational Transparency

Patrice Cloutier

We are in a transformational phase that will affect the work of emergency managers, business continuity planners and crisis communicators. Simply put, emerging technologies and trends have brought about a generalized "democratization" of these fields.

Three factors are driving this change:

- The growing importance of social networks and mobile technologies
- The overwhelming realization that speed is everything
- Greater public participation and input

The consequences of this are numerous but they all add to the workload of EM personnel and crisis communicators when an incident or disaster occurs. You must respond, alert/warn, monitor and then engage/communicate. In all this, social networks and mobile tech play crucial roles.

Second, the speed at which incidents and crises (whether in the physical or virtual world) occur means that delegation of authority and the automation of communications response processes become absolutely necessary.

Third, social networks bring greater participation from your stakeholders and audiences. That's the great democratization factor. Online communities coalesce rapidly over topics, crises, and disaster recovery, for example. Emergency managers and officials now have to deal with all sorts of newcomers to the EM table: crisis mappers, crowdsourcing groups, and online volunteers.

How do leaders adapt to this new reality where the response structure becomes somewhat more diffuse? They survive and even thrive, if they learn how to harness the power of the crowd. This entails a willingness to delegate authority more widely and an absolute commitment to openness and continuing dialogue with all stakeholders.

However, this is only possible when trust is shared; when the leader trusts his or her people and audiences and vice versa. Without reciprocity, nothing is possible.

The impact of social networks that have brought emergency management to an era of greater public participation is tremendous. The very definition of command must be re-examined, as should the current incident management doctrines. When response becomes more diffuse and activities are decentralized, does command retain the same meaning? Where in the doctrine should social media monitoring be placed and what value should be given to the data, analysis and mapping provided by the crowd?

So, again, we're back to the issue of trust. And trust can only be built on ongoing, two-way conversations. Communication is at the very heart of trust and should be a primary concern for any leader, incident commander, EOC director, or CEO.

Every single emergency management, business continuity, or response plan should have a crisis communications component to it. And every leader should know the basics of that art.

In a way, the very role of the crisis communicator has been transformed. Crisis planners are "facilitators" more than "spindoctors." Without the understanding and support of command and the people at the top, the facilitation efforts and the channels to communicate with audiences will be useless. Leaders need to understand public and stakeholder motivations during a crisis.

There are pitfalls on the way to successful leadership. The following five failure points are avoided by effective leaders:

1. *Being unprepared:* Leaders ensure their organizations have plans in place (and should be familiar with them) and they

ensure that their staff knows them. Having no procedures in place, no pre-approved messaging often means unorganized, ill-advised improvisation that leads to a lack of strategic vision. This damages trust.

2. *Not having a firm grasp of the situation:* Real leaders are decisive. Effective mid-level leaders don't "push things upstairs"; they act. They take a stand when they're facing a directive that is obviously misguided. Weak leaders, wherever they stand in the hierarchy, don't see the "big picture" and ignore established principles of good crisis management. Worse, they focus on process rather than on people.

3. *Micromanagement and interference:* These lead to complacency, a lack of innovation, and mediocrity. Leaders who don't trust their people get involved in operational details they shouldn't worry about and insist on an approvals process that handicaps any hope for a successful and quick crisis response.

4. *Lack of collaboration and outreach:* Ignoring key stakeholders means building a tall, empty silo. Shunning joint efforts, not maximizing their organization's reach, and not establishing solid relationships in favor of a "go alone," "we have our own agenda" approach, leads to a fragmented, uncoordinated response which serves no audience well.

5. *Lack of social media and web presence:* Leaders and their organizations need to occupy the public space and move at the speed of their stakeholders, clients, and audiences. Social media and constant web updates allow them to do that. Putting obstacles in that process hurts their image. Having a stale website in a crisis shows incompetence or a blissful ignorance of the needs of the audience.

Leaders and organizations operating under any of the five points above seriously hamper their response. Dealing with more than one is a critical wound, having to suffer under more than two means they will soon become irrelevant to their internal and external audiences.

In conclusion, to gain the trust of their audiences, leaders act quickly, communicate openly, and delegate the implementation of their crisis or response plans. They do so because they understand that in today's emergency management or business world, the speed of the response and how it's perceived by the public determine its eventual success.

ENDNOTES

1. Nadler, Judy and Schulman, Miriam. (2006) "Open Meetings, Open Records, and Transparency in Government." Markula Center for Applied Ethics – Santa Clara University. http://www.scu.edu/ethics/practicing/focusareas/government_ethics/introduction/open-meetings.html. Accessed March 31, 2012.
2. "Transparency and Open Government." (n.d.) White House Memorandum. http://www.whitehouse.gov/the_press_office/TransparencyandOpen Government. Accessed March 31, 2012.
3. Korbe, Tina. (2012) "Report Card: Most Transparent Administration Ever Receives a C- in Transparency." HotAir. http://hotair.com/archives/2012/03/19/report-card-most-transparent-administration-ever-receives-a-c-in-transparency/. Accessed March 31, 2012.
4. "Open Government Directive." (2009) OMB Memo M10-06. http://www.whitehouse.gov/open/documents/open-government-directive. Accessed April 1, 2012.
5. Holtz, Shel, Havens, John C., and Johnson, Lynne D. (2008) *Tactical Transparency: How Leaders Can Leverage Social Media to Maximize Value and Build Their Brand*. New York: Jossey-Bass.
6. Godin, Seth. (2012) "Transparent or Translucent?" Seth Godin's Blog. http://sethgodin.typepad.com/seths_blog/2012/02/transparent-or-translucent.html. Accessed April 1, 2012.
7. "2011–2012 Proposed Budget—Expenditures Allowance by Budget Control Level (BCL)." City of Seattle Open Data. https://data.seattle.gov/dataset/2011-2012-Proposed-Budget-Expenditures-Allowance-b/55z8-f4gi. Accessed April 2, 2012.
8. "Texas Transparency." (2012) Texas Comptroller's Office. http://www.texastransparency.org/local/cities.php. Accessed April 3, 2012.
9. "Coffee Statistics Report 2012 Edition." (2012) Coffee Statistics. http://www.coffee-statistics.com/coffee_statistics_ebook.html. Accessed April 4, 2012.
10. "The Difference between Arabica Bean and Robusta Bean Coffee." Coffee.org. http://www.coffee.org/articles/index.php?art=79. Accessed April 4, 2012.
11. Patnaik, Dev. (2009) *Wired to Care: How Companies Prosper When They Create Widespread Empathy*. New York: FT Press.
12. Patnaik, Dev. (2008) "Maxwell House Destroys Coffee." *Wire to Care* Excerpt. http://www.wiredtocare.com/?p=429. Accessed April 4, 2012.
13. Schneider, Bill. (1997) Cynicism didn't start with Watergate. *CNN/Time* Special Report. http://www.cnn.com/ALLPOLITICS/1997/gen/resources/watergate/trust.schneider/. Accessed April 4, 2012.
14. "The Post Investigates." *Washington Post* – Post Politics. http://www.washingtonpost.com/wp-srv/politics/special/watergate/part1.html. Accessed April 4, 2012.

15. "The Government Acts." *Washington Post* – Post Politics. http://www. washingtonpost.com/wp-srv/politics/special/watergate/part2.html. Accessed April 4, 2012.
16. "Nixon Resigns." *Washington Post* – Post Politics. http://www.washingtonpost. com/wp-srv/politics/special/watergate/part3.html. Accessed April 4, 2012.
17. Crowe, Adam. (2012) *Disasters 2.0: The Application of Social Media in Modern Emergency Management.* Boca Raton, FL: CRC Press.
18. "Newsroom: Fact Sheet." Facebook Newsroom. http://newsroom.fb.com/ content/default.aspx?NewsAreaId=22. Accessed April 5, 2012.
19. Bennett, Shea. (2012) "Twitter on Track for 500 Million Total Users by March." Mashable. http://www.mediabistro.com/alltwitter/twitter-active-total-users_b17655. Accessed April 5, 2012.
20. "More Americans Using Social Media During Emergencies." American Red Cross Press Release. http://www.redcross.org/portal/site/en/menuitem.9 4aae335470e233f6cf911df43181aa0/?vgnextoid=7a82d1efe68f1310VgnVCM 10000089f0870aRCRD. Accessed April 5, 2012.
21. Kaplan, Andreas M. and Haenlein, Michael. (2010) Users of the world, unite! The challenges and opportunities of social media. *Business Horizons.* 53: 59–68.
22. Lowenthal, Patrick R. (2010) Chapter 1.11: Social presence. *Social Computing, Concepts, and Methodologies.* http://www.patricklowenthal.com/publications/ socialpresence%20reprint.pdf. Accessed April 7, 2012.
23. "Media Richness Theory." (2009). Time Barrow Blog. http://blog.timebarrow. com/2009/09/media-richness-theory/. Accessed April 7, 2012.
24. Sutton, Jeannette. (2009) The public uses social networking to verify facts, coordinate information. *Emergency Management Magazine.* http://www. emergencymgmt.com/safety/The-Public-Uses-Social-Networking.html. Access April 8, 2012.
25. Glionna, John M. (2011) Post disaster, Japanese are less trusting of authority. *LA Times.* http://articles.latimes.com/2011/dec/18/world/la-fg-japan-distrust-20111218. Accessed April 8, 2012.
26. Grimmelihuijsen, Stephen G. (2010). Transparency of public decision-making: Towards trust in local government?" *Policy & Internet*, 2: 1, Article 2. http:// www.psocommons.org/policyandinternet/vol2/iss1/art2/. Accessed April 8, 2012.
27. "Five Former New Orleans Cops Sentenced in Hurricane Katrina Shootings." (2012). FoxNews. http://www.foxnews.com/us/2012/04/04/ five-former-new-orleans-cops-sentenced-in-hurricane-katrina-shootings/. Accessed April 9, 2012.
28. "Reducing Secrecy." (n.d.) Open the Government. http://www. openthegovernment.org/node/2917. Accessed April 11, 2012.
29. "The Clery Act." (n.d.) Higher Education Center. http://www.higheredcenter. org/mandates/clery-act. Accessed April 11, 2012.
30. "Citizen Co-Sponsor Project." (2012) House Majority Leader. http://www. majorityleader.gov/CITIZENS/. Accessed April 11, 2012.

31. "The FEMA Think Tank." (2012) Federal Emergency Management Agency (FEMA). http://www.fema.gov/thinktank/. Accessed April 11, 2012.
32. "Emergency Preparedness Townhall Gatherings at Johnson County Community College." (2011) Johnson County – A Community Prepared Blog. http://www.jocoprepared.blogspot.com/2011/09/emergency-preparedness-townhall.html. Accessed April 12, 2012.
33. Knell, Noelle. (2012) "5 Best Practices for Open Government." Government Technology. http://www.govtech.com/policy-management/5-Best-Practices-Open-Local-Government.html. Accessed April 12, 2012.
34. "Kiowa County – Greensburg Recovery." (2007) Blog. http://greensburgks.blogspot.com/2007_05_01_archive.html. Accessed April 12, 2012.

3

Instantaneous

Evolution is really slow. [It is] hard to demonstrate it in real time during a school board meeting. Gravity is instantaneous. Baseball players use it every day.

Seth Godin[1]

THE FUNDAMENTALS OF CONVERSATION

The instantaneous exchange of information via social media systems and related emerging technologies is the second component of the fundamental shift that is occurring in the expectations of the general public. Because of the widespread use and manipulation of social media systems by the general public, community organizations, and traditional media outlets, there is a growing expectation that information is distributed by everyone in ways that are nearly instantaneous. This far exceeds traditional expectations and utilizations of scheduled information engagement through television, print media, and radio programming. Consequently, this chapter discusses how social media accomplish this instantaneous information exchange and what the fundamentals of social media are that support this phenomenon. This includes real-life disaster examples, media adoption, and new techniques that can be leveraged by emergency management professionals to adopt a new paradigm of leadership that will function to help address growing challenges of social media engagement.

Social media are fundamentally about conversations between two entities. Unlike traditional physical conversations, social media occur in a variety of virtual environments through technological media including Internet-based computers, tablet computers, and mobile devices. Interestingly, there are literally thousands of different social media systems that help facilitate these types of conversations both within the given system and often interconnected with others. Some of the sites are even integrated into standard websites and traditional news pages. However, regardless of the technology platform utilized, the process of communication is the same as the fundamental components of conversations.

In a physical environment, conversations can be defined by a range of complexity that includes characteristics such as the number of participants, type of participants, length of engagement, personalization, comfort-level of participants, and quality of engagement (see Figure 3.1). For instance, a conversation between two individuals is far more personal (and often more private) than it would be when multiple people are involved. As discussed in Chapter 2, these types of conversations create higher levels of trust and intimacy and thus levels of engagement and resulting action are often higher as well. However, given certain circumstances, conversations with multiple parties are often equally as beneficial. For example, many support groups (e.g., Alcoholics Anonymous) often create high levels of trust and open discourse when there are shared and common challenges, issues, or connectivity among the members. Likewise, this can often occur

Figure 3.1 Conversation between two individuals is a fundamental means to build trust and exchange information whether it is face-to-face or in a digital environment. (From FEMA/Andrea Booher. With permission.)

with disaster survivors or families of victims as they share similar, highly emotional, experiences of a given situation.

COMPONENTS OF CONVERSATION

1. Number of participants
2. Types of participants
3. Length of engagement
4. Personalization
5. Comfort level of participants
6. Quality of engagement

The length of engagement is also a critical element of conversations. For instance, an unexpected conversation between two individuals who meet haphazardly or coincidentally will often result in casual conversation with limited (if any) added trust or confidence between the two parties. Conversely, individuals who engage in longer conversations—especially during shared or similar highly emotional events such as disasters— create instant credibility (or lack thereof) between each other. The length of engagement is often directly tied to the level of personalization between the two parties. Specifically, there is a limit to the number of casual topics that can be discussed between two unengaged parties before the questions (and corresponding answers) begin to delve into matters of greater personalization or importance to one (if not both) of the parties involved. It is almost impossible for the levels of trust not to be increased when conversations become personalized.

The last two components of conversation are also closely related. The comfort level of participants in a conversation is often wholly dependent on the quality of engagement provided by the parties involved. The quality of engagement in conversations is based on a variety of components, but is fundamentally built around a give-and-take exchange between the two parties. For instance, a conversation with two individuals is framed by statements and questions offered back and forth between the two in conversations. When this back and forth fails, the quality of the conversation drops. When the quality of the engagement drops significantly, the conversation is typically over. This is clearly understood by most people when they are engaging with other people. However, this dynamic is not as clearly defined or understood when organizations or governmental entities try to engage in conversations with individuals or groups of constituents. See Figure 3.2.

Figure 3.2 When government agencies create one-direction communications, the local constituents often feel disconnected and disenfranchised from their community. (From FEMA/Andrea Booher. With permission.)

This conversation failure point is one of special note, particularly in light of the way social media are utilized by governmental organizations such as emergency management offices. Much as with any conversation conducted in a traditional physical environment, social media conversations must abide by the same components. Although most of the components addressed earlier are controllable by emergency managers and other governmental agencies, there are significant challenges when it comes to the quality of engagement and pacing utilized by the emergency managers. Because of limited staffing, constricting budgets, and a diversity of mandated (and often unexpected) responsibilities, many emergency management offices struggle to create high-quality conversations primarily due to the timeliness necessary to engage in social media conversations. Much as in a traditional conversation, a social media conversation with a constituent must be reciprocated in a timely manner or else risk the loss of engagement and the potential trust that is closely tied to this relationship.

SPEED OF SOCIAL MEDIA

It is almost unfathomable to understand just how fast information is disseminated and redistributed via social media systems. For example, since Twitter was founded in 2006, the number of users and the corresponding number of tweets has grown exponentially. By 2007, Twitter users were tweeting more than 5,000 times per day. Over the next three years tweets per day rose to 300,000, 300 million, and 500 million, respectively.[6] The number of tweets for a particular event is also important to note. For example, during the Super Bowl in 2012, there were almost 14 million individual tweets about the game.[2] This number represents more people than any state in the United States other than New York, California, Texas, and Florida.[3] It is difficult to comprehend a conversation that involves nearly 14 million people simultaneously, but it is very possible when the topic is popular and centered around a particular issue and focused during a limited period of time.

Although the aggregate number of tweets for an event such as this is impressive, it is also important to measure how quickly these tweets are exchanged within the system. For example, during that same Super Bowl the social media conversation peaked at 12,233 tweets per second.[4] This is extremely impressive, however, this number was quickly surpassed a mere few weeks later at the Oscars™ ceremony where more than 18,000 tweets per second were noted during a show performance.[5] Interestingly, this pace is tremendously faster than just three years prior when the death of Michael Jackson generated a peak of only 493 tweets per second.[7] This pace on Twitter is not just limited to major events and movements of pop culture, but occurs relative to the area and degree of impact.

WHAT IS . . . THE SPEED OF SOCIAL MEDIA?

Social media are nearly instantaneous as a format to exchange information about a particular event. During some disasters and other public events such as the 5.8 magnitude 2011 Virginia earthquake, the distribution of tweets actually traveled faster than the earthquake waves.[25] This speed is achievable because of ideal connectivity between technological, interpersonal, and infrastructure capabilities.

Significant emergencies and disasters have generated similar pacing on Twitter and other social media outlets. For example, in 2011, three of the 16 highest tweets per second events were emergencies or incidents of international security.[8] Specifically, the Japan earthquake (March 2011), Virginia earthquake (August 2011), and death of Osama Bin Laden (May 2011) all generated peaks of more than 5,000 tweets per second.[8] People throughout the world conversed at incredible speeds about a variety of issues that made up the complexity of the event response and recovery efforts. Moreover, these conversations were not controlled or limited by any predefined parameters. People asked questions, sought answers, challenged results, and ultimately engaged in the event in whatever way they could. Likewise, people with personal connections to the incident sought clarification and others outside the event sought methods to begin to provide aid and support through donated monies and supplies. All of these conversations happened instantaneously in an organic fashion that was facilitated without formal government intervention.

For instance, unbeknownst to the world, in early May 2011, United States Special Forces performed a raid on a Pakistani building thought to be the residence of notorious international terrorist Osama Bin Laden. During the skirmish, Bin Laden was shot and killed. This information was reported back up the chain of command to President Barack Obama (see Figure 3.3). At approximately 9:45 p.m. EST on May 2nd, the White House Communications Director announced that President Obama would be addressing the nation at 10:30 p.m.[9] Although the major news outlets were initially unsure what the topic was about, some veteran political journalists suspected it was about Bin Laden.

Figure 3.3 President Barack Obama, Vice President Joe Biden, Secretary of State Hillary Clinton, and various other government officials await news of the Navy SEAL strike on the compound where Osama Bin Laden was hiding. (From Executive Office of the United States/Unknown. With permission.)

However, before any formal announcement was made by the president or hinted at by traditional media, social media messages began to appear on Twitter, Facebook, and other sources that Bin Laden had in fact been killed. More accurately, some five minutes before President Obama was scheduled to speak and while he was still completing his speech, a tweet from Keith Urbahn (Chief of Staff to former Secretary of Defense Donald Rumsfeld) wrote, "So I'm told by a reputable person they have killed Osama Bin Laden. Hot damn."[9] Thus within 45 minutes social media had deduced from well-informed, yet unofficial sources, the information that was about to be released in traditional fashion.

OPENING THE BOX: PRESIDENT OBAMA VERSUS TWITTER

In early 2012, President Barack Obama prepared a surprise trip to Afghanistan to sign a post-war agreement with Afghan President Hamid Karzai. Unfortunately, his arrival and intention were almost spoiled by the speed and spread of Twitter. Early in the day a local Afghan news agency posted to Twitter that President Obama had arrived in Kabul which was quickly retweeted by other Twitter accounts of political observers. The U.S Embassy in Kabul quickly sent out a tweet denying President Obama's arrival while White House communications staff quickly worked with official media to squash the rumor. Online observers continued to push that the story was accurate, with the Associated Press eventually tweeting that the story was accurate, as well. Interestingly, the Afghan news agency that originally posted the story later removed the tweet and replaced it with a statement that it was false. Although seemingly irrelevant, this story is a classic example of how the speed and instantaneous nature of social media nearly created a security breach in the protection of the president of the United States.

SOCIAL MEDIA AMPLIFICATION

This instantaneous nature of social media is not necessarily directly related to the type of event in question either. In other words, the speed of the information exchanged related to the death of a major international figure is not necessarily driven by the size and scope of the actual event. Due to the ubiquitous nature of portable computing devices and the plethora of social media systems available in mobile forms, social media information truly only needs one source with clear and legitimate information such as photos, videos, or eyes on the particular event. These eyewitness reports get shared through directly related social media contacts who then share among their followers and friends. This amplification is a secondary characteristic of the speed of social media that is difficult to match even for some of the most fundamental forms of sharing such as in-person word of mouth.

Amplification is the component of social media that creates a "crowd-sourced megaphone."[10] The impressive speed of exchange and interaction is magnified tremendously with no additional cost or resources necessary. For example, when Apple co-founder Steve Jobs passed away in late 2011, the social media response was, as expected, significantly large and instantaneously spread throughout the world of intense and casual users of various emerging technologies that Jobs helped develop. But the response was not just fast; it grew quickly and with significant acceleration. Specifically, information about his death peaked at 50,000 tweets per minute within 30 minutes of the announcement, with tweets about Jobs accounting for nearly 25% of all global tweets at that particular moment. (See Figure 3.4.)[10] Understanding elements of how to manage this amplification is a key component of the new leadership paradigm, and is established later in this chapter and throughout the book.

SOCIAL MEDIA VELOCITY

In addition to speed and amplification, there is a third component necessary to fully understand how social media are instantaneous. In a physical sense velocity is defined as how far something travels (distance) over a given period of time. For instance, automobiles maintain odometers that report velocity as mileage per hour (mph). However, some social media experts have applied this general concept to social media. Specifically, social media velocity has been defined as the "measurement of how fast an idea, embed, widget or other like unit spreads over web properties . . . [that are] benchmarked over time."[11] This measurement reflects relevancy when the velocity accelerates or decelerates about a particular issue or concept.[11]

Figure 3.4 Apple co-founder Steve Jobs and former Russian President Dmitri Medvedev looked at an iPhone 4. (From President of the Russian Federation (www.kremlin.ru)/Unknown. With permission.)

WHAT IS . . . SOCIAL MEDIA VELOCITY

Social media velocity is a leadership concept that evaluates relevancy by measuring how fast a social media unit (e.g., idea, widget, concept, etc.) spreads through social media outlets such as Facebook, Twitter, and various blogs. This is an important consideration for emergency managers to measure as they seek out validation for response actions.

For emergency managers and other disaster response managers, understanding this velocity is important particularly during an emergency or disaster. For example, during the April 2011 tornadoes that affected much of the southeastern United States there were widespread needs for community support and mass care in various areas (see Figure 3.5). During the response and recovery phases, needs of the community shifted and changed from day to day to include home needs, basic childcare needs (e.g., diapers, formula), emergency food stamps, sheltering, food, and other items. Some organizations such as Toomers for Tuscaloosa were able to leverage certain hashtags (e.g., #alneeds) to monitor the acceleration and deceleration of these incident needs

Figure 3.5 Damage from the widespread tornadoes that affected much of the southeast United States. (From FEMA/Christopher Mardouf. With permission.)

and adjust volunteer and donation management to better address the requirements of the event.

This amplification of social media information is also facilitated by the overlapping and integration of one social media system with another. Many social media systems (particularly those with media formatting such as YouTube) have built-in sharing features for social networks and microblogging sites including Facebook and Twitter, respectively. Likewise, many traditional news outlets and other online media have sharing buttons that allow for cross-linking to other sites that are socially connected. These built-in share buttons are easily integrated and encourage amplification by allowing easier access to social systems and thus the distribution of information.

TRADITIONAL MEDIA VALIDATION

Because of the instantaneous nature of social media information and the prime ability to exchange information in a timely manner that is quickly amplified, traditional media outlets have wholly embraced the functionality of social media as a primary method to gather and disseminate information during a newsworthy event. Traditional media formats such as newspapers, radio, and television have now integrated Twitter, Facebook, YouTube, and various other social media outlets into information gathering (e.g., reporting technology) and dissemination (e.g., websites) tools to ensure that news can be quickly shared and amplified by users and followers. In some cases, traditional media have safely integrated their social media content to where the models presented are blended or solely social.

Before the rise of social media, there were four major types of media: print, radio, television, and the Internet. With the printing of 200 Bibles in 1452 by Johannes Gutenberg on the first printing press, the concept of print media was initiated.[12] Over the next several hundred years printed periodicals such as newspapers, magazines, flyers, and various other types of print media were developed and distributed at various intervals to communities typically geographically centered around the location of the physical printing. This model of news distribution remained the sole source of distributed news until the late nineteenth century with the invention of the radio.

HISTORY OF TRADITIONAL MEDIA

59 BC – Julius Caesar has "Act Diurna" (Daily Events) posted daily around Rome.[13]

1452 – Invention of the printing press by Johannes Gutenberg.[13]

1690 – First American newspaper, *Publick Occurrences*, appears in Boston.[13]

1896 – Guglielmo Marconi granted the first patent for the radio.[14]

1920 – Pittsburgh station KDKA is issued first commercial radio license.[14]

1928 – The Federal Radio Commission issues the first television station license as W3XK.[15]

1933 – Edwin Armstrong is granted patent for frequency modulation (FM).[14]

1936 – There are 200 televisions in the world.[16]

1937 – Station W1XOJ becomes the first experimental FM radio station.[14]

1941 – FCC releases first standards for black and white television.[16]

1948 – Cable television is first introduced in Pennsylvania to help reach rural communities.[14]

1951 – The first computer is sold commercially.[13]

1967 – Most televisions in the United States are in color.[16]
1980 – Creation of 24/7 Cable News Network (CNN).[17]
1990 – Tim Berners-Lee invents the World Wide Web, HTML structure, and a text browser to engage the Internet.[18]
1994 – The American government releases control of the Internet.[13]
1997 – The term "weblog" is coined to describe online journals.[13]
2003 – The term "podcast" is conceived when certain types of audio files are placed into simple syndication.[13]

Meanwhile radio was developed in multiple forms toward the end of the nineteenth century, with Guglielmo Marconi ultimately granted the first patent and generally considered the father of radio. Over the next half century, radio quickly grew in its use and popularity with the addition of the frequency modulation (FM) option and commercial operations throughout the world. It quickly became the second major provider of information to the world.

By World War II, the television was beginning to be introduced throughout the United States and several other parts of the developing world. Specifically, by 1941, the U.S. Federal Communications Commission (FCC) released a standard for black and white televisions. Within the decade more than one million homes in the United States had television sets. As television's use grew, so did its utilization by news channels and other media outlets. Some historians have suggested that John F. Kennedy won the 1960 Presidential election over Richard Nixon primarily because of how he performed in televised debates. By 1996, there were an estimated one billion television sets throughout the world. See Figure 3.6.

In 1980, businessman and entrepreneur Ted Turner started a television station called the Cable News Network (CNN) that ran news and coverage of national events 24 hours of every day. Within 10 years, CNN had become a national staple as a trusted source that would provide information any time of day, any day of the week.[17] This "24/7" model of news coverage was quickly adopted by most radio, television, and eventually Internet providers. Print media lagged, as the setup and production time were so significant that 24/7 coverage was impossible. In the most ideal situations, print media were able to provide information twice each day. Regardless, media agencies and news wires such as the Associated Press were able to continue to be the primary and in some cases sole source of information related to emergent events.

Figure 3.6 The transition to television was a major shift in how families not only received information, but engaged in the experience of the process. (From National Archives and Records Administration/Unknown. With permission.)

With the advent of the World Wide Web in 1990, the Internet revolution started.[18] Internet pages and various kinds of websites began to be developed and quickly were transitioned for use by organizations and businesses looking for new ways to engage their audiences and customers. Most of these sites were fairly static, primarily utilizing text with some embedded photos. This type of interaction was fairly simple, with individuals having to seek out the website by knowing and engaging the particular Internet web address through a particular browser. Although not identified as such at the time, this type of interface is now referred to as Web 1.0.

In contrast to the Web 1.0 format discussed above, the second version of the web or Web 2.0 was ushered in with the rise of social media. As discussed in Chapter 1, the first successful social media outlet was Friendster, which was started back in 2002. Many other sites quickly followed, with MySpace, Facebook, and Twitter getting started in 2004, 2004, and 2006, respectively. Although these sites also were engaged through specific web addresses, they allowed for push and pull engagement where notifications of internal system actions could be driven to the users as well as the users seeking that information at their discretion. As has already been discussed and is evaluated in the chapters to come, this shift toward Web 2.0 style engagement revolutionarily changed how people engaged in information and news, particularly during emergencies and disasters.

BEYOND 24/7

Because of this information shift, many news agencies quickly adapted their output mechanisms to include not only websites, but social media systems such as microblogs and social networking to both monitor event activities and push critical information. Because social media sites require no setup and delivery time (unlike the traditional media of newspapers and television studios), the time it takes to push information to the general public has now exceeded the 24/7 model established by the constant news channels such as CNN, FoxNews, and MSNBC. In the past, this news cycle has been suggested to be a 60/60 news cycle, where information must be distributed and shared 60 seconds of every minute and 60 minutes of every hour.[19] Regardless of what it is ultimately called, it is clear there is a fundamental shift in how traditional news engages emergent information.

In addition, many media outlets—particularly those driven by photos and videos—have begun to embrace an altered standard in quality. Specifically, because of the instantaneous need and expectation for information about emergent events, most media outlets were not able to provide staff or equipment to the emergency scene in a timely manner. Consequently, professional media quickly realized that no matter where an event occurs there will be eyewitnesses, citizens, and other bystanders who are close to the scene and able to share information, photos, and videos with the news agencies. To facilitate this, many media organizations (particularly television outlets), have established areas on their websites and social networks to allow for citizen-generated content (e.g., CNN's iReport).[20] Although this process has improved the traditional delivery of news, it has also created questionable uses of incident information (e.g., pictures of dead bodies) for the sake of faster delivery of information.

One of the best examples of this phenomenon was the so-called "Miracle on the Hudson" which occurred during the emergency landing of US Airways flight 1549 in New York's Hudson River in 2009. In this particular event, Captain Chesley "Sully" Sullenberger and his crew successfully landed the Airbus A320 in the Hudson River with 150 souls on board. In the end, there were no deaths and only limited injuries. The defining imaging of this event was a picture taken by Janis Krums, a Florida marketer who happened to be in New York walking near the river when the plane went down. He quickly snapped photos of the plane in the water and posted them to Twitter via TwitPic. Because major media outlets were monitoring Twitter, they quickly found Mr. Krums' photo and began to use it as primary information about the crash. Likewise, they contacted and interviewed him repeatedly throughout the day as a key witness to the amazing events. Only later did professional media crews arrive and begin to cover the response activities related to the "Miracle on the Hudson."[20] Now information such as Mr. Krums' picture is commonplace and accepted for all primary sources and helps create and feed the instantaneous nature of social media.

OPENING THE BOX: THE DEATH OF NEWSPAPERS

Newspapers, magazines, and other print periodicals were truly the first major source of news and community information that was shared in America and countries throughout the world. The first newspaper published in America was called *Publick Occurrences*. It was published by Richard Pierce and edited by Benjamin Harris. Its first and only issue was released September 25, 1690, and filled only three sheets of paper measuring six by ten inches (roughly half of the front page of a modern newspaper; see Figure 3.7). Nearly 14 years later, John Campbell, postmaster of Boston, became the editor of the *Boston News-Letter* which became a weekly periodical of news and community interests. The *Boston News-Letter* became the *Boston Gazette,* and then later the *New England Courant,* as publishers and ownership changed hands and legal control of entities and names became muddled.

Printing methodologies were decidedly slow and inconsistent, as they were based on the printing techniques developed by Johannes Gutenberg more than 250 years before. By the early 1800s, printing technology improved with the use of continuous rolls of paper along the traditional press. This development created added efficiency in printing with a tremendous drop in the per unit costs and the development of the so-called "penny press." This phrase actually originated when the *New York Sun* dropped its price to a penny per copy in 1833. This change created the first true mass medium due to its availability and price.[26]

Starting at this point, newspapers became commonplace throughout the country with editions available in most cities throughout the world and with some major cities maintaining multiple editions (e.g., morning and afternoon). Journalists supported various community components including politics, government, sports, entertainment, lifestyles, investigative reporting, and much more. Major world events were reported via print publications, including activities such as the *Washington Post's* investigation of the Watergate scandal, Truman's defeat of Dewey, the Japanese attacks on Pearl Harbor, and many others.

However, as technologies such as television, and later the Internet and social media, rose in prominence so did the speed and pace of the delivery of news and emergent information. Circulation of newspapers and other print media forms slowly declined in the 1990s and precipitously in the 2000s. The major turning point came in 2009 when two major newspapers, the *Rocky Mountain News* and the *Seattle Post-Intelligencer*, shut down with little notice.[27] These closings and many more afterward led to more than 2,900 and 4,100 newspaper layoffs in 2010 and 2011, respectively.[28,29] A 2012 report by the USC Annenberg Center for the Digital Future states that "Circulation of print newspapers continues to plummet . . . [and] the only print newspapers that will survive will be at the extremes of the medium—the largest and smallest," with most newspapers being completely "dead" in the next five years.[30]

Ultimately, newspapers were a highly effective medium for the transportation of information when speed was not part of the equation. However, as other media presented options that were faster and now nearly instantaneous, newspapers not only became an inferior option, but ultimately began to disappear. Emergency managers must be aware of this type of shift in the types of information used and how fast the information is processed to ensure major mistakes are not made with emergency management going the way of the newspaper.

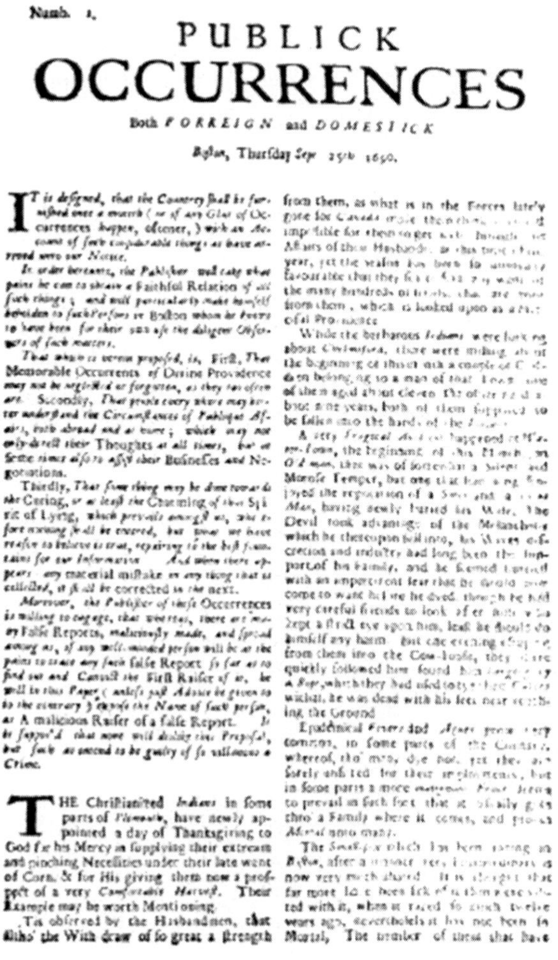
Numb. 1.

PUBLICK
OCCURRENCES

Both FORREIGN and DOMESTICK

Boston, Thursday Sept. 25th. 1690.

IT is designed, that the Countrey shall be furnished once a moneth (or if any Glut of Occurrences happen, oftener,) with an Account of such considerable things as have arrived unto our Notice.

In order hereunto, the Publisher will take what pains he can to obtain a Faithful Relation of all such things; and will particularly make himself beholden to such Persons in Boston whom he knows to have been for their own use the diligent Observers of such matters.

That which is herein proposed, is, First, That Memorable Occurrents of Divine Providence may not be neglected or forgotten, as they too often are. Secondly, That people every where may better understand the Circumstances of Publique Affairs, both abroad and at home; which may not only direct their Thoughts at all times, but at some times also to assist their Businesses and Negotiations.

Thirdly, That some thing may be done towards the Curing, or at least the Charming of that Spirit of Lying, which prevails amongst us, wherefore nothing shall be entered, but what we have reason to believe is true, repairing to the best fountains for our Information. And when there appears any material mistake in any thing that is collected, it shall be corrected in the next.

Moreover, the Publisher of these Occurrences is willing to engage, that whereas, there are many False Reports, maliciously made, and spread among us, if any well-minded person will be at the pains to trace any such false Report so far as to find out and Convict the First Raiser of it, he will in this Paper (unless just Advice be given to the contrary) expose the Name of such person, as A malicious Raiser of a false Report. It is suppos'd that none will dislike this Proposal, but such as intend to be guilty of so villanous a Crime.

THE Christianized Indians in some parts of Plimouth, have newly appointed a day of Thanksgiving to God for his Mercy in supplying their extream and pinching Necessities under their late want of Corn, & for His giving them now a prospect of a very Comfortable Harvest. Their Example may be worth Mentioning.

'Tis observed by the Husbandmen, that altho' the With draw of so great a strength

Figure 3.7 A copy of *Publick Occurrences,* the first newspaper published in the United States. (From unknown source.)

TECHNOLOGICAL CHANGES

In addition to philosophical and structural changes that contribute to the instantaneous nature and expectation of social media, technological changes and adaptations have also affected this capability. For example, according to a recent survey, more than 50% of those sampled had received breaking news from social media via mobile devices. Likewise, 46% of those surveyed had received information via online sources about emergencies and disasters. Depending on the source, social media outlets are routinely noted as the second or third most popular source for news and emergent information. Events such as the Egyptian uprising (2011), Mumbai terrorist attacks (2008), British royal wedding announcement (2010), Osama Bin Laden's death (2011), Whitney Houston's death (2012), and many other major new events first broke via social media channels such as Facebook, Twitter, and YouTube.[21] See Figure 3.8.

This mobile engagement occurs through smartphones and tablet devices. According to a 2011 Pew Internet survey, nearly 35% of American adults own smartphones.[22] This number jumped to 46% in 2012.[23] It is interesting that 41% of Americans reported having cell phones that were not smartphones, which means that smartphones are more pervasive

Figure 3.8 Major international events such as the death of terrorist and 9/11 mastermind Osama Bin Laden were first announced on social media systems such as Twitter. (From U.S. Federal Bureau of Investigation/Unknown. With permission.)

than traditional cell phones in America.[23] The prevalence and growth in the use of smartphones is even higher in Europe according to some sources.[24] For example, 87% of smartphone users access the Internet or e-mail via their device, with 68% doing so on a daily basis.[22] This Internet access (either through browser or phone app) allows access to a variety of social media sites including Facebook, Twitter, YouTube, Tumblr, WordPress, and many more. With interaction and access to mobile data literally at their fingertips, citizens instantaneously can report, observe, comment, and provide eyewitness media such as photos and videos to any observed event.

In addition to the access to social media outlets, the use of all cellular devices for text messaging is also significant. Text messaging allows for individuals to send 140-character (or less) messages to each other utilizing small packets of information. This exchange of messages occurs in real-time, often in a conversational format of question and answer between the two parties involved. This process has grown significantly since its introduction with the mobile cellular phone in the 1990s. For instance, according to a 2011 Pew Internet study, more than 73% of adult cell phone users utilized their phones for text messaging at least occasionally. Moreover, text messaging users send or receive an average of 41.5 messages per day, with the median user sending or receiving 10 texts each day.[22] In both cases, this number has significantly increased since 2010 and continues to rise each year as the use and availability of text messaging through mobile devices becomes nearly ubiquitous.

Because of this nearly instantaneous interchange, many businesses and organizations have begun to leverage this type of technology, both commercially and via social media, to provide information in real-time to customers and constituents. See Figure 3.9. Some emergency management organizations have begun to leverage this technology as well, but it is often expensive to implement fully. For example, the city of Philadelphia utilizes a community alerting system to notify the public. Unfortunately for emergency management leaders, the public expectation for not only utilizing this technology, but also engaging at a pace that is quick and nearly instantaneous is growing exponentially. The overwhelming utilization of technologies such as social media and texting are grossly challenging when, where, and how emergency managers at all levels of government and across all disciplines must engage their constituency to prepare communities for the hazards they face.

Figure 3.9 Disaster survivors routinely utilize mobile devices to access social media systems to receive and share information during disasters. (From FEMA/David Fine. With permission.)

DIGITAL ALTRUISM

The emergency management community has long seen the value of engaging the public in the processes that ready a community for an emergency or disaster. Unfortunately, this philosophy has been focused on internal considerations, including how this engagement should be controlled or influenced to reap predetermined results that support current preparedness considerations. Clearly, this type of internally focused approach is time-intensive and difficult to manage when a significant number of people are engaged in the process or event. Consequently, one of the major changes related to the instantaneous nature of social media is the rise of digital altruism.

Digital altruism is a loose process that modifies traditional emergency management volunteerism by incorporating emerging technologies in nonspecific geographic locations. Traditionally, emergency managers leverage local and spontaneous volunteers physically in the affected environment to do basic response and recovery activities that can be accomplished with limited training and technical skill. Digital altruism is the polar opposite of this traditional approach. Volunteers from anywhere in the world come together to supplement technological infrastructure and communication systems to facilitate emergency response and recovery needs. Moreover, this nonspecific geographic assistance is often outside the review, approval, and commission of formal emergency management and response processes within the community. This fact has been one of the most controversial for emergency management leaders attempting to adapt to social technologies.

This digital altruism has been extremely effective at supporting affected communities. For example, after the April 2011 outbreak of tornadoes in Alabama, a digital altruism group called Toomers for Tuscaloosa quickly arose with more than 80,000 followers on Facebook discussing and coordinating the exchange of basic needs items like food, water, diapers, and shelter (see Figure 3.10). In comparison, the State of Alabama Emergency Management Agency only had slightly more than 3,000 followers at the time and struggled to find ways to quickly and adequately address basic needs in the local community that were brought up via the social media sites. Much as did newspapers mentioned earlier, the State of Alabama struggled to maintain the speed of information exchange that the public was expecting. The Toomers for Tuscaloosa digital altruism group quickly filled the needs gap by facilitating both organizational and peer-to-peer response at the nearly instantaneous pace necessary. The possibility of this type of collaboration and magnification of response is further discussed in Chapters 6 and 7.

Figure 3.10 The significance of the widespread damage from the tornadoes that affected Alabama in April 2011 resulted in the rise of volunteerism groups such as Toomers for Tuscaloosa. (From FEMA/Christopher Mardouf. With permission.)

DEDICATED STAFF AND RESOURCES

One of the only solutions to address the challenges of the instantaneous nature of social media is for emergency management leaders to find ways to dedicate staff and resources to engage their constituency before, during, and after emergencies and disasters. Although the most direct method to address this is to hire or dedicate full-time emergency management staff to address social media issues, this may not always be a possibility. This may create an initial connectivity with the social media community, but it is not a sustainable solution to the constant engagement considered and expected by the general public.

If full-time staff are to be considered, a more manageable option is to incorporate the use of social media into the functions of each available staff member so as to ensure that social media engagement can be maintained during all phases of emergency management and facilitate the exchange and monitoring of information for incident intelligence. For example, in 2012, Philadelphia's police department implemented a new strategy of allowing a small contingent of field officers to tweet while on duty about the policing activities currently being conducted.[32] Not only was this a cost-effective alternative to limiting communications to one (or two) staff members, it gave a genuine "face" to the information being shared via social media.

There are two challenges to this particular model. The first is that the number of emergency management professionals engaged and comfortable with social media technologies is growing, but still relatively limited. Instituting this level of resource dedication would require a commitment to education, training, and exercises that is currently unprecedented. It would need to parallel commitment levels with communications interoperability, GIS integration, and other similar critical functions. The second challenge to this implementation strategy is that it is not possible in smaller emergency management organizations that may only support one full-time staff person. This is a challenge that cannot and will not be overcome by hiring additional staff or distributing duties.

Consequently, additional committed resources will only be available through the use of general or technical volunteers to support a local emergency management function. Locally trained volunteers such as Community Emergency Response Teams (CERT), Medical Reserve Corps, amateur radio operators, or other similarly trained emergency volunteers could be leveraged to maintain support for the instantaneous conversations and exchange of information necessary during emergencies and disasters. Alternatively, technical volunteers (similar to the locally trained volunteers mentioned above) can be leveraged not only after an event, but before it as well. One example of this is the Virtual Operations Support Team (VOST) concept first introduced by Jeff Phillips, an emergency manager from Los Ranchos, New Mexico. Phillips states that VOST is the creation of "a virtual team whose focus is to establish and monitor social media communication, manage communication channels with the public, and handle matters that can be executed remotely through digital means."[31] This type of approach has been very effective in regional and major disasters and is growing in popularity and use among forward-leaning emergency management and preparedness organizations. Although not the only model, this is certainly a strong model for smaller organizations who struggle with the dedication of staff and resources necessary to fulfill the need for speed.

DIGITAL OPERATIONS CENTER

The most profound adaptation yet adopted to address the instantaneous nature of social media and its impact on the exchange of information during real-time events is the establishment of a digital operations center. Some private companies such as Dell and Gatorade have leveraged social media command centers to monitor activity about the quality and brand of their company, however, the utilization of this type of digital operations center was first widely recognized during the 2012 Super Bowl, when the National Football League (NFL) used analysts and technology specialists to monitor digital engagement related to the game and brand on social media systems including Facebook and Twitter. The NFL utilized a 2,800 square foot space in downtown Indianapolis (location of the game), which was activated on the Monday before the game and was operational throughout the week. More than 20 people supported the activity for more than 15 hours per day. From an infrastructure standpoint, the social media command center utilized more than one mile of Ethernet cable and more than 150 square feet of networked screen space.[33]

The first of this kind of center within the emergency management community was the digital operations center that was announced by the American Red Cross in early 2012. In partnership with Dell, the American Red Cross dedicated space within their Washington, DC headquarters to monitor social activities 24/7 using volunteers and trained personnel. Among their many methods to monitor social media, the American Red Cross's Digital Operations Center primarily focused on utilizing heat maps, community profiles, keyword growth, and the volume of conversation over the observed time. At the time of the announcement of the new center, the American Red Cross stated that the goal was, "To be informed by and to become a social liaison for people, families, and communities to support one another before, during, and after disasters."[34]

Although a very new concept in the monitoring and engagement of social media, there is a strong possibility that digital operations centers will be highly effective options for monitoring and engaging social media systems at the instantaneous pace expected. Unfortunately, much as with the approach of dedicating staff to addressing social media, the capability of establishing a digital operations center is impractical if not an impossibility for average emergency management organizations. Many of these jurisdictions already struggle to maintain and support emergency operations centers (EOCs), much less additional facilities that are formatted in a similar way. The key to this may be how the American Red Cross (and other response agencies) utilizes volunteers to magnify the results and efficiency of social media monitoring. Clearly, a one-size-fits-all option is not available for such monitoring in an attempt to address the instantaneous nature of social media. However, it is equally evident that the problem is real and must be addressed by leaders today and tomorrow as emergency management continues to address the implementation of social media before, during, and after emergencies.

LEADERS IN THE OPEN: TODD JASPER

Todd Jasper is an emergency management and strategic planning consultant who has supported planning and preparedness for organizations at all levels of government with a particular focus on federal government agencies and private sector organizations. He is also certified as a Master Professional Continuity Practitioner, Master Exercise Practitioner, and Master Training Practitioner. Todd is active in social media and a charter member of the Emerging Technology Caucus of the International Association of Emergency Managers (IAEM). In the following essay written for this book, Mr. Jasper discusses the economics of information in emergencies.

The Informational Black Market

Todd Jasper

Since the beginning of time, humans in emergency situations have required information quickly. Indeed, studies have shown that when seconds count and life is potentially threatened, information can be more valuable than food or water. With the advent of social media (including all technology and systems that enable rapid information exchange among a network of individuals), the way society seeks and collects information in an emergency has changed significantly.

Social scientists call the natural response to want to learn more about an immediate threat or emergency "information-seeking behavior." Information-seeking behavior is changing to include reliance on social media. As social media proliferate, it is evident that information-seeking behavior and the information collection process are shifting to favor more immediate (but potentially less reliable or accurate) information.

During emergencies, there is an overwhelming demand for quick information. People want to know if they are in danger, how to get to a safe area, and even learn from mistakes other people have made. Using the standard economics supply and demand model, during an emergency we can see that there is a deficit of supply of information at the same time that demand is surging. Under normal circumstances (equilibrium), demand is met by adequate supply. But emergencies are clearly not normal circumstances.

During emergencies, there is an initial lack of information as provided by traditional media. For instance, if a fire were to start in an occupied building, its occupants would be forced to seek immediate information about the incident. Traditional media journalists may have heard about the fire and might be en route, but no actionable information would be available to the building's occupants via traditional media. Naturally, in the period of time until traditional, trusted media reports are available, people are now turning to more immediate forms of information via social media. During information deficits in emergencies, social media are filling the void.

In other words, the immediacy of emergencies tends to create a black market for information, and social media act to fill the void. Social media have been successful as an alternative to traditional media. For example, the U.S. eastern seaboard was jolted by an earthquake in August 2011. As the tremor moved away from its point of origin in Virginia, people in New York received tweets about the earthquake in the seconds before they felt the earthquake themselves. Twitter estimates that approximately 40,000 tweets were sent per minute during the earthquake (over 600 per second). The media were quick to report the earthquake, but social media were even faster.

Crisis and emergency managers are accustomed to press releases and interviews with traditional news media, but the market is casting its vote for immediate information. As information-seeking behavior shifts to favor more rapid social media, the emergency management field must adopt risk communication and crisis communication strategies that include social media or risk irrelevance. See Figure 3.11.

In fact, as technology improves, the definition of immediate notification is changing as well. Prior to the horrific Virginia Tech massacre, few campuses had adopted text messaging for notifications. Just 10 years prior, notification was usually made using bulletin boards in residence halls. Following the Virginia Tech massacre, the U.S. Department of Education fined the school over $50,000 because it failed to notify its students and staff of the initial shootings on a timely basis.

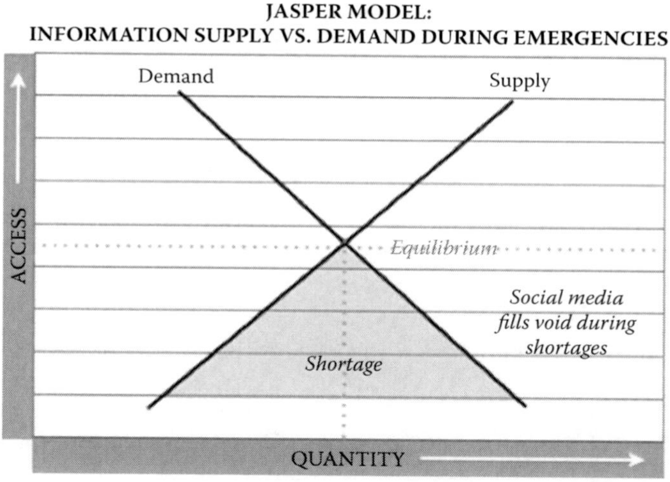

JASPER MODEL:
INFORMATION SUPPLY VS. DEMAND DURING EMERGENCIES

Figure 3.11 The "Jasper Model of Information Economics" states that supply and demand have a specific relationship to each other especially during a disaster. (From Todd Jasper. With permission.)

94

Expectations and information-seeking behavior are changing. As the emergency management field learns to gauge the new information marketplace better, it is easy to misunderstand how competitive social media can be. In the new marketplace, speed is allowed to trump accuracy, spelling, and even formality. As a lesson learned post-Virginia Tech, St. John's University in New York had an incident with a male carrying a gun on campus. The university issued a text alert. Their text message was sent soon after the first report of the gunman: "From public safety. Male was found on campus with a rifle. Please stay in your buildings until further notice. He is in custody, but please wait until the all-clear." According to the Associated Press, "At St. John's, the [text] 'messages were sent so quickly that a student who helped subdue the suspect felt his cell phone vibrate with the information while he was restraining the gunman.'"

In the new information marketplace, emergency managers are responsible for being entrepreneurial. The emergency manager of the future will have to understand how to engage constituents via social media, sometimes in the middle of an emergency. It is no longer enough to just passively send out press releases during an emergency or hours later. Consumers of information want to interact with those who are sending the information. Indeed, with the development of the "Whole Community" approach and with the National Preparedness Goal establishing "Public Warning and Information" as a core competency across all NIMS phases, it is clear that the emergency management field is moving toward embracing new technology to communicate more openly and rapidly with our constituencies.

The information marketplace is a competition of information. Some information may be incorrect, some information may be rumor, and other postings may even be malicious misinformation (intended to complicate or worsen emergency response). This new marketplace can be strange and daunting, but the emergency management field is currently in the process of recognizing that it cannot sit on the sidelines as consumers turn to social media during emergencies.

The future of successful emergency management includes shaping discourse, rumor management, and engaging with the community when they need information quickly. In the new marketplace of information, emergency management must be prepared for the awesome demand from modern information consumers. When seconds

count and traditional media are absent, the right information provided immediately may mean the difference between life and death.

ENDNOTES

1. Godin, Seth. (2008) "Gravity Is Just a Theory." Seth Godin's Blog.http://
   sethgodin.typepad.com/seths_blog/2008/12/gravity-is-just.html. Accessed
   April 16, 2012.
2. Olanoff, Drew. (2012) "Most Viewed US Program Ever, Super Bowl
   46, Had 13.7 Million Tweets." TheNextWeb. http://thenextweb.com/
   socialmedia/2012/02/06/highest-rated-us-television-program-ever-super-
   bowl-46-saw-13-7m-related-tweets/. Accessed April 19, 2012.
3. "States Ranked by Size and Population." (2012) iPl2. http://www.ipl.org/
   div/stateknow/popchart.html. Accessed April 19, 2012.
4. Olivaraz-Giles, Nathan. (2012) Super Bowl XLVI sets new tweet-per-second
   record. *LA Times*. http://www.latimes.com/business/technology/la-twitter-
   super-bowl-46-new-york-giants-new-england-patriots-eli-manning-tom-
   brady-madonna-20120206,0,1184572.story. Accessed April 19, 2012.
5. Dugan, Lauren. (2012) "The Oscars on Twitter: 18,718 Tweets Per Second
   Record." Media Bistro. http://www.mediabistro.com/alltwitter/the-oscars-
   on-twitter-18718-tweets-per-second-record-but-dwarfed-by-grammys_
   b19005. Accessed April 19, 2012.
6. Weil, Kevin. (2010) "Measuring Tweets." Twitter Blog. http://blog.twitter.
   com/2010/02/measuring-tweets.html. Accessed April 19, 2012.
7. Hajj, Flemings. (2012) "#WhitneyHouston's Impact on Twitter."
   Black Enterprise. http://www.blackenterprise.com/2012/02/15/whitney-
   houstons-death-impact-on-twitter/. Accessed April 19, 2012.
8. "Tweets Per Second." (2011) Twitter Blog. http://yearinreview.twitter.com/
   en/tps.html. Accessed April 19, 2012.
9. Stelter, Brian. (2011) How the Bin Laden annoucement leaked out.
   New York Times. http://mediadecoder.blogs.nytimes.com/2011/05/01/
   how-the-osama-announcement-leaked-out/. Accessed April 20, 2012.
10. McGuire, Seth. (2011) "Why Traders Use Social Media: Speed &
    Amplification." GNIP Blog. http://blog.gnip.com/why-traders-use-social-
    media-speed-amplification/. Accessed April 21, 2012.
11. Owyang, Jeremiah. (2008) "Social Media Measuring Attribution:
    Defining Velocity." Web Strategy Blog. http://www.web-strategist.com/
    blog/2008/03/06/social-media-measurement-velocity/. Accessed April 21,
    2012.
12. "Johnannes Gutenberg." (2007) Media History Project. http://www.
    mediahistory.umn.edu/timeline/gallery/gutenb.html. Accessed April 22,
    2012.

13. Andrlik, Todd. (2012) "A Brief History of Traditional and Social Media." ToddAnd Blog. http://toddand.com/2006/11/23/a-brief-history-of-traditional-and-social-media/. Accessed April 22, 2012.

14. "A History of Radio." (2012) Voices.com. http://www.voices.com/articles/broadcast-radio/marconi-to-today-100-years-of-radio. Accessed April 23, 2012.

15. "The Invention of Television." (2012) About.com Inventors. http://inventors.about.com/od/tstartinventions/a/Television_Time_3.htm. Accessed April 23, 2012.

16. "Important Dates in Television History." (n.d.) Chicago Entertainment Law. http://www.entertainmentlawchicago.com/introbroad/Important%20Dates%20in%20Television%20History.pdf. Accessed April 24, 2012.

17. "Cable News Network." (2012) The Museum of Broadcast Communications. www.museum.tv/eotvsection.php. Accessed April 25, 2012.

18. "A Brief History of the World Wide Web." (2011) University of North Carolina— Pembroke. www.uncp.edu/home/acurtis/courses/resourcesforcourses/webhistory.html. Accessed April 25, 2012.

19. Crowe, Adam. (2012) Disasters 2.0: *The Application of Social Media in Emergency Management*. Boca Raton, FL: CRC Press.

20. "CNN iReport." (2011) CNN. www.ireport.cnn.com. Accessed April 25, 2012.

21. Laird, Sam. (2012) "How Social Media is Taking Over the News Industry." Mashable. www.mashable.com/2012/04/18/social-media-and-the-news. Accessed April 25, 2012.

22. Smith, Aaron. (2011) "Smartphone Adoption and Usage." Pew Internet. http://pewinternet.org/Reports/2011/Smartphones.aspx. Accessed April 26, 2012.

23. Siwicki, Bill. (2012) "Smartphone Adoptions Soars to 46% in February." Internet Retailer. http://www.internetretailer.com/2012/03/01/smartphone-adoption-soars-46-february. Accessed April 26, 2012.

24. Hansberry, Ed. (2012) Smartphone adoption higher in Europe. *InformationWeek*. http://www.informationweek.com/news/mobility/smart_phones/232500674. Accessed April 26, 2012.

25. Plummer, Brad. (2011) Tweets move faster than earthquake. *Washington Post*. http://www.washingtonpost.com/blogs/ezra-klein/post/tweets-move-faster-than-earthquakes/2011/08/25/gIQA4iWHeJ_blog.html. Accessed April 27, 2012.

26. "Newspaper: The History." (n.d.) Oracle Think Quest. http://library.thinkquest.org/18764/print/history.html. Accessed April 28, 2012.

27. Gillin, Paul. (2012) "The Power of One." Newspaper Death Watch. http://newspaperdeathwatch.com/the-power-of-one/. Accessed April 30, 2012.

28. "2010 Layoffs". (n.d.) Papercuts Blog. http://newspaperlayoffs.com/maps/2010-layoffs/. Accessed April 30, 2012.

29. "2011 Layoffs." (n.d.) Papercuts Blog. http://newspaperlayoffs.com/maps/2011-layoffs/. Accessed April 30, 2012.

30. Irvine, Don. (2012) "New Study Predicts the Death of Newspapers in 5 Years." Accuracy in Media. http://www.aim.org/don-irvine-blog/new-study-predicts-the-death-of-newspapers-in-five-years/. Accessed April 30, 2012.
31. Stephens, Kim. (2012) "New Case Study – Virtual Operations Support Teams: Trial by Fire." http://idisaster.wordpress.com/2012/02/24/new-case-study-virtual-operations-support-team-trial-by-fire/. Accessed May 1, 2012.
32. Mulholland, Jessica. (2012) "Philadelphia Police Officers to Start Tweeting at Work." Government Technology. http://www.govtech.com/public-safety/Philadelphia-Police-to-Start-Tweeting-at-Work.html. Accessed May 2, 2012.
33. Laird, Sam. (2012) "Super Bowl XLVI Gets a Social Media Command Center." Mashable. http://mashable.com/2012/01/21/super-bowl-xlvi-social-media/. Accessed May 3, 2012.
34. Stephens, Kim. (2012) "American Red Cross Digital Operations Center: Your Questions, Your Answers." iDisaster Blog. http://idisaster.wordpress.com/2012/03/16/american-red-cross-digital-ops-your-questions-their-answers/. Accessed May 3, 2012.
35. Fitzpatrick, Alex. (2012) "How Twitter Nearly Ruined Obama's Secret Trip to Afghanistan." Mashable. http://mashable.com/2012/05/01/obama-afghanistan-twitter/. Accessed May 15, 2012.

4

Entrepreneurism

Those who fear risk also begin to fear movement of any kind. People act as though . . . the movement of people or ideas or anything else that is unpredictable exposes us to risk, and risk exposes us to failure. The fearful try to avoid collisions, so they avoid movement.

Seth Godin[1]

PUBLIC ADMINISTRATION FLAW

Rarely do governmental operators such as emergency managers and first-responders consider the application of business principles in the operation of their organization. Rather, on the contrary, they tend to run organizations or events based on the sole-source model where only one entity has the knowledge, influence, and power to accomplish a specific task. This model has been studied significantly and is in many ways a fundamental concept of public administration and affairs. Although beneficial in some ways, it creates a leadership perspective that is limited to avoiding a risk-and-reward balance for fear of making mistakes or appearing incapable.

The challenge with the traditional public administration model is that it is fundamentally flawed in many ways. Government is the only entity that can provide governmental services, however, there are numerous jurisdictions that have begun to dabble in the provision of community resources that otherwise might be provided by the private sector (e.g., solid waste services, water supplies, and utility providers; see Figure 4.1). However, when this engagement occurs it is often to the detriment of the greater competitive market and severely limits open competition and the engagement of citizens' capitalistic privilege to choose providers based on supply and demand.

Similar challenges occur when government agencies—including emergency management organizations—attempt to control and manipulate communication systems. Under traditional media approaches, emergency managers have been taught methods of engagement and deference to measure and control (to some degree) when and how a particular media message is disseminated. Although always dicey, the ability to control messages this way is completely eliminated by social media. Government information, particularly during a disaster, can no longer be treated as a sole source controlled only by those in authority.

Figure 4.1 Some community programming such as utility services are often provided by government even though there are private or pseudo-private alternatives that may be driven more by entrepreneurial benefits. (From FEMA/Holly Latimer. With permission.)

Information is freely given and exchanged by those experiencing the event directly, secondarily, and through tertiary means. These citizens and constituents (as traditional media quickly have become) are now the owners of the conversation, where information is exchanged with or without government interaction.

CONSUMER CHOICE

Government represents its constituents and ostensibly wants to engage them in the process, however, it is a far different experience as a constituent than as a customer. When citizens are treated as customers they are provided not only choices of products, but ultimately choices of companies or providers as well. These choices are based on a variety of factors including supply, demand, price, actual quality, perceived quality, location, and customer service just to name a few. If any individual or related combination of these qualities fails to satisfy, or collectively is found to be more satisfactorily provided by another, customers have the opportunity to (and often do) leave to procure their goods from that provider.

To address this consumer choice, businesses have to make significant decisions about how to engage their products with the marketplace. They seek out innovative and attractive options that are cost effective and often new to the marketplace. The risk that is necessary to accomplish this feat is often directly correlated to the potential reward of more customers and more clients (i.e., risk versus reward). This is the fundamental concept of entrepreneurial activities and is a foundational component of social media and the public expectations from social media and similar emerging technologies.

DEFINITION OF ENTREPRENEURSHIP

Entrepreneurship is built around the premise that an operational decision must take risk to receive any outcome that is greater than the components that were input into the process. In the simplest purely financial terms, if $1 is buried in the ground it will still only be $1 when it is dug up. However, if the $1 is invested in a system that has some risk it may result in $0, $5, $10, or more when the investment is liquidated. Clearly, this is oversimplified and only begins to define the complexity that is traditional entrepreneurship. In reality, entrepreneurship is comprised of six characteristics that include measured impacts, opportunity driven, embracing failure, engaging people, constant innovation, and step-by-step success.

CHARACTERISTICS OF ENTREPRENEURSHIP

1. Big idea versus big impact
2. Risk averse versus opportunity driven
3. Embrace failure
4. Step-by-step success
5. Enroll clients
6. Nonstop innovation

In many ways, social media have generalized the expectations and stigma of who and what constitutes entrepreneurism. For instance, a simple idea such as a website asking, "What are you doing?" (Twitter's initial question) and sharing it with your friends now has millions of active users and an estimated $100 million in annual revenue.[3,4] The possibility of small ideas now having equal impact empowers all modern entrepreneurs. Likewise, so many social media systems have built-in access points (advanced programming interfaces or APIs) that any computer programmer (or visionary) with a concept can be an entrepreneur by building another small idea on top of the previous small idea. This cascading phenomenon is not devoid of failures though. Many of these small ideas fail, but these failures continue to help refine thoughts and ideas that were built with a small risk, but big possibilities.

Unfortunately, this type of entrepreneurial social media where efforts are constantly evolving with leveraged risk and reward has not yet been embraced by emergency managers. Because governmental operations such as emergency management functions are often based on little risk, these types of entrepreneurial behaviors are rare. The status quo of a given operation is often what has defined its characteristics for far too long under the guise of "best practices" and "model programming." In almost no case are citizens engaged in leadership and operational decisions of a governmental organization. Moreover, when citizens are engaged it is often through highly measured situations or limited in exposure (e.g., public forums). This contrasts significantly with the growing expectation of the public that they be intimately and actively engaged in the process. Therefore, each component of entrepreneurism must be considered for government adaptation.

BIG IMPACT VERSUS FEAR OF FAILURE

This first foundation of entrepreneurism is the concept of something commonly called the "big idea." Great leaders of innovation and industry including Bill Gates, Henry Ford, Thomas Edison, J. P. Morgan, and others are noted mostly for significant ideas and concepts that they introduced and that were revolutionary for the sociological time or industry in which they were engaged (see Figure 4.2). These big ideas were in reality "big impacts" that leveraged personal, professional, and economic risk to affect the community in ways that did not simply make progress, but facilitated significant leaps in the community or world. The exception to this rule is the so-called "lone genius" who moved and worked so far outside the managed risk spectrum that the results simultaneously were big ideas and ultimately big impacts. An example of the lone genius is someone like Steve Jobs, co-founder of Apple, who certainly ushered in revolutionary changes; they are not necessarily people to copy because they are the exceptions to the rule. The influence of Steve Jobs is not reviewed as entrepreneurship, but is highlighted in Chapter 8 as the influence of creativity and public relations, and is evaluated within the consideration of this new emergency management leadership paradigm.

The second component of entrepreneurism is the incorporation of risk. Most people in the general public assume that an entrepreneur must seek out risk to maximize the possibility of an increased reward.

Figure 4.2   Great leaders of innovation, such as Thomas Edison (pictured), were willing to take risks that could lead to significant rewards rather than simply seek out the one big idea that changes society. (From U.S. Library of Congress/ Unknown. With permission.)

Risk is certainly a component of entrepreneurism, but engaging in risk is driven by opportunities rather than the inherent nature of risk. In other words, entrepreneurs are willing to take risk when the opportunity or potential result creates an opportunity that is ultimately more valuable to the organization or community. This risk-averse, opportunity-driven component is contrasted sharply with the average citizen who is unwilling to take the risk even when an opportunity for a positive outcome is possible.

For example, there was a study conducted by psychologists Jonathan Baron and Ilana Ritov that proposed a hypothetical vaccination decision to the general public. Their study revealed that a majority of participants expressed an unwillingness to vaccinate children against a hypothetical disease that was projected to kill 10 out of 10,000 children when the vaccine itself would kill 5 out of 10,000 through the side effects. Respondents were unwilling to accept any risk from the "commission" of vaccination even if there was an opportunity to actually save five lives[1] (see Figure 4.3). Clearly this is an extreme case that has significant ethical underpinnings that play a part; however, it is this opposing willingness to accept risk when a beneficial opportunity exists that is part of what defines entrepreneurism.

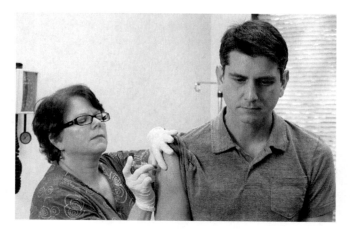

Figure 4.3 Studies have shown participants are occasionally unwilling to engage in activities such as disease prevention through vaccination where risk from commission occurs, but is less than the risk from not taking the vaccination. This type of hesitation is often present among emergency management leaders as well. (From U.S. Centers for Disease Control and Prevention (CDC)/Jordan Douglas, M.A. With permission.)

In addition to the willingness to leverage risk for opportunities, entrepreneurism is also defined by the need to embrace failure. Specifically, those with entrepreneurial tendencies know that every concept, idea, or program developed will not be a success. As established earlier, the inherent risk that is necessary ensures there are no guarantees. If opportunity fails to materialize, loss and failure are strong possibilities and simply provide fertile ground for future opportunistic directions. Thomas Edison is perhaps the most well-known example of this concept. He was quoted as saying: "I have not failed 700 times . . . I have not failed once . . . I have succeeded in proving that those 700 ways will not work . . . when I have eliminated the ways that will not work, I will find the way that will work."[2]

Unfortunately, governmental operators and especially emergency managers do not engage in these components of entrepreneurism with any regularity or skill. Conversely, there is a significant, often paralyzing, fear of failure and mistakes. Much as with the vaccination example mentioned earlier, emergency managers and first-responders often associate leadership mistakes and failure within an overall mission failure, which is most often associated with life safety and property protection. However, the reality is that the risk versus reward balance of emergency management and first-responder decisions is often a collection of individual successes or failures and must be accounted for accordingly. The reality is that these decisions are based on components that have transactional values, which must be understood and established to measure risk and reward in a timely manner.

EMERGENCY MANAGEMENT TRANSACTIONAL VALUES

The conception of transactional value is potentially one of the most accurate yet controversial components in this book. Regardless of the model adopted, the function and purpose of emergency management have products, costs, and losses. The products generated in emergency management are plans, products, programs, and procedures that prepare an organization to support a community to respond and recover from emergencies and disasters. As with traditional products, these emergency management products also have costs. In *Action Trumps Everything: Creating What You Want in an Uncertain World*, these types of costs are defined as money, time, reputation, missed opportunities, and personal/community time.[5] Likewise, there are losses from these products due to insufficient planning, misappropriated resources, and other secondary causes. The challenge for emergency managers is determining how to gauge whether these products are profitable in light of these identified costs and losses.

Profitability for emergency managers can be defined as more than simply by traditional financial measures. Although certainly there are financial elements in emergency management (e.g. local budgets, grants, etc.), they poorly reflect the true spectrum of how transaction value should be measured. According to Seth Godin, profitability can be measured as the equity stored in cultural, social, and community components.[6] These various types of profitability and equity are of value and benefit to a community without any direct costs. For example, when local government organizations invest in areas or facilities in the community that are otherwise undervalued or considered a blight on the community, the value to the community is increased for a variety of reasons including real estate values and community pride, among others.

On the other end of the spectrum is the necessary and acceptable loss that is inherently tied to the possibility of profitability. Within emergency management, there is a variety of potential losses that help comprise this equation, but essentially they are based on the foundations of emergency management and crisis response: protection and preservation of life and property. All plans, procedures, trainings, exercises, mutual aid agreements, and other planning and preparedness components are ultimately centered on these two goals. However, in reality, no level of planning and preparedness can ever fully achieve these goals. In other words, emergencies and disasters will continue to happen with some loss of life and effect on property (e.g., no walls can be built strong enough to stop a hurricane). Although extraordinarily unfortunate, this reality is part of the threat of manmade and natural disasters. The question is what level of personal and property impact is acceptable to community emergency managers.

Unfortunately, the vast majority of emergency management professionals are unwilling to acknowledge or admit that there is some effective line. Rather a majority of traditional emergency management professionals would push an increasing amount of costs—both financial and metaphorical—in an attempt to improve the readiness of their community and reduce the number of lives affected. The problem with this approach is that it is an asymptotic model. In mathematics, asymptotes are curved lines that approach other lines in a reducing fashion without ever touching that line. Seth Godin explains the business application of this concept in his book *Linchpin*. He describes a widget manufacturer who generates one error in every 10 manufactured widgets who invests an insignificant amount of money in the operation to improve efficiency to one error in every 100. This level of increased productivity is worth the cost. If this process is continued to improve efficiency to one in 1,000, then one in 10,000, then one in 100,000, with costs exponentially increasing, the question has to be asked whether the improved efficiency creates added value considering the growing costs for only minor improvements. Thus there must become an acceptable amount of loss or error for the organization.[7]

This is true for emergency managers as well. Equipment, resources, and personnel time can be poured into activities to improve planning and preparedness and reduce loss of life and the impact on preparedness. However, at some point, there is an asymptotic return on this investment that ultimately is not worth the effort. Property often has a discrete value that is covered by insurance (either commercial or governmental) for replacement or repair. Likewise, many people would argue that an individual life is priceless and therefore every effort must be made to save and protect it. But in practical terms this statement is erroneous. Individuals and families routinely take out life insurance policies that provide a certain amount of money to identified beneficiaries. Moreover, according to a 2008 *Time Magazine* report, insurance providers and governmental agents often value a life at approximately $50,000 per quality year of life. Similarly, a Stanford University student reported that this value should be closer to $129,000.[8] Regardless, it is clear that there are real and practical financial values to a human life.

One emergency management methodology that lowers the costs of localized personnel, equipment, and resources is the application of technological volunteer groups such as Crisis Commons, Humanity Road, and Virtual Operations Support Team (VOST). This type of approach eliminates the need for local infrastructure, personnel, and associated costs by utilizing volunteers across a nonspecific geographic area and often outside the jurisdiction of primary response. This can help shift the equilibrium between needs and costs and potentially allow local resources to be refocused on more critical local issues on which technology has little to no impact. These components are further discussed in Chapter 7, when a broader consideration of collaboration is considered.

EMBRACING FAILURE

Entrepreneurs in all fields acknowledge that failure is a significant part of any current or future entrepreneurial success. It is an important consideration for emergency managers to adopt this principle. In application for emergency management, failure is again measured against the prism of saving lives and protecting property. Major failures in emergency response litter the history of disasters, particularly since the rise of the Federal Emergency Management Agency and the contemporary era of emergency management in 1979.[9] In some ways public perception about emergency management activities are almost completely defined by perceived failures such as Hurricane Katrina, the Fukushima Daiichi nuclear power plant meltdown, and the Deepwater Horizon oil spill (see Figure 4.4). Emergency response disciplines of all kinds have learned from these mistakes, but in truth these changes were often embraced begrudgingly due to sweeping legislative changes, unfunded mandates, and difficult implementation.

In reality, the truly opportunistic failures of entrepreneurism when applied to emergency management are at smaller levels. Those failures of preparedness can be in campaigning, training programming, planning teams, and a variety of products as discussed earlier. Social media systems and utilization apply to this principle. Thousands of different social media systems have been developed in the last 10 years, with nearly as many being shuttered or funneled into niche social engagement areas. However, the best and worst components and characteristics of these systems are quickly identified and incorporated or eliminated from newer versions.

Figure 4.4 Major disasters such as the Deepwater Horizon oil spill often affect public perception about the effectiveness of formalized emergency management activities. (From U.S. Coast Guard/Unknown. With permission.)

Figure 4.5 Emergency plans often stay "in process" or as a "living document" to avoid legal concerns about the finality of the document rather than to ensure a dynamic and efficient process. (From FEMA/Savannah Brehmer. With permission.)

This type of step-by-step growth, where small steps are built upon small failures, is vital for emergency managers to understand. Likewise, social media developers and users do not wait for the system to be wholly perfected. Rather, a smaller and more manageable version of the product is introduced into the system with ongoing changes and updates happening as quickly as failures and successes can be identified and incorporated.

Ironically, emergency managers and governmental operators often use the phrase "living document" to describe a process of continual planning (see Figure 4.5). However, in most cases, this is a misrepresentation that more accurately reflects whether the document says "Final" or "Draft" on it rather than as an ever-changing process. Consequently, emergency managers must embrace this changing paradigm to put their products into the community market in a truly constantly evolving process instead of the static and linear process that often defines the development and distribution of planning and preparedness activities.

TRADE IDEAS AND LEVERAGE PEOPLE

Another principle of entrepreneurism is the need to sell ideas to people who will spread and magnify their utilization. Particularly in light of the constant development process mentioned above that leverages small successes and failures, it is important to leverage others outside the organization to be advocates and carriers of the products or messages being delivered. This creates higher operational efficiencies due to the fact that the personnel costs (e.g., contractors) are reduced without any impact on the ultimate result. In a relatively small and specialized field such as emergency management, it is important to maximize the efforts that can be delivered by each component of the operation including all resources, equipment, and personnel.

Traditionally, this maximization is extremely difficult due to the high level of time necessary to invest the knowledge, skills, and abilities to leverage opportunities into products and results within emergency management and thus affect the basic philosophy of the protection and preservation of life and property. Malcolm Gladwell explains this point through his "10,000-hours" rule. His theory is that true proficiency in any one field is only accomplished after spending 10,000 hours practicing, performing, and perfecting it through trial and error.[10] For perspective, an emergency manager would have to work 250 40-hour work weeks or slightly less than five years to achieve proficiency. This example ignores those administrative and managerial tasks that are unrelated to the direct proficiency of an emergency manager, but are often required for daily program or jurisdictional preservation. As such this window grows significantly and creates further challenges to true entrepreneurial activity.

WHAT IS . . . THE "10,000-HOUR" RULE?

The 10,000-hour rule is a sociological and cultural theory that states proficiency in a given area can only occur after a person has spent 10,000 (or more) hours practicing, performing, and perfecting the actions required.

On the other hand, social media and emerging technologies help counteract this challenge. Instead of one emergency manager trying to achieve full competency over an extended period of time, an online and social community can be sold on ideas and grow a collective competency that can aid a community in seeking quicker and more efficient emergency preparedness. This collective capability is primarily accomplished through the sharing and magnification components of social media systems such as Twitter, Facebook, and YouTube. These systems allow ideas to spread from person to person and group to group in a consistent and exponential way. This type of magnification is further discussed in Chapter 6.

Seth Godin refers to this phenomenon as an "ideavirus." Similar to biological viruses, he argues that social media and other emerging technologies allow for individual and connected ideas to spread easily and often without intentionality. To accomplish this, he suggests that individuals play several roles including "sneezers" who spread the word within their direct or extended community and, most important, are believed when information is shared.[13] Similarly, Malcolm Gladwell in his book, *Tipping Point*, refers to these ideavirus participants as connectors, mavens, and salespeople with a specific role and purpose of identifying the idea, bridging it to others, and selling it to others.

By leveraging social media, emergency managers may also be able to present innovative ideas in a more effective manner, as long as the engagement allows for the virus to spread naturally and organically through the various components of the virtual community. This is particularly challenging as these types of individuals are not easily identified or utilized. However, when individuals within a community rise to fulfill these roles, emergency managers need to encourage and promote their roles and involvement. By advocating for this process, the magnification possibilities allow for the 10,000-hour rule mentioned above to be achieved by hundreds or thousands rather than the one individual emergency manager (see Figure 4.6). Although Chapter 6 further discusses this magnification concept, it is important to consider as it reduces the threshold of commitment needed for entrepreneurial activities in emergency management.

NONSTOP INNOVATION

Another critical element of the application of entrepreneurism in modern emergency management is the need for nonstop innovation. As established earlier, emergency management in all disciplines is highly based on best practices and standardized approaches. Although major failures do lead to modifications (most of them minor) of these best practices, the common approach is to stay in a comfort zone that often lacks true innovative approaches. Those organizations and practitioners who serve as innovators often operate on the fringe of their individual industries and are often treated as outliers and outcasts

Figure 4.6 Emergency managers must leverage nontraditional volunteers and the possibilities of social magnification to reduce the challenges of reaching so-called 10,000-hour proficiency. (From FEMA/Steven Zumwalt. With permission.)

who are innovating in rebellious rather than productive ways. Without broad-ranging support of innovation within the organization and professional structures, a "recognized opportunity is [like] a tripod with [only] two legs."[12]

WHAT IS ... INNOVATION?

Innovation is the entrepreneurial characteristic that fundamentally shifts the "trajectory of development" and ultimately serves as an incredibly powerful force for change.[11]

Innovation within entrepreneurism ultimately creates learning and training environments that are unmatched. Seeking out methods of improvement ultimately leads to testing and evaluation of current practices and procedures. In turn, this process partners with the need to create small incremental changes and improvements to operational standards. Therefore, rather than have to wait until major mistakes or oversights are determined in real-life emergencies and disasters, constant changes and improvements can be implemented in a more controlled and sustained fashion.

OPENING THE BOX: THE TREATMENT
AND ERADICATION OF MALARIA

According to the U.S. Centers for Disease Control and Prevention (CDC), Malaria is a mosquito-borne disease caused by a parasite. Those infected with malaria often experience fever, chills, and flu-like illness, and if left untreated many develop severe complications and die. In 2010, there were an estimated 216 million cases of malaria with more than 650,000 associated deaths. Of those deaths, nearly 91% occurred in Africa.[15]

The effects of malaria were first described in ancient Chinese medicinal writings in 2700 BC (see Figure 4.7). By the fourth century BC, symptoms similar to malaria were noted by Hippocrates as the cause of the decline of many of the city–state populations. During the age of Pericles, there were extensive references to malaria with additional notes about depopulation of rural areas. Historians and medical observers routinely noted the symptoms and effects of malaria throughout time.[16]

By the time Spain arrived in the New World, Spanish Jesuit missionaries learned from local native tribes about medicinal bark and other ethnobotanical treatments for the reduction of fevers (see Figure 4.8). One of these barks ultimately became known as the anti-malarial drug, quinine. Since that time quinine has served as the major source of treatment along with a drug classification known as artemisinins which was first identified by Chinese scientists in 1971.[16]

The control of malaria was also a critical factor during the Industrial Revolution and certain international war efforts. For example, malaria significantly affected the speed of construction of the Panama Canal because a majority of the workers were initially stricken by the disease (see Figure 4.9). By 1947, the CDC established the National Malaria Eradication Program as a cooperative under-taking by state and local health agencies as well as the CDC. Over the next four years, the number of cases in America dropped significantly with most health experts considering malaria eliminated from the United States by 1951.[16]

Unfortunately, international efforts have not been as successful. With the continued development of antimosquito treatments, antimalarial medications, and international efforts coordinated through the World Health Organization (WHO), eradication in nations with temperate climates and seasonal malaria is complete. Some nations such as India and Sri Lanka have seen a significant reduction in the number of malaria cases, whereas other nations such as Indonesia, Afghanistan, Haiti, and Nicaragua have seen little or no progress due to emerging drug resistance, environmental concerns over pesticides, and unstable government structures. Consequently, WHO and CDC have moved away from eradication in these areas with greater focus on control.

It is interesting that over the last decade entrepreneurial and innovative practices have led to a variety of new treatment approaches to control and, it is hoped, eradicate malaria. For example, insecticide-treated bed nets have been developed as a personal protection that in several communitywide trials in Africa have shown to reduce early childhood deaths by 20%.[17] Furthermore, the treated nets not only kill the mosquitoes they also repel mosquitoes and other insects from entering the area. This creates both a singular protection and crowd treatment through some very simplistic and inexpensive innovations. Likewise, in 2010, pharmaceutical manufacturer GlaxoSmithKline published the structures of more than 13,500 chemical starting points for antimalarial drug identification with an open invitation for collaborative innovation.[18] This public leveraging of people is estimated to reduce the research and development time significantly with an estimated delivery of a clinically tested and internationally viable treatment by 2015.[19]

However, as social media have become more common not only with citizens but also within the field of emergency management, the need to innovate and ultimately collaborate is extraordinarily important. The conversational connectivity of social media systems as well as the inherent creation of community allows for an immediate and effective feedback mechanism for any concept or idea that is presented. This ability of the crowd is not new to social media, but rather is amplified by the available technology. Likewise, social media and related emerging technologies have also reduced the expected time and frequency of innovative activities. The news is littered with projects and possibilities

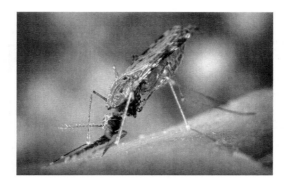

Figure 4.7 As a mosquito-borne disease, malaria has been a health challenge for nearly 2,700 years in cultures throughout the world. (From U.S. Centers for Disease Control and Prevention/James Gathany. With permission.)

Figure 4.8 As Spanish Jesuit missionaries arrived in the New World, they learned from local native tribes about medicinal bark and other botanical treatments for the reduction of fevers and other ailments. (From Public Domain/ Unknown.)

that have come from the private process of innovation and success. Moreover, the public is not only impressed by the number of innovations, but the perceived jumps in progress and purpose. Specifically, functions and programming that have previously only been possible in science fiction are now commonplace.

Figure 4.9 Major construction projects such as the building of the Panama Canal were nearly suspended due to the high rate of infection from malaria. (From U.S. Coast Guard/Unknown. With permission.)

ENTREPRENEURIAL CHARACTERISTICS IN EMERGENCY MANAGEMENT

To fully integrate entrepreneurial characteristics within an emergency management organization and throughout the industry as a whole, there needs to be a clear set of customer expectations, opportunities for learning and improvement, and a cyclical process of when, where, and how to leverage failures and innovation to improve emergency management processes.[12] As stated previously, the rise and integration of social media into mainstream culture have significantly affected public expectations for this process. Likewise, maintaining a constant environment of incremental changes will quickly create a culture of success that is sustainable over the long term. The remaining challenge is what process can be integrated to help achieve these markers of success and ultimately create a more successful organization.

According to Richard Goossen, this process should be opportunity-driven, resource creative, team-centric, organizationally integrated, and holistic in its approach.[12] These characteristics are not always present in emergency management, as there is a perceived breakdown between their associations with business activities that lack involvement with emergency management functions. However, as this chapter has continually reiterated, the change in public perception due to the strong influence of social media is significantly influencing the need to be more progressive and pragmatic with when, where, and how information and programming are implemented.

For example, emergency management organizations must be opportunity-driven. This is accomplished by being attractive, durable, timely, and anchored in products that add value to the community served. Because people want and expect information quickly and effectively, the need to be attractive is very real. People are overwhelmed every day with information that is asking, pushing, and cajoling them to take certain actions such as buying a particular product or signing a certain petition. For example, a 2009 report from the University of California, San Diego suggested that an average American consumes 34 gigabytes of content and 100,000 words of information every single day.[20] This makes it very clear that emergency management information needs to be clear, concise, interesting, and attractive. Traditional emergency public information models have suggested the need for focusing on clarity and consistency, however, emergency managers in general have not considered how to make disaster information—before, during, and after an event—interesting and attractive (see Figure 4.10). Conversely, most emergency managers merely "preach to the choir" by adding emphasis and consideration only for those individuals already engaged and interested in emergency preparedness issues.

The second major component often underutilized by emergency managers is the quality of the product provided. Much like traditional entrepreneurs, emergency managers are ultimately only successful if their products are interesting, engaging, and ultimately easier and more effective to use than other options available to the consumer. As established earlier in this chapter, emergency management products such as

Figure 4.10 Although some political and cultural leaders such as President Barack Obama have recognized the need to leverage emerging and social technologies to reach the general public, most emergency managers are simply underutilizing the free and dynamic tools available to their organizations. (From White House/Unknown. With permission.)

plans, campaigns, personal preparedness, and the like not only have to be presented in an engaging way (see Chapter 9), but also legitimately have to add value to a public constituency. This added value means that those engaged must be more prepared (either via community or personal efforts) than they were before the product was offered or responded to more quickly.

A prime example of this type of added value concept is gluten-free bakeries. At the turn of the twentieth century, the relative awareness of individuals with allergies to the baking protein gluten was relatively unknown. An estimated 1.3% of the population is afflicted by celiac disease which prevents them from being able to digest gluten. Unfortunately, gluten is a critical "sticky" factor in most bakery items including breads and cookies, as well as pasta, and many other food items. This means there were nearly no alternatives for those with celiac disease to eat and enjoy these types of items. Although a small portion of the population, the number of cases began to rise significantly.[21] Consequently, many chefs and bakers began adopting gluten-free recipes which led to the need for gluten-free local bakeries. Because of the appeal to those afflicted with gluten allergies as well as some of the recently identified secondary health benefits to everyone, the business application moved from niche to mainstream with nearly 19,000 gluten-free establishments throughout the world.[22] The gluten-free approach clearly provided added value to the consumer and is a model of success for emergency managers and other entrepreneurial models, particularly when considering components or changes that might be perceived as insignificant or only serving niche markets (see Figure 4.11).

The final component of entrepreneurism in emergency management is the need for a holistic approach. At the broadest level, this holistic approach is achieved by integrating the principles of entrepreneurism discussed here throughout all components of emergency management operations and all phases of disaster response. Although personnel challenges to entrepreneurism in emergency management have already been mentioned, it is important that the integration be achievable, opportunity-driven, and benefit-oriented. Much as discussed earlier, while it is not necessarily prudent to have every component embrace these challenges, it is important that the effects of entrepreneurial decisions have tertiary impacts throughout the organization and served community.

For example, after the 2010 Haiti earthquake that caused significant loss of life and impact on local infrastructure, there was a significant outcry from countries throughout the world to help (see Figure 4.12).

Figure 4.11 Traditional organizational models such as baking have had to innovatively shift their products and processes to address growing changes in their consumer bases. Emergency managers must make the same modifications as public expectations change. (From U.S. Navy/Petty Officer 3rd Class Paul J. Perkins. With permission.)

Figure 4.12 Major disasters such as the earthquake in Haiti in 2010 drive the general public to want to donate goods, services, and money to support response and recovery efforts. (From U.S. Navy/Daniel Barker. With permission.)

The United States was no different, as traditional nonprofit organizations including the American Red Cross immediately started support missions and fundraising to address issues in Haiti. By 2010, more than six trillion text messages were sent annually, which meant that nearly 200,000 messages were exchanged every second.[23] To maximize the public's vast (and growing) utilization of cell phones and to incorporate text messaging, the American Red Cross released a text-to-donate campaign that allowed people to text a message to a certain number to donate $10 in support of the Haiti earthquake relief. This donation campaign was a unique and entrepreneurial partnership between the American Red Cross, U.S. Department of State, and all major cellular providers. The campaign was so successful that the American Red Cross raised $5 million within the first two days and $32 million over the course of the first month.[24,25] This phenomenal innovation led to a permanent and ongoing practice not only by the American Red Cross, but by numerous nonprofit organizations.

LEADERS IN THE OPEN: JEFF PHILLIPS

Jeff Phillips is a volunteer emergency management coordinator for the Village of Los Ranchos in Albuquerque, New Mexico and the vice president and chief operating officer of Specialized Emergency Management Solutions, LLC. He has previous experience with both state-level emergency management and national mutual aid and assistance. He is well versed in the application of social media in emergency management and is the founder of the Virtual Operations Support Team (VOST) concept. Mr. Phillips speaks about his experience with entrepreneurial behavior in emergency management in the following essay written for this book.

Force Multiplication through Innovative Behavior

Jeff Phillips

Until late 2009 I had only dabbled with social media and new technology in my private affairs. That changed when at a weekly staff meeting my mayor said, "You ought to get on Facebook and Twitter." From that day forward I have been a full-fledged practitioner, experimenting, learning, and improving at every opportunity.

I have always believed that, at its core, emergency management is "all about the network," and I quickly discovered that this belief is supported and augmented when fully utilizing the power of social media to engage the community and our stakeholders. I immediately had new avenues to share preparedness and incident-related information and there was a community that wanted it.

We determined to follow a policy of full engagement and not see social media as "one-way traffic." This approach allowed me to interact and develop relationships with local individuals who in turn amplified the information I was sharing, provided me with information from the field, and perhaps most important, offered a range of technical assistance and support. Engagement also allowed me to find other emergency managers and enthusiasts who had embarked in the social and new technology realm.

The earthquake in Haiti was a major event in spurring me to go beyond simply practicing in my corner of the world. It was at that time I became aware of Crisis Commons and the concept of crisis camps. Shortly after that event, a group of interested people came together in person and virtually to form what we call EMCampNM. This public–private partnership continues as a brand on multiple social media platforms and as a virtual and sometimes in-person mechanism to bridge community and emergency management through social media.

Throughout 2010 I continued to follow and engage with people locally and nationally that were interested in advancing the concept of transforming the emergency management enterprise through social media and new technology. I had established many great new virtual relationships by the Fall when the IAEM conference was held. Many of us were interested in seeing how social media and new technology would be integrated into the conference and in participating remotely and interacting with attendees, but were frustrated by the lack of opportunity.

In early 2011, active members of the #SMEM initiative decided to conduct a one hour #SMEMChat on a Friday lunch hour. The Twitter-based chat was very well attended and instantly became a weekly event with various topics and continuously growing participation. In March 2011 we hosted what we called SMEM Camp at NEMA11, the association's mid-year conference in Washington, DC. This day-long "unconference" was unprecedented for the emergency management community and certainly for NEMA. We arranged to make the camp open to anyone who was interested, so there a great mix of EM and non-EM alike. Participants decided the session topics and moved around throughout the venue discussing topics ranging from Social

Media 101 to engagement strategies and policy issues. Live tweeting, Facebooking, and ustreaming were provided from the venue to extend the reach to those wishing to participate from afar. A research team was on-site to capture discussions, issues, and conclusions that were later published in a white paper. The SMEM Camp was very well received and provided an important benchmark for the #SMEM initiative.

One of the things I'm most proud of is the concept of Virtual Operations Support Teams (VOST); the idea of recruiting and integrating teams of trusted agents into the emergency management operation to support an emergency management entity on a full range of tasks. I realized early on that by practicing #SMEM on a daily basis I was creating expectations within the community that I would not be able to fulfill when my focus shifted to more traditional emergency operations tasks.

I developed and implemented the VOST concept as a force multiplier relying on basic emergency management and incident command system (ICS) principles. I convened my first VOST (actually three teams working under a VOS group supervisor) to support the SMEM Camp at NEMA11 and to demonstrate the concept.

The first activation of VOST for an actual event was in support of the Portland National Incident Management Organization (NIMO) public information officer on the Shadow Lake wildfire in Oregon. I convened and led the team for a 19-day mission focused on monitoring for situation awareness, delivery of approved messages, message amplification, archiving, and technology assistance for the NIMO. The University of Colorado Project EPIC analyzed this activation and wrote a white paper examining the concept, eventually delivering it to ISCRAM 2012 in Calgary.

I don't consider myself a technologist or early adopter of technology but I also do not fear it. Since undertaking this new open approach to emergency management I have been exposed to dozens of social media platforms and virtual collaboration tools by colleagues in and out of emergency management. Some tools and platforms have transformed the way I do business, enhancing efficiency and enabling greater involvement with the community.

I'm proud to have played a role in integrating social media and new technology in the emergency management realm. My approach from the outset has been guided by the idea that I am bound only by my imagination and by my willingness to trust others. This approach has served me very well.

ENDNOTES

1. Bazerman, Max H. and Watkins, Michael D. (2008) *Predictable Surprises: The Disasters You Should Have Seen Coming and How to Prevent Them.* Boston: Harvard Business School Press, p. 88.

2. "Thomas Alva Edison Quotes." (n.d.) http://www.fadedgiant.net/html/edison_thomas_alva_quotes.htm. Accessed May 6, 2012.

3. Bennett, Shea. (2012) "Twitter on Track for 500 Million Users by March, 250 Million Active Users by End of Year." All Twitter Blog. http://www.mediabistro.com/alltwitter/twitter-active-total-users_b17655. Accessed May 7, 2012.

4. Gobry, Pascal-Emmanuel. (2011) Twitter is obscenely profitable. *Business Insider.* http://articles.businessinsider.com/2011-06-30/tech/30012755_1_twitter-advertisers-revenue. Accessed May 7, 2012.

5. Kiefer, Charles F., Schlesinger, Leonard A., and Brown, Paul B. (2010) *Action Trumps Everything: Creating What You Want in an Uncertain World.* New York: Innovation Associates.

6. Godin, Seth. (2006) *Small Is the New Big: And 183 Riffs, Rants, and Remarkable Ideas.* New York: Portfolio Hardcover.

7. Godin, Seth (2011) *Linchpin: Are You Indispensable?* New York: Portfolio Trade.

8. Kingsbury, Kathleen. (2008) The value of human life: $129,000. *Time* Magazine. http://www.time.com/time/health/article/0,8599,1808049,00.html. Accessed May 14, 2012.

9. "FEMA History." (2010) Federal Emergency Management Agency (FEMA). http://www.fema.gov/about/history.shtm. Accessed May 14, 2012.

10. Gladwell, Malcolm. (2008) *Outliers: The Story of Success.* New York: Little, Brown.

11. "The Paramount Importance of Innovation." (2012) Bill and Melinda Gates Foundation. http://www.gatesfoundation.org/g20/pages/importance-of-innovation.aspx. Accessed May 17, 2012.

12. Goossen, Richard J. (2008) *ePreneur: From Wall Street to Wiki: Succeeding as a Crowdpreneur in the New Virtual Marketplace.* New York: Career Press.

13. Godin, Seth. (2000) "Unleashing the Ideavirus." Do You Zoom. http://www.sethgodin.com/ideavirus/downloads/IdeavirusReadandShare.pdf. Accesseed May 18, 2012.

14. Gladwell, Malcom. (2002) *Tipping Point: How Little Things Make a Big Difference.* New York: Back Bay.

15. "Malaria." (2012) U.S. Centers for Disease Control & Prevention. http://www.cdc.gov/MALARIA/. Accessed May 18, 2012.

16. "The History of Malaria, an Ancient Disease." (2010) U.S. Centers for Disease Control & Prevention. http://www.cdc.gov/malaria/about/history/. Accessed May 18, 2012.

17. "Insecticide Treated Bed Nets." (2010) U.S. Centers for Disease Control & Prevention. http://www.cdc.gov/malaria/malaria_worldwide/reduction/itn.html. Accessed May 19, 2012.

18. Calderon, Felix, et. al. (2011) An invitation to open innovation in malaria drug discovery: 47 Quality starting points. *ACS Medicinal Chemistry Letters.* 2(10). http://pubs.acs.org/doi/abs/10.1021/ml200135p. Accessed May 19, 2012.

19. "GSK's Commitment to Fighting Malaria." (n.d) GlaxoSmithKline Newsletter. http://www.gsk.com/media/downloads/gsk-malaria-factsheet-Apr-2012.pdf. Accessed May 19, 2012.

20. Bilton, Nick. (2009) The American Diet: 34 Gigabytes a Day. Bits: *New York Times* Blog. http://bits.blogs.nytimes.com/2009/12/09/the-american-diet-34-gigabytes-a-day/. Accessed May 20, 2012.

21. Adams, Jefferson. (2011) "Are Estimates of Celiac Disease Too High?" Celiac. com. http://www.celiac.com/articles/22423/1/Are-Estimates-of-Celiac-Disease-Rates-Too-High/Page1.html. Accessed May 20, 2012.

22. Stout, Hillary. (2011) Looking for plan B? Make it gluten-free. *New York Times.* http://www.nytimes.com/2011/06/05/fashion/gluten-free-bakeries-and-cafes.html?_r=2&pagewanted=all. Accessed May 20, 2012.

23. Lilly, Paul. (2010) Report: 6.1 trillion messages sent in 2010. *MaximumPC.* http://www.maximumpc.com/article/news/report_61_trillion_text_messages_sent_2010. Accessed May 20, 2012.

24. Van Grove, Jennifer. (2010). "Red Cross Raises $5,000,000+ for Haiti Through Text Messaging Campaign." Mashable. http://mashable.com/2010/01/13/haiti-red-cross-donations/. Accessed May 20, 2012.

25. Health, Thomas. (2010) U.S. cellphone users donate $22 million to Haiti earthquake relief via text. *Washington Post.* http://www.washingtonpost.com/wp-dyn/content/article/2010/01/18/AR2010011803792.html. Accessed May 20, 2012.

Section II

The Effects of Leading through Engaged Social Media: Efficiency, Collaboration, and Magnification

Chapters 2–4 of this book focused on identifying and accepting the changing public expectations about social media and the fundamentals of how social media have affected emergency management. In the first section, the structure was built upon the fact that public presumption of transparency drives the expectations of instantaneous exchange of information. This combination of transparency and instantaneous exchange of information combines with the need for entrepreneurism within the emergency management community.

These expectations and characteristics necessitate the need for efficiency, which is discussed in Chapter 5. The need for efficiency drives the facilitation of programming and leadership that necessitates the magnification of preparedness and collaboration with the community.

These two components comprise the focus of Chapters 6 and 7 and begin to establish what leadership characteristics and programming may be necessary for emergency managers of all disciplines to begin to leverage social media and related public expectations to create the new paradigm proposed within this book.

5

Efficiency and Effectiveness

Unexpected events—natural disasters, terrorist attacks, pandemics—make us frantic. In the aftermath, we obsess about learning from our mistakes and pour resources into predicting what might happen tomorrow. We turn to experts, asking them how we might do things differently next time. The problem is that the experts were part of the system that failed in the first place, and their recommendations almost always get filtered through large, top down bureaucracies that are poorly suited to deal with radical change.

Rafe Sagarin[1]

EXTERNAL FORCES AFFECTING EFFICIENCY

The beginning of the second decade of the twenty-first century is an extremely difficult time for emergency managers across all disciplines. Organizations of all sizes and types as well as each level of government are challenged by extraordinarily poor economic conditions not only affecting the respective organizations, but the individuals of the community as well. Organizations have made difficult decisions to cut costs including, but not limited to, the reduction (if not elimination) of training opportunities, exercises, resources, equipment, and personnel. These cuts have come without corresponding cuts or reductions in legal, political, executive, and requirement levels. Consequently, the emergency management community is at an emergency preparedness crossroads that may or may not succeed at mitigating risk in a given community.

For example, with every major domestic or international disaster, a plethora of new preparedness and response requirements are established into law, often with legal and compliance requirements. These new requirements are often a mixture of practical and political characteristics with minimal to no funding to support the new initiatives. These so-called "unfunded mandates" can often be extraordinarily difficult for the average emergency manager to implement effectively. For example, after the Fukushima Daiichi nuclear plant meltdown in 2011 due to the Japan earthquake, there were significant pushes from environmental and emergency preparedness organizations to mandate changes to nuclear protection procedures. The U.S. Nuclear Regulatory Commission strongly considered extending the nuclear evacuation zones from 10 miles to 25 or 50 miles and expanding the "ingestion pathway zone," which monitors food, milk, and water sources, from 50 miles to 100 miles.[2] This type of expansion would add exponential burdens to emergency managers who are already struggling to provide adequate preparedness for nuclear planning zones. Although this type of response may ultimately prove correct, it was perceived by many in the response field as a knee-jerk reaction to the tragedy.

The challenge is that these types of reactions often overlook simpler solutions or considerations that could address the issue at hand. In the example of the Fukushima incident, the risk created by the impact of the earthquake to the nuclear power plant was related more to the location and response characteristics of the particular power plant (e.g., building a nuclear power plant on an earthquake fault and by the ocean) rather than an overarching flaw in nuclear and radiological emergency planning issues. These types of overcommitments lead to excessive impacts on the possibility of emergency managers maintaining a high level of efficiency and effectiveness (see Figure 5.1).

Likewise, as discussed in Chapter 4 on entrepreneurism, emergency managers also tend to cycle endlessly toward common priorities, with more and more resources dedicated to a particular effort. For example, the need for and importance of individual and family preparedness is universally agreed upon by the emergency management community as critically important due to the inherent need to bridge the gap between immediate response challenges and formalized short-term recovery. However, the reality is that not every individual or family within the community will embrace and execute on the concepts of

Figure 5.1 Regulatory requirements for nuclear power plants often change in reaction to emergencies and other political directives causing undue pressure on emergency preparedness and response organizations. (From U.S. Nuclear Regulatory Commission/Unknown. With permission.)

emergency preparedness. Consequently, pushing additional resources through more educational materials, public presentations, or formalized campaigning is not efficient. Rather, it is asymptotic with a diminishing return on the increased investment. This type of approach, which is not limited to personal preparedness, is counterproductive and inefficient.

SOCIAL MEDIA EFFICIENCY

On the other hand, social media are inherently efficient on nearly all levels. For example, the fact that many social media systems are functional across multiple platforms (e.g., computer, tablet, mobile, etc.) means they leverage virtual cloud technologies to decentralize data and thus make them available from literally anywhere that supports Internet access. This structural component creates a sense that social media are so diffused that they are available for use at any time of day or night. As discussed in Chapter 3, this is one of the phenomena that leads to the expectation for nearly instantaneous reception and distribution of information via these systems.

Likewise, social media systems such as social networks and microblogs have established content limits within the given structure. For example, Twitter posts are limited to 140 characters or less. Although this was initially established to ensure compliance with SMS texting requirements, it has helped create a fundamental efficiency due to the need for users to utilize language efficiently to translate understood messages within the Twitter community. To further help accomplish this, the Twitter community organically has adopted specific Twitter "language" rules that minimize the characters utilized within the message. For examples, the letters "RT" may be utilized in a repeated message to indicate that it is being reposted (aka retweeted). Similarly, hashtags (Twitter-specific classifications) are leveraged to give context and clarity to the short 140-character messages. See Figure 5.2. Although not nearly as restrictive, Facebook and other social media sites have similar limited content boxes that force efficiency in messaging.

COMMON TWITTER "LANGUAGE" TERMS

RT   Retweet (message is reposted by another user)
MT   Modified tweet (message is reposted with modifications for space)
D Direct message (communication between individual users rather than broadcast)
@ User designation (used to specifically identify message recipient)
# Hashtag (trigger for categorical system)

femaregion5 @femaregion5   14 Sep
#FF Did you know that the Administrator of @fema is on Twitter?
Follow Craig Fugate here: @CraigatFEMA
Expand

Figure 5.2 This example Twitter post from FEMA Region V contains some of the common language and efficiently presents its message. (From Screenshot.)

SOCIAL MEDIA SELF-CORRECTION

Interestingly, one of the fundamental concepts of social media is self-correction. This self-correcting mechanism is based on a variety of characteristics, but ultimately allows for misinformation or inconsistent activities to be quickly and efficiently identified by the community of users. This is done both to purify knowledge (e.g., Wikipedia) and clarify information (e.g., Twitter conversations). In both cases, there is a clear improvement in the efficiency and exchange of information.

WHAT IS . . . A WIKI?

A wiki is a type of public or private website that allows for combined content contributions of users within the system to ultimately magnify the knowledge and information holdings of any one individual user. It is a particularly effective strategy for crowdsourcing knowledge and information and is widely utilized in systems like Wikipedia.

For example, wiki sites like Wikipedia are based around combined contributions and editing of information by users of the system (open or closed). This collective information exchange ultimately allows one person's knowledge and holdings of information to be magnified, and thus improves the time and resources needed at the origin to understand the information. Likewise, during a disaster event erroneous information (intentional or unintentional) is often interjected into the flow of information, which can cause confusion and be resource intensive to emergency management personnel who need to clarify such information. In traditional media management, this type of rumor management has been handled by public information officers monitoring media reports and providing clarification for future media cycles. The self-correcting mechanism does this process for the broader community and helps eliminate, via the collective knowledge and information capacity, the erroneous information regardless of whether it was placed there intentionally or simply as part of the flow of disaster information.

In some instances, this type of collective information occurs through geographic mapping interfaces. This is particularly valuable during disasters, as they inherently are connected to an event that happened

131

at a particular location or locations in a given period of time. Those individuals who are directly affected by the disaster or who are nearby observers provide event commentary with a corresponding geo-tag that is then uploaded or laid over a mapping interface. Because the mapping interface is often set up to accept this information via multiple communication systems including phone, text, web comments, e-mail, and social media, there is an efficiency created that is only available through the utilization of emerging technologies and leveraging the growing uses of mobile and wireless devices as discussed earlier in this book (see Figure 5.3).

This type of geographically based efficiency is available through a variety of mechanisms, but is perhaps most profoundly observed through the various uses of a crowd-based application called Ushahidi. Ushahidi is a website that was initially established to map reports of violence during the 2008 elections in Kenya. At that time, there were 45,000 users in Kenya, which was significantly more than anticipated by the founders of the system and ultimately served as the impetus to push the system to become more widely available.[3] Since that time, Ushahidi has been used during numerous disasters to track a variety of disaster-related information during response and recovery activities. For example, during the 2010 Haiti earthquake, Ushahidi was quickly established by various emergency technological volunteer groups to collect and geo-tag response needs of local survivors in the area who lacked other formal

Figure 5.3 Mapping interfaces such as this one from the Haiti earthquake of 2010 often efficiently gather disaster-related information via multiple channels such as text messages, phone, web submissions, and social media. (From: Screenshot.)

mechanisms to report basic needs. Likewise, affected and currently available infrastructure needs could also be reported.[4] Ushahidi was utilized later that same year by a group of students at Tulane University who referred to themselves as the Louisiana Bucket Brigade. Specifically, days after the explosion on the Deepwater Horizon oil drilling platform, this group of students immediately utilized Ushahidi.[4] However, in contrast to the Haiti earthquake, Ushahidi was utilized to improve the collection of information related to environmental impacts from the spill and thus improve the efficiency by which both formal emergency response organizations could respond and traditional media agencies could increase the accountability of those responsible for the spill itself and the clean-up.

WHAT IS . . . USHAHIDI?

Ushahidi is a web-based platform that allows geospatial visualization of emergent information and incident news, particularly in high-risk or vulnerable communities. It was initially utilized to monitor democratic elections in Kenya, but has since been utilized in major disasters throughout the world by virtual technology groups.[21]

EFFICIENCY: MORE WITH LESS

Efficiency is an intricate process with many degrees of complexity. At its most fundamental level, efficiency is an action-oriented process of how an activity can be performed or a resource achieved with fewer resources than initially considered. In all measurements of efficiency, there must be an initial consideration and a second evaluation that occurs after some change in process or procedure. For instance, Chapter 4 discussed a company that produced a certain number of widgets with a pre-determined error rate (e.g., one faulty widget per 1,000 produced). Hypothetically, the company would make changes to its manufacturing process or quality control measures to improve the ratio of correctly produced widgets to those that were faulty. By comparing the initial measurement with the secondary measurement, it was clear that the widget manufacturer achieved improved efficiency as they were able to achieve more with less.

OPENING THE BOX: HENRY FORD AND
THE FIVE-DOLLAR WORKDAY

Henry Ford is considered the father of efficiency. With his foresight and planning, he released the Model T in 1908 as the first mass-produced automobile in the United States. See Figure 5.4. To achieve this feat, Ford improved manufacturing precision by standardizing interchangeable parts, dividing labor into specialized functions, and ultimately automating a moving assembly line. Because of the improved manufacturing efficiency, Henry Ford achieved his personal goal of producing a reasonably priced, reliable, and efficient mode of family transportation that was easy to operate and could be handled on the rough roads most common in the predominately rural communities of America. This process was so efficient and effective that more than half of the cars owned and operated in America by 1918 were the Model T.[12]

It is interesting that Henry Ford's manufacturing improvements were perhaps not his most profound example of leveraging efficiencies. Specifically, on the morning of January 5, 1914, Henry Ford announced a new economic model that he called "profit sharing." Within his proposal, Ford announced that his motor company would be increasing the salary of all of his employees to a minimum of $5 per eight hours of work (up from the common $2.34 for the same period) and instituting eight-hour shifts to maximize the effectiveness of the manufacturing plants.[13] Ford instituted this process to better incentivize his workers to remain with the company and become more productive and efficient both at home and work (see Figure 5.5). Unfortunately, Ford's so-called "Five Day Work Week" plan was not well received, with the *Wall Street Journal* calling it "blatant immorality."[14] In the end, the profits of the Ford Motor Company doubled from $30 million to $60 million between 1914 and 1916 upon the institution of this new plan, leading Henry Ford to state that "The payment of five dollars a day for an eight-hour day was one of the finest cost-cutting moves we ever made."[14] In the end, Henry Ford's attempt to utilize various techniques to improve efficiency—even when counterintuitive—are fine examples even in the face of criticism and ridicule.

Figure 5.4 Henry Ford implemented various strategies to improve the efficiency of the automobile manufacturing process. (From Public Domain.)

Figure 5.5 Henry Ford's efficiency standards affected his workers at the factory and their homes. (From Public Domain.)

The concept of more with less is not as simple and straightforward as it appears, particularly for emergency managers. Unfortunately, emergency managers are often limited in the staffing and resources available to perform all functions necessary to fulfill responsibilities related to preparedness, response, recovery, and mitigation with their particular community. Consequently, traditional emergency management professionals have taken an approach of putting more time and resources into operational processes in an attempt to get more out, especially to improve operational efficiency. This approach is equivalent to putting additional fuel into an automobile with the hopes and expectations of it going faster. Although it is an admirable trait to maintain a strong work ethic with the dedication and willingness to put forth extra effort to accomplish a greater good, it is no longer sufficient to meet the public expectations established by the use of social media.

As established in the earlier chapters of this book, the public has grown to expect a significant increase in the speed and delivery of information in a similar format to that which can be acquired via social media systems such as Facebook and Twitter. These systems have truly allowed the general public to be more engaged with fewer resources required to engage initially and continually with the system. Specifically, it only takes an e-mail address (often from free sources such as Yahoo or Google) to sign up for a Facebook account. This, in turn, allows that individual user to have access to information, pictures, videos, and posts from the more than 900 million active users currently on the Facebook system.[5] The same is true for Twitter and various other social media systems. This level of efficiency in accessing information is the quintessential definition of getting more for less.

Clearly emergency managers cannot duplicate the size and scope of social media efficiency of systems such as Facebook. However, emergency managers can adopt philosophies of approach and institute protocols that seek out opportunities to leverage social media and other emergency technologies as opportunities to truly achieve an operational efficiency that is capable of achieving more with less. Some emergency management organizations have begun to take on this approach, but still only in limited or inconsistent ways. However, the organizations adopting this type of strategy lack venues to transmit or share it with those who are not. In many cases, emergency management organizations effectively adopting appropriate strategies or leveraging social media to improve efficiency are ostracized or isolated within the broader professional community.

EFFICIENCY: PERSONNEL AND RESOURCE ELASTICITY

An additional form of efficiency revolves around the concept of personnel and resource elasticity. In the physical sense, elasticity is the material property of a substance that reflects on its ability to change dimensions, volume, or shape in response to an external force and then return to its original form.[6] This concept is particularly important in emergency management, as each emergency or disaster will always require new considerations or applications that may not have previously been considered or planned for within the community. This is a major justification for adopting an all-hazards approach to community hazards. Rather than try to maintain a fully detailed plan for every hazard, a community will organize its planning and preparedness efforts around similar capabilities and thus find efficiency and flexibility in the execution and delivery of services and resources.

Unfortunately, this type of efficiency often erodes when an emergency management organization is addressing new challenges and technologies such as those that social media and other emergency technologies present. Much as with the more-with-less style of efficiency described earlier, many of these challenges arise from difficulties in personnel elasticity. Bill Hybels, leadership guru and founder of the Global Leadership Summit, refers to this concept as "talent elasticity." Specifically, he talks about the need for individuals within a healthy organization to be willing to adopt and maintain flexibility at all times to move with the dynamic challenges that face an organization as well as growth and evolution within the organization.[7]

WHAT IS ... TALENT ELASTICITY?

Talent elasticity is a term coined by Bill Hybels that suggests individuals need to be willing to adopt and maintain flexibility at all times when facing dynamic challenges.

Hybels encourages leaders to evaluate talent elasticity quickly within their teams and swiftly reassign underperformers to alternative duties that may be a better fit. He has specifically stated that "If you don't deal with underperformers, you discourage and demotivate your best people."[8] In addition, Hybels strongly suggests that those who have sufficient talent elasticity are those who should be the focus of organizations.

137

This is fairly atypical in emergency management organizations. In most cases, the personnel who primarily engage in these operations are strongly influenced by repetitious operations and behaviors that have previously been shown to be best practices, but may not be flexible enough in light of social media changes. Likewise, managerial and supervisory roles are more often based on seniority or professional experience than inherent superior qualities.

In contrast, the adaption and integration of social technologies into so many aspects of everyday life have created an expectation that only those things which are optimized and socially efficient are retained. For example, in the mid-2000s, MySpace was the most influential social network in the burgeoning world of social media. By 2008, MySpace peaked at slightly more than 75 million users as other social media systems, including Facebook and Twitter, grew in popularity and now has become nearly defunct as a significant social player.[9] The failure of growth in MySpace did not simply occur because of a competitive marketplace. Rather, it was due to a lack of flexibility. Sean Parker stated that the failure of MySpace was because "They weren't successful in iterating and evolving the product enough [because] it was basically this junk heap of bad design that persisted for many, many years."[10] This is a potential fate for emergency management in this new social paradigm if efficiency and effectiveness through organizational and personnel flexibility are not strongly embraced.

OPENING THE BOX: M-PESA (MOBILE MONEY IN KENYA)

The invention and persistent growth of the mobile phone market and related decrease in the size and costs of mobile technology has had a tremendous effect on global communication and interaction. This impact is no more apparent than in sub-Saharan African where traditional fixed-line communications and related physical infrastructure have often been inadequate and unreliable. However, mobile phone growth in most of Africa has been remarkable. For instance, in 1999 there were 15,000 mobile subscribers in Kenya, but by the end of the next decade that number had reached nearly 8 million and has continued to grow since then.[18] Consequently, mobile devices have allowed many African communities to skip over the landline issues and leverage mobile devices to their full potential.

In March 2007, the leading cell phone company in Kenya launched M-PESA, which leveraged the SMS technology available on mobile phones to transfer money. This system quickly created a framework for individuals to deposit, send, and withdraw funds using only their cell phone. Since that time, M-PESA has grown rapidly, with approximately 38% of Kenya's adult population utilizing the service.[17] This implementation rate is particularly critical when more than 80% of the local people are excluded from the formal financial sector for one reason or another.[18] The M-PESA system allows Kenyans to keep up to 50,000 shillings in a "virtual account" with transfer potential of 100 to 35,000 shillings per text message transaction.[18]

This efficiency is particularly relevant in Africa where money is often sent (usually by personal delivery) to other family members who are in need or lack the resources at that particular time. This is where the amazing efficiency begins to arise with M-PESA. Not only do mobile system providers generate revenue from a relatively simple process with only technological overhead (i.e., no buildings to support and few employees), but citizens are empowered with a tool that can make their lives easier and faster within an environment that otherwise would not support such engagement. M-PESA may not be supported forever (although it has grown and expanded into other countries including Afghanistan, Tanzania, and South Africa), however, this is a profound example of how pre-existing systems, when leveraged in a flexible manner, can be extraordinarily efficient.[19,20]

EFFICIENCY: THE BIOLOGY OF ORDER

The third mechanism to help achieve efficiency is simply by abiding by the organic and biological drive toward order and structure. Studies have shown that when there is no organization within a group or project the human brain works much harder to decipher the disorganization and thus affects the efficiency and effectiveness of the given operation. Specifically, the prefrontal cortex is challenged, which influences the control areas for anxiety, fear, and impulse control. This lack of order significantly affects the overall capability to maximize operational decisions and considerations (see Figure 5.6).[15]

Most emergency managers are not biologists, therefore striving to maintain order is clearly a mechanism to improve efficiency

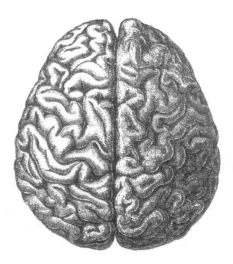

Figure 5.6 The human brain works harder when faced with disorganized and inefficient processes. (From Public Domain.)

and effectiveness. For decades, there have been suggested behavior patterns (e.g., Steven Covey's *Seven Habits of Highly Effective People*) or activities to help improve this inefficiency, but no one process has ever significantly improved efficiency for more than a short period of time. However, organizing the chaos of life has been a primary focus of social technologies and has been exponentially improved through these technologies. An entire class of social productivity systems including Evernote, Google Docs, and DropBox have been developed and leveraged by users of all disciplines to improve their individual and organizational efficiency. These systems utilize a combination of mobile, tablet, and desktop access through cloud-based technologies to create nonstop synergy that not only supports the drive for instantaneous information (see Chapter 3), but also improves efficiency.

For example, Evernote is a note-capturing social software that provides a variety of organizational resources for free to users. According to the Evernote website, "Our goal . . . is to help the world remember everything, communicate effectively and get things done . . . [including] saving thoughts and ideas to preserving experiences to working efficiently with others . . . [by making] it easy to stay organized and productive."[16] This drive toward building an efficient tool is primarily based on two foundational principles: that the vast majority of services are free and thus eliminate any cost hurdles, and that Evernote as an organization is attempting to build primary and secondary tools that add to the efficiency of the system in time and space. Unlike traditional processes that might help build or encourage efficiency in an office or personal setting only, tools such as Evernote help transcend this process and create efficiency when the biological drive is highest, specifically, transcending applications during both personal and business uses. Consequently, striving for efficiency and leveraging the social tools available will help emergency managers become more efficient and effective as this new paradigm becomes clear to industry leaders.

Much as with Evernote, many other social media and emerging technologies also have free or so called "freemium" versions that allow for quick access, easy use, and cost effectiveness. This includes communication tools such as online video chats (e.g., Skype), webinar programming (Adobe Connect), and collaborative editing tools (Google Docs or Pirate Pad) that are extremely useful to emergency management organizations. Without these tools, most emergency management organizations would simply utilize older methodologies that may be ineffective in the broader application and may create inefficiencies as the organization engages the broader community.

WHAT EFFICIENCY IS NOT

It is also important to understand what efficiency is not in light of growing public expectations related to the use and integration of social technologies. Specifically, efficiency is not arbitrary reductions, mandatory control, or inherent industrialization. Unfortunately, like many of the examples shared in this chapter and throughout the book, these are operational tactics and approaches that are characteristics that have long been held as best practices and industry standards for emergency managers. Moreover, these techniques have occasionally been veiled as efficiency generators or may even provide temporary efficiency, but are not intrinsically drivers of long-term and sustainable efficiency (see Figure 5.7). The need to avoid these characteristics is particularly reinforced in social media systems such as Facebook and Twitter for a variety of reasons, which are discussed in greater detail in the following. Understanding how these characteristics interfere with true efficiency is vital.

Arbitrary reductions is one of the first incorrect mechanisms that is utilized to try to achieve efficiency. The rationale is based around

Figure 5.7 Long-held best practices and industry standards in emergency management can often be disorganized processes that do not support long-term and sustainable efficiency. (From FEMA/Dave Saville. With permission.)

the concept similar to the efficiency philosophy of more with less described earlier. If an organization simply reduces the amount of resources, equipment, personnel, or other measurable component of emergency management, then the output ratio will automatically be increased when compared to the input amount. The challenge to this approach is that it is almost never achievable. The remaining components are almost never able to maintain the level of output that was accomplished before or, if they do achieve some efficiency, there is a point of no return where services are diminished or the quality of action is significantly impaired. If cuts are made, they must be focused and strategic to ensure efficiency is created. This type of process is mirrored by social media systems that routinely review and update their systems to make strategic reductions and changes that ultimately improve efficiency.

Likewise, best practices can be equally contrary to matters of efficiency. This is initially counterintuitive, as best practices are inherently based in repeated operational and administrative packages that have been shown to be more efficient and effective at performing the feature under consideration. This is particularly true in emergency management, as some best practices such as the National Incident Management System (NIMS) and the emergency management cycle (preparedness, response, recovery, and mitigation) have become so ingrained in the leadership that any faults or shortcomings are often overlooked or ignored, even when they are logically plausible. For example, since 2010, emergency management personnel comfortable with the rising influence of social media have pointed out that the speed and pace of social media systems do not fit properly or appropriately within the command and control status of NIMS; however, no clear sense of change is being discussed or appears to be on the horizon as national professional organizations and emergency management organizations continue to support the status quo (see Figure 5.8).

Beyond emergency management, this phenomenon is clearly documented in a simplistic, yet effective experiment that is annually conducted by Professor Max Bazerman of Harvard Business School. The premise is that he conducts an auction for one $20 bill. The only unusual rules are that the auction winner and runner-up must both honor their final pledge, but only the winner receives the $20 bill. Logical and rational behavior would suggest that there is a defined value ($20) that would not only limit bidding, but also cause the secondary bidders to stop in order not to lose more money than necessary. However, this assumption is often overwhelmed because the individual bidders get caught in the cycle

Figure 5.8 Adjustments have yet to be made to the instruction or application of best practice standards such as the National Incident Management System to address changes related to social media. (From FEMA/Amanda Bicknell. With permission.)

of repetitious behavior and the fear of failure from altering the course and changing the behavior. On the contrary, Bazerman has conducted this experiment over 180 times over the years and has taken less than $39 combined in the auction only once. Seven times the auction pushed past $100 individually and once generated $407 between the two finalists.[23,24] Unfortunately, this is the same type of behavior exhibited by some emergency management organizations that continue to conduct operations based on outdated methods.

LEADERS IN THE OPEN: SARA ESTES COHEN

Ms. Cohen has 10 years of professional experience in public relations, outreach, and communication with a specific focus in crisis communications including online communities, social media, and digital strategies. She is an expert on data analysis and the application of strategic integration of emerging technologies. In the following essay written for this book, Ms. Cohen discusses the need for greater efficiency through the use and application of social media and emerging technologies within emergency management.

Social Media Make Everything Easier

Sara Estes Cohen

In the days and hours leading up to first Tropical Storm and now Hurricane Isaac, I reflect on the changes and advances in the use of social media for preparedness and emergency response. Having first noticed its importance during Katrina, the juxtaposition of its place in society for this event is mind-blowing. For the last seven years, I've worked specifically on the use of social media for public safety purposes, encouraging individuals, schools, government agencies, companies, and nonprofit organizations to leverage the tools to encourage participation, collaboration, and preparedness. However, in the last seven years, we have run into a series of snags, from unfamiliarity with new technologies to liability, lack of funding, legal and human resources concerns, and more.

Although the process and methodology behind social media begin to advance, the concept remains the same: social media make everything easier. They enable information sharing on a viral level, provide the means to communicate with an exponential number of people, for any reason, at any time, and they empower individuals to participate in events and communicate with each other. In an event such as Hurricane Isaac, I can't help but notice the changes in my community with respect to the use of social media; it's obvious we've learned a few things since the last time we "battened down the hatches."

First, the City of New Orleans and surrounding parishes, as well as the Governor's Office of Homeland Security and Emergency Preparedness have been very active on social media tools such as Facebook and Twitter. I personally am aware of and follow many accounts on a daily basis, and notice that many in the community do as well. By establishing and maintaining a visible presence within the community on an ongoing basis, city officials are able to share information quickly and easily about preparedness, safety tips, and other important data. Second, in using social media to communicate directly with the community, city officials empower individuals to participate in their own preparedness and safety, leading to community resilience, or a community that is able to prepare for, respond to, recover from, and thrive after a disaster, on their own, removing some of the strain on government resources and funding.

Finally, community organizations, from healthcare clinics to clothing and food stores to special interest groups to the New Orleans Saints, who all use social media on a daily basis for marketing and public relations purposes, share important messages from city officials through their own networks, by reposting, retweeting, adding jokes, anecdotes, and additional details, to make the sometimes dry information a bit more "digestible." Collaboration is inherent in a tightly knit community; social media are a natural reflection of that behavior. Not using this to your advantage would be a wasted opportunity, not to mention hours of additional work.

ENDNOTES

1. Sagarin, Rafe. (2012) Sink or swim: When confronted with catastrophe, emulate the octopus. *Wired Magazine.* April 2012.
2. "Press Update." (2012) CleanEnergy.org. http://www.cleanenergy.org/index.php?/Press-Update.html?form_id=8&item_id=273. Accessed May 21, 2012.
3. "Press Kit." (2012) Ushahidi. http://ushahidi.com/about-us/press-kit. Accessed June 2, 2012.
4. Crowe, Adam. (2012) *Disasters 2.0: The Application of Social Media in Modern Emergency Management.* Boca Raton, FL: CRC Press.

5. "Facebook Key Facts." (2012) Facebook Newsroom. http://newsroom. fb.com/content/default.aspx?NewsAreaId=22. Accessed June 2, 2012.
6. "Elasticity." (n.d.) Dictionary.com. http://dictionary.reference.com/browse/ elasticity?s=t. Accessed June 5, 2012.
7. Hybels, Bill. (2011) Global Leadership Summit. Speech. Heard August 2011.
8. Perman, Matt. (2012) "What's Best Next." God-Centered Leadership Blog. http://www.whatsbestnext.com/2011/08/what-do-you-do-when-someone-lacks-the-talent-elasticity-to-stay-in-the-organization/. Accessed June 5, 2012.
9. Kindelan, Katie. (2011) MySpace on the auction block: What happens to user data? *SocialTimes*. http://socialtimes.com/myspace-on-the-auction-block-what-happens-to-user-data_b34636. Accessed June 5, 2012.
10. Horn, Leslie. (2011) Sean Parker: MySpace could have been Facebook. PCMag. http://www.pcmag.com/article2/0,2817,2387799,00.asp. Accessed June 5, 2012.
11. Atack, Jeremy, Haines, Michael R., and Margo, Robert A. (2008) "Railroads and the Rise of the Factory: Evidence for the United States: 1850-1870." National Bureau of Economic Research. http://www.nber.org/papers/w14410.pdf?new_window=1. Accessed June 6, 2012.
12. "The Life of Henry Ford." (n.d.) The Henry Ford Museum. http://www. hfmgv.org/exhibits/hf/. Accessed June 6, 2012.
13. Raff, Daniel M.G. (1988) Wage determination theory and the five-dollar workday at Ford. *The Journal of Economic History*. http://www.jstor.org/ stable/212117. Accessed June 6, 2012.
14. "Five Dollar Day." (n.d.) Bryant University Blog. http://web.bryant. edu/~ehu/h364proj/summ_99/armoush/page3.html. Accessed June 6, 2012.
15. Steele, Tara. (2011) "Why Disorganization Hurts the Brain's Capacity to Function Properly." AGBeat. http://agbeat.com/real-estate-news-events/ why-disorganization-hurts-the-brains-capacity-to-function-properly/. Accessed June 6, 2012.
16. "About Us." (2012) Evernote. http://evernote.com/corp/. Accessed June 6, 2012.
17. Jack, William and Suri, Tavneet. (2010) "The Economics of M-PESA." MIT Sloan. http://www.mit.edu/~tavneet/M-PESA.pdf. Accessed June 7, 2012.
18. Rice, Xan. (2007) Kenya sets world first with money transfer by mobile. *The Guardian*. http://www.guardian.co.uk/money/2007/mar/20/kenya. mobilephones. Accessed June 7, 2012.
19. "M-PESA Launched in South Africa." (2010) How We Made It in Africa. http://www.howwemadeitinafrica.com/m-pesa-launched-in-south-africa/3611/. Accessed June 7, 2012.
20. "M-PESA Disappoints for Vodacom SA." (2011) Tech Central. http://www. techcentral.co.za/m-pesa-disappoints-for-vodacom-sa/23167/. Accessed June 7, 2012.
21. "Ushahidi". (n.d.) Ushahidi webpage. http://www.ushahidi.com/. Accessed June 7, 2012.

22. Crowe, Adam. (2010) The elephant in the JIC: The fundamental flaw in emergency public information within the NIMS framework. *Journal of Homeland Security & Emergency Management*. 7: 1.
23. Finley, Mike. (1994) "The Five Hundred Dollar Twenty Bill and Other Negotiated Pleasures." Max Bazerman: What is Strategy? Blog. http://mfinley.com/experts/bazerman/bazerman.htm. Accessed June 11, 2012.
24. Schenk, Robert (n.d.) "Nasty Auctions." http://ingrimayne.com/econ/info_risk/NastyAuction.html. Accessed June 11, 2012.

6

Magnification

Effective leaders view and treat the people around them as partners or potential partners. Being an ally to others means using the principles of reciprocity: as we do things for others in the organization, they become more likely to help in return.

Naim Kapucu and Alphaslan Ozerdem[1]

SOCIAL MAGNIFICATION

As discussed in the first section of this book, social media systems such as Facebook, Twitter, Tumblr, Pinterest, and YouTube are inherently built upon community, conversations, and relationships between individuals and organizations. These connections are vastly widening the natural, virtual, and occasionally artificial networks between people. In turn, these networks have created individual and interconnected communities that share similar and sometimes divergent ideas about particular issues that are either of local importance or more global in nature.

This interaction within these social networks and communities is what creates value and purpose within social media and creates a system that is distinctively different from other forms of traditional and digital media (e.g., print, television, radio, and websites). The connectivity and convenience of the mobile tools to engage social systems allows for participation and engagement that often exceed the level of engagement seen in traditional (and physical) community activities such as town halls, elections, forums, and parades. Malcolm Gladwell says, "Social networks are effective at increasing participation—by lessening the level of motivation that participation requires."[2] Because of the lowered level of motivation required, the availability of access tools, low cost of engagement, and wide range of topics, social media can quickly magnify messages, content, quality, and effectiveness of engagement within the system.

Within emergency management, the magnification of social media systems has profoundly increased since early 2010 after the earthquake in Haiti (see Figure 6.1). Starting with that event, all emergencies and disasters have been defined by the organic and often spontaneous involvement of citizens engaged through digital communities. Meaningful engagement is a critical element of how volunteers and donations are managed during disasters, as well as how incident intelligence is gathered and reviewed. Likewise, emergency preparedness and educational messages have also been radically changed (for both good and bad) by the level and significance by which they are carried and magnified by the engaged communities. Consequently, a new leadership paradigm within emergency management is necessary to embrace this magnification and leverage it for successful response and recovery efforts.

Figure 6.1 Dynamic scenes of response during the 2010 earthquake in Haiti often are redistributed via digital communities and help establish dynamically engaged online communities. (From US Navy/Mass Communication Specialist 2nd Class Justin Stumberg. With permission.)

EPIDEMICS: HOW INFORMATION SPREADS

To further understand the magnification possibilities for the field of emergency management, the sociological and psychological considerations of how this happens must be further evaluated. There are several theories that can help frame this issue, but fundamentally it is critical to understand that individuals share content, messages, programming, and passion with other individuals who in turn share with other individuals and so on, all without the oversight or control of formalized government. This exponential pattern is what creates the magnification possibilities for any organization leveraging social tools such as Facebook and Twitter. Moreover, as we show throughout the remainder of this chapter, this concept is particularly important for emergency management organizations struggling to maintain planning and preparedness in light of financial cutbacks in tough financial times.

To conceptualize this process, the biological phenomenon of epidemics outlines this process. In his book *Tipping Point: How Little Things Make Big Differences*, Malcolm Gladwell describes epidemics as "A function of the people who transmit infectious agents, the infectious agent itself, and the environment in which the infectious agent is operating."[3] Because of the interconnectedness of the participant, agent, and environment, epidemics are often widespread due to contagiousness. Interestingly, contagiousness and epidemic conditions do not abide by typical cause and effect relationships. Rather, small changes have large, dramatic, and often uncontrollable results. Much as with local epidemics or the global H1N1 pandemic, these conditions are often only identified after the results have been dramatically observed and are consequently difficult to manage. Social media magnification results in much the same way during a disaster. See Figure 6.2. The activity and distribution of information is often only noticed by professional emergency management organizations after they have grown to epidemic proportions and are thus very difficult to handle after the fact.

Within web-based and social systems, this concept is often referred to as a *meme*. The term originates from the 1976 book by Richard Dawkins called *The Selfish Gene*. Dawkins describes a meme as a "Unit of cultural transmission or imitation," however, no complete definition has ever been settled upon in light of the Internet and social media.[25] Anecdotally, a meme is an online social concept that is established via social media systems such as Facebook, shared by e-mails, posted on websites and

151

Figure 6.2 Contagious conditions are not limited to public health crises, but can serve as excellent examples of how digital information can grow and spread during all types of emergencies or disasters. (From U.S. Centers for Disease Control & Prevention (CDC)/Unknown. With permission.)

blogs, or otherwise made available to the world through digital interfaces. More important, a meme acts as an epidemic or quickly transmits an idea or concept that can replicate, spread, and evolve very quickly. This evolution also includes the adaptation and cross-over of its use to other information sources or pieces of technology.[25] This spread (much like a virus) occurs without any formal intervention or official acknowledgment. Understanding the foundations of epidemics and memes as well as how they spread will be critical for emergency management leaders to begin to understand when, where, and how social technologies are and will be leveraged during a disaster to magnify the possible response and recovery protocols.

WHAT IS . . . A MEME?

A meme is an idea or concept that rapidly spreads most often through social media or the Internet and evolves into a humorous, poignant, or practical concept. Much as a virus or epidemic, memes often spread, mutate, and cross over to new applications as they are shared.

An additional visualization of social media magnification is the so-called "Zuckerberg's law." Mark Zuckerberg, co-founder of Facebook, said in November 2008, "I would expect that next year people will share

152

twice as much information as they share this year, and [the] next year they will share twice as much as they did the year before."[4] Since that time, Zuckerberg's theory has held true with exponential growth in the users and content available not only on Facebook, but Twitter, YouTube, and nearly all social media systems. To put this into perspective, as of Spring 2012, Facebook had more than 125 billion friend connections that generated more than 300 million uploaded photos and 3.2 billion "likes" and comments generated every day.[5] Likewise, YouTube supports nearly 72 hours of video uploaded every minute with more than 3 billion hours of videos watched each month.[6] With this level of social media sharing and engagement, the possibility of Zuckerberg's law influencing the possibility of magnification is significant, particularly during emergencies and disasters.

OPENING THE BOX: McKAYLA IS NOT IMPRESSED

During the Summer Olympic games of 2012, the United States women's gymnastics team was highly regarded, with both individual and collective medals projected. This was especially true of 16-year-old McKayla Maroney who was considered one of the best gymnasts on the vault in the world. Therefore, on August 5, 2012, when Maroney performed a nearly flawless vault many fans and prognosticators projected her to win individual gold. Unfortunately on her second vault she failed to get high enough and ultimately fell down on the landing. Because of her fall, Maroney's combined score left her with the silver medal for the competition. Although certainly a worthwhile result, Maroney's disappointed facial expression was caught by Bryan Snyder of Reuters who photographed a now notorious scowling expression. By August 7th, a Tumblr blog was established showing photoshopped images of Maroney's scowl set against famous or historical individuals or feats of grandeur with the phrase, "McKayla Is Not Impressed" emblazoned across the bottom. When similar photos were posted to Reddit (an online news aggregator) there were more than 170,000 views of the images. Likewise, the Tumblr site received thousands of followers within hours of being established. This is a classic example of a meme that originated accidentally after a legitimate and highly watched international sporting event.[44,45] As with nearly all memes that rise in the digital environment Maroney clearly had no intention, understanding, or acknowledgment of what happened in response to her real-life situation.

153

VOLUNTEERISM: TRADITIONAL AND UNAFFILIATED

Volunteerism in emergencies and disasters has long been important to professional emergency management and response professionals. In 1881, the recently established American Red Cross responded to the Michigan "Thumb Fire" (named after the shape of the Michigan peninsula) that killed nearly 300 people, caused nearly $2.5 million (unadjusted figure) in damages, and left thousands of rural survivors homeless or without crops or livestock (see Figure 6.3).[7] Since that time, the use of individual and collective groups of volunteers has become a staple of response organizations. The importance and influence of

Figure 6.3 Clara Barton's recently established American Red Cross first responded to a disaster in 1881 after a large fire in the Thumb peninsula of Michigan killed nearly 300 people and left thousands more homeless or without crops or livestock. (From Public Domain.)

professional emergency volunteerism is focused and profiled through state and national groups referred to as volunteer organizations active in disaster (VOAD). For example, the National VOAD website lists 52 different professional volunteer groups active in emergency response including (but not limited to) the United Methodist Committee on Relief (UMCOR), Islamic Relief USA, Feeding America, and Catholic Charities.[8]

Unfortunately for professional emergency managers, not all individuals seeking to volunteer during an emergency or disaster affiliate with professional volunteer organizations such as those listed above. On the contrary, so-called unaffiliated or spontaneous volunteers can become significant challenges to formalized response. These volunteers (often common citizens with little to no formal training) are willing to help but because they are not associated with any part of the existing emergency management structure are often underutilized and problematic to effective event management. To put this in perspective, after the terrorist attacks on 9/11, New York City had to manage more than 25,000 unaffiliated volunteers who arrived from throughout the country and ultimately had to be integrated with more than 53,000 trained American Red Cross volunteers (see Figure 6.4).[9] NVOAD presents this as a paradox: people's willingness to volunteer versus the system's capacity to utilize them effectively.[10]

Figure 6.4 More than 25,000 unaffiliated volunteers responded after the 9/11 terrorist attacks to help support survivors and recovery activities. (From Public Domain/Don Halasy.)

VOLUNTEER MANAGEMENT 2.0

The presence of spontaneous volunteerism has grown significantly through the use of social media tools. Most often individuals or groups of like-minded citizens gather virtually via social networks or blogs to find opportunities to engage in disaster response and recovery. This virtual volunteerism occurs both within the traditional emergency volunteer structure and in parallel with spontaneous unaffiliated activities. For example, in 2009 during flooding in North Dakota along the Red River near the Fargo–Moorhead area, local response officials were struggling to generate enough volunteers to maintain the levee dike. However, after a local citizen posted a message to his Facebook page about the need for more volunteers, the number of volunteers jumped from a few hundred to nearly five thousand by the next day (see Figure 6.5). Because of the significant success of the use of social media, city officials quickly approved the use

Figure 6.5 Local leaders in Fargo utilized social networking to exponentially increase the number of volunteers who were available for sandbagging during their 2009 flooding event. (From U.S. Airforce/Senior Master Sgt. David H. Lipp. With permission.)

of Facebook to create the Fargo-Moorhead Flood Volunteer Network to continue to recruit and maintain volunteers.[11]

Likewise, after the 2010 and 2011 earthquakes in Canterbury, New Zealand, a group of students at the University of Canterbury began to organize an emergency group of volunteers via a Facebook page. At the peak of their engagement, they maintained more than 25,000 "likes" via Facebook and thousands of volunteers. However, they provided information and engagement only through the established Facebook page. The group, which became known as the University of Canterbury Student Army (UCSA), quickly integrated into formal civil defense and emergency management operations and became part of the official response mechanisms.[12] The UCSA mission was so effective that local leadership in Canterbury ultimately honored the group with the Royal New Zealand Anzac of the Year Award for 2012 based on a "single act . . . or significant service to New Zealanders or the international community."[13] Ultimately, the UCSA defeated the paradox mentioned above because the skills and tools provided by the group were leveraged within the formalized system rather than as a spontaneous and unaffiliated group.

Although the Fargo-Moorhead Volunteer Network and UCSA examples successfully integrated into the formalized volunteer recruitment and management systems being leveraged within the given communities, this does not always occur during emergencies and disasters. For example, after the tornado outbreak in April 2011 in the southeastern United States, an emergent volunteer group called Toomers for Tuscaloosa quickly galvanized and became a clearinghouse of information and survivor supplies related to the disaster. According to one of its founders, the Toomers for Tuscaloosa came about because of a public perception that traditional response systems were insufficiently responding to the needs of those citizens who had been affected by the event. These included mass care and sheltering issues as well as special care items such as baby formula, diapers, water, and food.[14]

Emergent Groups Addressing Unique Needs

Toomers for Tuscaloosa was headed up by Holly Hart who served as their chief executive officer. Since the emergence of Toomers for Tuscaloosa in April 2011, the group has provided more than 82,000 meals, distributed 400 free helmets to kids for tornado safety, bought a man a mobile home, and remodeled disaster-damaged houses not only in Alabama, but also in Missouri (Joplin) and Kentucky (West Liberty). Hart and her team used more than 9,000 cell phone minutes each month to process requests and volunteer activities and leveraged a $60,000 budget without any salaries. All funding (much as with traditional volunteer organizations) came from private donations.[15] In many ways, the results and structure appear to be very similar to other traditional volunteer organizations active in emergencies and disasters, but in reality the engagement and exponential growth were substantially different.

Toomers for Tuscaloosa (see Figure 6.6) was an emergent and organic group that spread the need and magnified its message primarily through Facebook, Twitter, and an integrated website. Within weeks of being established, the Facebook and Twitter pages had more than 80,000 and 2,500 followers, respectively. To put this into comparison, the official Alabama Emergency Management Agency/FEMA Facebook page for the tornado outbreak had approximately 3,500 followers at the same time.[12] The emergent nature of the group leveraged pre-existing relations and local passions (Toomers referenced Auburn University and Tuscaloosa was a reference to the University of Alabama). Clearly people in the state of Alabama (and eventually 23 other states) identified Toomers for Tuscaloosa as a place to receive information about the disaster and as an easy and effective way to help respond.

Figure 6.6 Emergent volunteerism groups such as Toomers for Tuscaloosa generate significant support for disaster survivors including distributing meals, providing safety equipment, and helping rebuild disaster-damaged homes. (From FEMA/Ruth Kennedy. With permission.)

As discussed later in this chapter, this type of relevant and compelling emergent group can generate an amazing amount of interest and be extraordinarily effective at meeting the needs and issues raised during response to the event. When disaster survivors needed diapers, Toomers for Tuscaloosa addressed the need. When shelter was needed (because of delays in formal federal and state aid), Toomers for Tuscaloosa found the shelter. Perhaps one of the most profound examples of the effectiveness of their system of people helping people outside of government control and intervention was when an Alabama woman ran to a tornado shelter in the middle of the night without any undergarments. The storm destroyed her home and blew away all of her possessions. She posted her need to the Toomers for Tuscaloosa Facebook page and was addressed within an hour by a woman in Florida who had recently had augmentation surgery and no longer needed her old undergarments.[14] Although an extremely non-traditional need, it is a quality of life support that has almost no traditional mechanism to be addressed.

Although Toomers for Tuscaloosa was perhaps an emergent organization that leveraged local passions under the right leadership during a devastating disaster, it is a prime example of a growing trend. Similar emergent groups arose after the EF5 Joplin tornado (2011) and Tokyo earthquake and tsunami (2011) and appear to be a growing trend in disaster volunteer management. Unfortunately, the vast majority of professional emergency managers have yet to move beyond cooperation with traditional volunteer organizations active in disaster. Likewise, only recently have some of the more active NVOAD leaders interested and passionate about social media begun to consider how traditional organizations can acknowledge, engage, and utilize emergency volunteer groups such as Toomers for Tuscaloosa. No best practices have yet been commonly accepted, however, it is clear that these groups exemplify the achievable magnification that is possible by leveraging social media and other emerging technologies.

Techno-Volunteers

In addition to the magnification of traditional disaster volunteerism and the rise of emergent groups of volunteer networks, the final type of magnification possibility resides in a group of technological volunteers who are geographically dispersed, but disaster focused. Perhaps the most well-known example of technological volunteerism is a group called Crisis Commons; however, other examples include CrisisMappers and Humanity Road. Although each organization's mission and purpose is unique, Crisis Commons states that their volunteers "are not only technical folks like coders, programmers, geospatial and visualization ninjas but . . . are also . . . super creative and smart folks who can lead teams, manage projects, share information, search the internet, translate languages, know usability, [and] can write a research paper."[17] It is this unique combination of technical and response experts that allows for the magnification of response capabilities through volunteerism.

The idea of technological volunteerism started in 2009 as a derivative of the so-called "bar" camp where individuals came together and leveraged open development technology to address solutions to problems being addressed. Due to the foresight and leadership of those involved with Crisis Commons, this bar camp idea was applied to disasters. Although small events occurred, the first major application of this concept occurred after the 2010 Haiti earthquake that displaced thousands of Haitians. Specifically, within five days of the earthquake more than 400 people in five American cities worked on 13 technology-related projects in support of victims and disaster response. By the next week, 14 additional camps (or groups of technology volunteers) were held to continue to address the needs, and within four months of the earthquake a total of 65 camps in 10 different countries were held. Among other activities, Crisis Commons and their hosted crisis camps helped create an app to aid in translating local messages posted in Haitian Creole and supported open source mapping of damaged areas throughout Haiti by using Ushahidi.[18]

WHAT IS . . . USHAHIDI?

Ushahidi is a nonprofit technology company that specializes in the creation of open-sourced and free software that helps collect information, visualize it graphically, and interactively map the collection. Ushahidi provides three different types of programs: Ushahidi, Swift River, and CrowdMap.[19] Although it was originally developed to monitor democratic elections in Kenya, it was quickly adapted for disasters and has been leveraged in disasters including the Haiti earthquake (2010), Deepwater Horizon oil spill (2010), Alabama tornadoes (2011), and Snowmaggeden (2010) just to name a few.[12]

The astounding possibility of technological volunteers is twofold. First, the availability and application of emerging and social technologies creates a virtual infrastructure that can support (and in the case of Haiti, replace) affected or nonexistent infrastructure. Needs that arise are quickly addressed based on need and application of the wide spectrum of technologies available at that particular time. This format creates a sense of "organized chaos" that lacks—intentionally—organized structure and hierarchy that is common in emergency volunteer organizations and the professional emergency management organizations that support them. This quickly allows for significant output and productive volunteerism that in many ways has outpaced the traditional process, particularly in highly affected areas. This possibility for magnification must be strongly considered and integrated whenever possible in local VOAD and emergency management organizations to ensure the significant possibilities that exist due to the format of technological volunteerism are not underutilized or misapplied.

OPENING THE BOX: WHY KETCHUP WORKS

Ketchup is the quintessential food condiment. People of many cultural and ethnic backgrounds use ketchup to aid and amplify the flavors of other foods. Mustard, mayonnaise, relish, and certain kinds of other condiments are also popular, but are very different from ketchup. For example, commercially available mustard is often available in at least three different varieties: standard, honey mustard, and spicy mustard. Likewise, over the last several years there has been significant growth in the variations of mayonnaise including standard forms, spiced and herb forms, and sweeter salad dressing alternatives. But this trend has not occurred with ketchup. Since Henry Heinz bottled fresh tomatoes, vinegar, and selected spices in glass jars back in 1890, the ketchup formula has basically stayed the same.[19] The only significant attempt at altering this was the limited time release of green and purple ketchup in 2000 to moderate success.[20] Regardless, the physical ingredients and formulation stayed the same with just additional food coloration added. Various manufacturers, both mass produced and locally generated, produce ketchup but the ingredients are consistent. So why is ketchup produced and consumed with such consistency in spite of the limited number of ingredients? In his article, "The Ketchup Conundrum," Malcolm Gladwell explains that there are five fundamental tastes in the human palate; salty, sweet, sour, bitter, and umami.[21] Most individuals are familiar with the first four, but may not be knowledgeable about umami. According to the Umami Information Center, umami is a Japanese term that refers to the pleasant and savory test that is generated from the presence of certain amino acids that naturally occur in many foods including meat, fish, vegetables, chicken soup, fish stock, aged cheese, and dairy products. Umami is also a broader description of subtle, blended, and magnified flavors and tastes that are perceived as delicious.[22] In other words, it's what "Turns a soup from salt water into a food."[21] Interestingly, once Heinz released his version of ketchup (which arguably became the industry standard), he created a potent source of umami. Specifically, sourness from the vinegar, sweetness from the added sugar, and natural saltiness and bitterness from the added seasonings hit four major human taste sensations and ultimately amplify each other to create umami. Clearly the ingredients of ketchup are strong individuals, but the effects are compounded when combined and magnify its value and purpose. It is truly an example of something that is greater than the combination of its parts. This same magnification is possible when emergency managers begin to apply leadership to ensure "ingredients" such as professional emergency management, traditional volunteer groups, social media, and the various components that have grown (and will continue to rise) are effectively combined after emergencies and disasters.

THE CHALLENGE OF DONATIONS MANAGEMENT

In addition to volunteer management during emergencies and disasters, the field of emergency management must also consider how to manage and deliver donated goods and resources (see Figure 6.7). People are inherently affected by emergencies and disasters, whether they have an impact on their local community or are witnessed from afar. For those within the affected community, needs and gaps in the system are quickly apparent and most often revolve around basic support including food, water, shelter, and specialized needs (e.g., baby formula or maintenance medications). Unfortunately, individuals outside the area are unsure (or simply forget) what fundamental needs are present in the affected area and begin to collect and donate items in support of disaster.

According to one study after Hurricane Katrina, there was a definite correlation between characteristics of the disaster and the type of

Figure 6.7 Donations management is one of the most challenging facets of short-term and long-term disaster recovery. (From FEMA/Tim Burkitt. With permission.)

donations generated. For example, characteristics including geographical proximity to the disaster event, income, education, unemployment status, and type of donor (e.g., organization headquarters, company, and individual) all had an impact on the magnitude of monetary, physical, and in-kind donations.[24] Likewise, disasters in and around highly populated areas of well-educated, wealthy, and married individuals corresponds to larger and often more complicated donations.[24] These considerations are evidence that donations management is already grossly affected sociologically and psychologically, and seems ripe to be leveraged and aided by social networks and technologies.

In addition to the natural sociological challenges, there are many logistical and planning considerations that influence donations management. For example, unsolicited donations create an extremely significant burden on local response organizations and emergency management agencies. For example, donated materials must first be logistically separated, stored, and assessed for quality and appropriateness, which often requires significant manpower and warehousing space that are difficult to manage during the disaster. Likewise, local infrastructure can often be damaged such that it is difficult for delivery trucks and other transportation systems to locate warehouses or drop sites. Consequently, loads of donated goods are often simply left on the side of the road in the disaster zone. For example, the damage from Hurricane

Andrew in 1992 was so significant that street signs and other geographic markers had been knocked down such that there was no way for people to know where to go. As a result, piles and piles of donated goods were simply left and ultimately had to be burned and discarded after they had been left for long periods of time in the warmth and humidity of south Florida.

Likewise, those seeking to help disaster victims often donate goods that are inappropriate for disaster zones. Rather than make a concerted effort to select and donate goods that will help those basic needs established above, it is often (subconsciously) seen as an opportunity to clean out closets and donate things that are no longer used or desired. As a result, sometimes goods are donated that are completely inappropriate, including bathing suits for winter storms, heavy coats for tropical areas, used underwear, expired or opened foodstuffs, perishable foods, and the like. One of the most outrageous examples was the opened chocolate body paint that was donated to a local church hosting a food drive for disaster victims.[23]

DONATIONS MANAGEMENT 2.0: TEXTING

In contrast to these traditional models of donations management, new social concepts have begun to influence how this process is conducted both within the formal structures and by emergent groups. Much as with volunteer management, these groups or processes have become highly beneficial and often result in real and perceived increases in productivity and impact to the affected communities. The challenges present in traditional donations management are still found in these new models; however, by leveraging certain technologies and social engagement, forward-thinking organizations, activists, and leaders have found new ways to magnify the possibilities and the potential of mass donations during emergencies and disasters.

Perhaps the most profound example of this was again after the 2010 earthquake in Haiti that ravished the already poor country. Much as with the forward leading actions of Crisis Commons discussed earlier in this chapter, the American Red Cross found a significant opportunity to leverage the magnification possibilities of social and emerging technologies through their text-to-donate campaign. Specifically, the American Red Cross worked with all the major cell phone providers to allow for $10 to be donated to earthquake relief every time a user

Figure 6.8 The American Red Cross utilized a text-to-donate campaign during the response to the 2010 Haiti earthquake that has become an industry standard for disaster relief organizations. (From Screenshot. With permission.)

texted "HAITI" to the number 90999[26] (see Figure 6.8). Within two days of the earthquake, this campaign generated $5 million and over the next month generated more than $32 million, which ultimately constituted nearly 10% of the total given to the American Red Cross for earthquake relief in Haiti.[12]

In a matter of days 10% of all donations raised by the American Red Cross were generated by thousands (if not millions) of users who had already embraced their cell phones and the related functionality, including SMS text messaging. In fact, by 2009 nearly five trillion text messages were sent annually around the globe. By 2010, cell phone texting had surpassed phone calls, e-mails, and face-to-face conversation as the primary mode of communication for 12–17 year olds, with the average teenager sending more than 3,330 text messages per month.[27,28] At nearly the same time, 72% of adults utilized SMS text messaging for communication and sent out an average of 10 text messages per day.[29] By late 2011, more than 95% of all 18–29 year olds used text messaging features on their mobile phones and sent or received an average of nearly 88 messages per day.[30] Given the pervasiveness of text messages, leveraging their usage for the quick and easy generation of response funds was extraordinarily effective. It has since become standard practice for the American Red Cross and many of the larger nonprofit volunteer and donations management organizations.

Although seemingly very successful, it is important to understand more of the sociological and psychological considerations that surround this type of event to ensure new leaders can embrace this phenomenon successfully. For instance, Pew Internet conducted a study two years after the Haiti earthquake and found that most of the text donations were made on impulse, primarily in response to media coverage about the disaster. Moreover, 75% of those surveyed indicated that it was the first time they had participated in a text donation campaign and only 33% of them made additional donations (via traditional mechanisms) to Haiti relief. On the other hand, more than 50% of those who texted a donation have repeated the act for disasters since the earthquake in Haiti, with nearly 40% donating via text message after the 2011 Japan earthquake and tsunami.[31] Clearly, utilizing text messaging has opened doors for beneficial new emergency preparedness and response activities and serves as a prime example that social and emerging technologies are extremely valuable when used creatively and appropriately to magnify the results and productivity of traditional processes.

DONATIONS MANAGEMENT 2.0: SOCIAL GIVING

On the other end of the spectrum from the ubiquitous nature of SMS text messaging is the small but growing social gaming market. According to a 2012 survey, more than 81 million people play games via social networks such as Facebook or via their mobile device every day, and more than 510 million are considered active users within social gaming.[32] These games include FarmVille, MobWars, Words With Friends, Bejeweled Blitz, CityVille, Sims Social, and other similar formats. In most cases, the game player is engaged in various challenges and earns a certain amount of reward for each activity which allows the game to expand and increase in detail. However, at some point in the game, a certain level is reached that is achievable given standard access and engagement. Beyond that point, users can purchase virtual currency with real currency to continue to move the game along. Although this may seem unusual and unnecessary for nongame players, Bloomberg News reported in 2012 that social games will generate $5.33 billion which is an increase of 39% from the year before, with a potential peak of nearly $9 billion by 2015.[33]

It is interesting that these purchased virtual goods and currency can also be donated to support disaster response activities. For instance, in 2011 after the Japan earthquake and tsunami, social gaming producer Zynga established funding strategies in cooperation with Save the Children to donate funds to victims of that particular disaster. Specifically, in their games FarmVille and FrontierVille, Zynga designated certain virtual products such as sweet potatoes and radishes that could be purchased to donate money to disaster relief.[34] Similarly, in 2010, Zynga offered a virtual "Gulf Coast Turtle" in its game FishVille that would generate proceeds that would be donated to the Audubon Society to support clean-up efforts after the Deepwater Horizon oil spill.[35]

Much as with the use of SMS text messaging to generate additional fund raising, the rise of so-called "social good" through social gaming is extraordinary. Traditional emergency management strategies are to utilize traditional voluntary organizations active in disasters to generate and manage donations generated in response to a disaster. However, as discussed earlier, this process is often extraordinarily cumbersome and resource intensive, but much of this process is alleviated if donations are made as money rather than items. Consequently, it is critical for both volunteer organizations active in disasters as well emergency managers at all levels to consider how to embrace social gaming as not only a fringe activity that has occurred in a limited number of major disasters, but also as a legitimate and real opportunity to magnify people's use and engagement of social media.

MOVING TOWARD SOCIAL INTELLIGENCE

Social media and emerging technologies also are affecting how emergency management and response leaders handle intelligence and information gathering during incidents and disasters. Law enforcement, homeland security, and other intelligence-gathering organizations have traditionally utilized a variety of means to seek out information that might benefit the response operation or investigation underway. Intelligence activities have always necessitated the collection of information from multiple trustworthy sources. Since the explosion of social media systems in the mid-2000s, the challenge to the intelligence community has been the difficulty in accepting social media as a trustworthy source of incident-specific information. However, as events like the Arab Spring of 2011 move from small-scale upheaval to full-scale revolution, it has become clear to the intelligence community that the information contained within social media has value and must be leveraged.

For example, in 2012, the Intelligence Advanced Research Projects Activity (IARPA) which is an arm of the Office of the Director of National Intelligence, issued a public solicitation to figure out how to use "Open Source Indicators" to help predict and foresee intelligence events using a method similar to how meteorologists perform weather predictions at specific and regular intervals.[36] Considering the anecdotal evidence of the significant impact of Twitter and Facebook during the Arab Spring, leveraging information openly posted in shared systems as well as complex patterns, this type of system would be highly beneficial. Likewise, the United States Institute of Peace initiated a "Blogs and Bullets" meeting to bring companies and experts who analyze social media data together with policy makers and other members of the intelligence community.

It is clearly evident that both users of social technology systems and significant components of the intelligence community have acknowledged that leveraging social media for intelligence is not only prudent, but necessary for the management and control of future time-sensitive information. Interestingly, the exchange of information via social media channels and the data and intelligence shared therein occurs with or without the intervention of formal emergency response and professional intelligence gathering. Therefore, utilizing these systems is a prime opportunity for organizations seeking out and in need of additional incident information to magnify their efforts without additional resources being pushed into the system.

Crowdsourcing Intelligence

One prime example of how intelligence is being leveraged (intentionally or not) to magnify information available during a particular event is through crowdsourcing. Crowdsourcing is a broad concept that allows the collective knowledge of a group of individuals (either as strangers or commonly known) to address certain challenges or needs for information. Wikipedia is perhaps the most well-known example of this phenomenon, with more than 17 million individuals registered as editors (or knowledge contributors) to the system. During an emergency or disaster, emergency managers comfortable with social media often use crowdsourcing to confirm or clarify incident-related information. Craig Fugate, FEMA administrator and social media maven, has often stated the importance of crowdsourcing information about events (see Figure 6.9). Specifically, prior to the 2011 Hurricane Irene, he stated that "individuals, families, and communities are our nation's first first responders . . . [and] the sooner we are able to ascertain the on-the-ground reality of a situation, the better we will be able to coordinate our response efforts in support of our [affected communities]."[38]

WHAT IS . . . CROWDSOURCING?

Crowdsourcing is a phenomenon where the collective knowledge, wisdom, experience, or availability of a group of people is greater than the individual components. Because of this collective capability, crowdsourcing lends itself to modern leadership in emergency management through its ability to amplify and magnify the capability of the individual emergency manager or response agency.

Figure 6.9 FEMA Administrator Craig Fugate provides situation report to President Obama during the response to Hurricane Sandy in 2012. (From FEMA/ Aaron Skolnik. With permission.)

In addition to disaster information, intelligence agencies also benefit from the magnification of intelligence information from crowdsourcing. For example, after the 2011 Stanley Cup hockey finals, individuals in Vancouver began to riot in response to their team losing (the Vancouver Canucks lost game seven to the Boston Bruins). As events progressed, the Vancouver Police Department posted a message on their website asking for pictures of the riots. Within hours an online Tumblr site called "Vancouver 2011 Riot Criminal List" appeared, where the general public quickly and consistently started posting pictures from the riots including individuals, groups of people, destruction, and other criminal activities. The creator of the Tumblr site posted the first message as: "Let's hold people accountable for their actions! Alright everyone, let's start posting pictures of the idiots setting fires and looting."[39] Similar other social media sites arose that collected and helped identify those who were guilty.

Ultimately, within one year, the Vancouver Police Department was able to bring 301 charges against 114 rioters.[40] Although the traditional investigative capabilities of the Vancouver Police Department certainly are on par with other major investigative organizations, the level of response from the public and the clear impact tremendously magnified the speed and delivery of law and order related to this particular event. It is unclear whether the Vancouver Police Department expected this level of response, but the department clearly was willing to leverage the crowd-sourced knowledge (through pictures and videos) of all criminal activity occurring. Much as with disaster response, the limited number of formal responders can only do so much and be in so many places, but the crowd is truly everywhere. There are certainly some ethical considerations for new leaders with using crowdsourcing for intelligence, and this is further discussed in Chapter 10.

TRADITIONAL PUBLIC EDUCATION

Public education and awareness have long been important to the traditional emergency manager. In many cases, state laws and statutes have been created specifically to require each legal jurisdiction to maintain some engagement with the general public. These campaigns are often divided into two major goals: public awareness and public engagement. Public awareness is often the consideration that the public needs to be aware of what risks exist in their community and what actions professional emergency response agencies take on their behalf. Likewise, armed with awareness, individuals and families are encouraged to take steps toward personal preparedness not only to maintain self reliance, but to take pressure off the formal response structure. This approach has traditionally been served through providing the public with printed educational materials (i.e., brochures and pamphlets), public gatherings, and most recently websites. This strategy is philosophically sound, however, it is built on assumptions that no longer work in a world built on the use and expectations of social technologies.

For instance, a 2012 RAND Corporation study revealed that current strategies in emergency preparedness are built on five faulty assumptions. The first of these is the assumption that a personally prepared citizen (or family) is the foundation for a resilient community. However, this type of individualism takes away from the strength of community networks, particularly those bearing witness through social media. The second assumption is that not preparing for a disaster is irrational, as numerous disasters happen regionally, nationally, or internationally every year. Unfortunately, this does not hold true as individuals and families simply do not make preparedness a major concern when they are rarely personally affected by such an event. Likewise, citizen assumptions about response time from professional responders and costs associated with preparedness often skew the commitment. The third assumption is that individual preparedness is constructive within the overall cycle of a disaster event. This consideration can be flawed, as some research has indicated that individuals who do commit to preparedness often think they can ride out major disasters (e.g., hurricanes) instead of responding to directed evacuations or other requested behavior changes that would better protect them. The fourth assumption is based on the presentation by most emergency management organizations of an evidenced-based approach to what should and should not be included in emergency preparedness kits. Unfortunately, the food, water, and supplies are very unique to the event and personal considerations of the individual or family. The final assumption is related to metrics of success. It is extremely difficult to quantify and measure what successful emergency preparedness looks like. Would it be food and water? Would it be making a plan? Must you have both? Looking at simple and one-directional measurements such as how many flyers are distributed is insufficient.

FAULTY ASSUMPTIONS RELATED TO TRADITIONAL EMERGENCY PREPAREDNESS[41]

Assumption 1: Prepared, self-reliant citizens are the foundation of a resilient community.

Assumption 2: There have been lots of disasters so it's irrational not to prepare.

Assumption 3: Promoting individual preparedness is constructive.

Assumption 4: Citizen preparedness campaigns are informed by evidence.

Assumption 5: Surveys of buying and planning activities are useful to gauge citizen preparedness.

Social Education Messaging

Instead of these traditional mechanisms, some emergency management leaders are beginning to utilize social technologies to magnify the otherwise challenging (and often ineffective) preparedness processes currently utilized as best practices. For example, if an emergency manager speaks with a small local community group he or she may spend an hour or more preparing for the presentation, collecting materials, traveling to the event, conducting the presentation, and heading back to the office, while only reaching a limited number of people. In contrast, if that same emergency manager spent the same amount of time communicating and in conversation on social media outlets such as Twitter, Facebook, and a blog, they not only could communicate with hundreds (instead of dozens), but those same messages can be redistributed and shared via those same systems. Consequently, the social media followers have become carriers of the message and significantly magnify the results of the original message. As was discussed in the chapter on entrepreneurism, it is critical that emergency managers seek out unique ways to maximize the results of the energy and resources initially deposited into the system.

One of the most profound examples of social media magnification for emergency preparedness is the Zombie Preparedness campaign that was run by the U.S. Centers for Disease Control and Prevention (CDC) in 2011. For a matter of less than $80, the public health emergency preparedness division created a blog that discussed what emergency preparedness activities would be necessary to become ready for the threat of a zombie invasion.[42] At no time did they declare there actually was a zombie invasion, but rather they simply stated the same standardized emergency preparedness messaging under the veil of zombies (instead of pandemic influenza and bioterrorism). Because of the unique presentation and the popularity of zombies, the posted CDC blog was visited and redistributed so many times that the CDC website servers crashed by the end of the first day it was posted. To put this into context, the CDC blog typically got 1,000 to 3,000 hits per day with a previous high of 10,000 daily visits; however, by the end of the first day (when the server first crashed) the site had more than 60,000 visits.[43] Since that time, the CDC has expanded this socially relevant format and pushed it into other formats such as graphic novels to continue to allow the natural interest and passion of citizens to carry the message and propel its success and acceptance to far greater audiences than ever before.

LEADERS IN THE OPEN: SARAH WATERMAN

In the hours after Tropical Storm Irene affected the state of Vermont, Sarah Waterman and several colleagues at Reality VC set up www.vtresponse.com to be an information resource for volunteers ready to help and those in need related to disaster response. Ms. Waterman has worked numerous disasters including Hurricane Katrina. In the following essay, written for this book, Ms. Waterman shares her views of how social media magnification affects emergency management leaders.

The Flexibility, Connectivity, and Adaptability of Social Media

Sarah Waterman

Imagine a hurricane hits your jurisdiction, bringing with it wind-driven rain, flooding, and the loss of power to most of the area. As emergency manager, you are focused on executing the emergency action plan. You are in close contact with police and fire officials, state officials, and members of county government and have a good sense of areas of major concern around the county. You provide information to television and radio stations about emergency shelters, safety around downed power lines, and water over the road, and contact numbers for those in need of assistance. By the end of Day 1, response is coordinated and a needs assessment is underway. By the morning of Day 2, however, your office has begun to receive calls about a Facebook page for a neighborhood that claims to be isolated and without assistance since before the storm. Residents of the neighborhood, other local citizens, and members of the media are actively posting on the wall of the page to get and spread the story. By 5 p.m., the nightly news is featuring the story about the forgotten residents of West Elm Lane.

The role of social media in emergency management is rapidly evolving. The flexibility, connectivity, and adaptability of social media make it an excellent tool for the emergency manager before, during, and after a disaster. These same qualities can also spread misinformation and spiral into a public relations nightmare. Harnessing the power of social media and mitigating the downsides starts with an understanding of the structure of social media platforms and how the magnification of message can work for the emergency manager.

The utility of social media in emergency management hails from two major structural features. First, social media networks connect people by a common thread. On Facebook, people connect with friends and family and like groups or businesses that are of interest. On Twitter, people follow other users who share interests or geography, those who entertain, and those who inform. Unlike brick and mortar networks, however, social media networks spread far beyond actual acquaintances and cross-over is greater than in a traditional network. For example, celebrities on social media are more accessible than in a traditional network. A tweet from a celebrity about a cause or issue spreads to millions of followers who can see the message and share it themselves. Second, social media make sharing simple. From liking a page to retweeting a link, social media platforms offer an easy mechanism for users to share information, indicate approval or alignment with an issue, and spread images and ideas from user to user. In the case of a disaster, both people in the affected area and with connections to that area use social media to gather and share information.

The magnification of message is one of the biggest benefits of social media. As many companies have learned, public relations nightmares can spark from a single tweet or post. Similarly, positive effects can be rapidly amplified. Because of the spider web structure, a message can be spread among a diverse audience in live time. In the wake of a disaster or emergency, the appearance of activity on a social media network can be as important as the substance. The ability to update information constantly on a Facebook page or a Twitter feed is a tool to communicate breaking information accurately and helps to quell accusations of inactivity. It also offers a way to communicate with citizens when power outages occur, as many social media platforms are readily accessible on smartphones.

When Tropical Storm Irene hit Vermont in 2011, residents from the governor to the average citizen turned to Twitter and Facebook. Towns set up Facebook pages to share pictures of damage, plan town meetings, and post road closures. Governor Shumlin used Twitter extensively from the day of the storm forward to communicate official updates from state government. Social media supplemented and further organized the small communities that dot the landscape of Vermont even with limited post-storm connectivity. Perhaps no experience illustrates social media magnification more succinctly than my own at the helm of VTResponse.com, a grassroots experiment in social media after Irene.

As a spontaneous volunteer following Hurricane Katrina, I was well acquainted with both the challenges and benefits of managing volunteers after a disaster. When Irene decimated my home state of Vermont, I was compelled to help. In 20 minutes on the morning after the storm, I built a blog called "VTResponse.com" and advertised it on my personal Twitter account and a Facebook page called "Vermont Flooding 2011." Intended as a place for people to connect to ask for and offer help, VTResponse became the clearinghouse for Irene-related information. By the end of Day 1, we had 8,000 views. On Day 2, we had 25,000 views and on Day 3, we had 44,000 views. All information was received via Twitter, Facebook, e-mail, or phone call and shared on the blog, where it was sent back out via Twitter and Facebook. In a state with an historically modest risk profile, social media offered a scalable inexpensive tool to harness volunteers and organize information following a major natural disaster.

ENDNOTES

1. Kapucu, Naim and Ozerdem, Alphaslan. (2011) *Managing Emergencies and Crisis*. New York: Jones and Bartlett Learning.
2. Gladwell, Malcolm. (2010) Small change. Articles from *The New Yorker/* Gladwell Blog. http://www.gladwell.com/2010/2010_10_04_a_twitter. html. Accessed June 18, 2012.
3. Gladwell, Malcolm. (2002) *Tipping Point: How Little Things Make a Big Difference*. New York: Bay Back Books, p. 18.

4. Hansell, Saul. (2008) Zuckerberg's law of information sharing. *New York Times*. http://bits.blogs.nytimes.com/2008/11/06/zuckerbergs-law-of-information-sharing/. Accessed June 19, 2012.

5. "Key Facts." (2012) Facebook statistics. http://newsroom.fb.com/content/default.aspx?NewsAreaId=22. Accessed June 19, 2012.

6. "Statistics." (2012) YouTube statistics. http://www.youtube.com/t/press_statistics. Accessed June 19, 2012.

7. "Responding to America's Wildfire." (n.d.) American Red Cross Museum. http://www.redcross.org/museum/history/wildfires.asp. Accessed June 19, 2012.

8. "National Members." (2012) National volunteer organizations active in disasters. http://www.nvoad.org/index.php?option=com_content&view=article&id=83&Itemid=65. Accessed June 19, 2012.

9. "Remembering 9/11: Ten Years Later." (2011) American Red Cross – Greater New York Region. http://www.nyredcross.org/?nd=remembering_911. Accessed June 20, 2012.

10. "Managing spontaneous volunteers in times of crisis: The synergy of structure and good intentions." (n.d.) National Volunteer Organizations Active in Disaster (NVOAD) Report. http://www.fema.gov/pdf/donations/ManagingSpontaneousVolunteers.pdf. Accessed June 20, 2012.

11. Condon, Patrick. (2009) Fargo uses social network to fight floodwaters. *MSNBC*. http://www.msnbc.msn.com/id/29901184/ns/technology_and_science-tech_and_gadgets/t/fargo-uses-social-networks-fight-floodwaters/#.T-KGQ7VYuSo. Accessed June 20, 2012.

12. Crowe, Adam. (2012) *Disasters 2.0: The Application of Social Media in Modern Emergency Management*. Boca Raton, FL: CRC Press.

13. "Student Volunteer Army Named Anzac of the Year." (2012) University of Canterbury Press Release. http://www.litarts.canterbury.ac.nz/rss/news/index.php?feed=news&articleId=369. Accessed June 20, 2012.

14. Hart, Holly. (2012) "Toomers for Tuscaloosa." Talk given at Midwest Disasters 2.0 Social Media Workshop. February 22.

15. Solomon, John. (2012) "Toomers for Tuscaloosa Still Gives Back One Year After Devastating Alabama Tornadoes." Al.com. http://www.al.com/sports/index.ssf/2012/04/toomers_for_tuscaloosa_still_g.html. Accessed June 21, 2012.

16. Lucas-McEwen, Valerie. (2012) Technical communities redefine disaster volunteerism. *Emergency Management Magazine*. http://www.emergencymgmt.com/disaster/Technical-Communities-Redefine-Volunteerism.html. Accessed June 22, 2012.

17. "About." (2012) CrisisCommons Blog. http://crisiscommons.org/about/. Accessed June 22, 2012.

18. "About Us." (2012) Ushahidi. http://ushahidi.com/about-us. Accessed June 23, 2012.

19. "Heinz Ketchup: 135 Years of Innovation." (n.d.) Heinz Blog. http://www.heinz.com/data/pdf/ketchuptimeline.pdf. Accessed June 24, 2012.

20. "It's Easy Being Green." (2000) About.com Pittsburgh. http://pittsburgh.about. com/library/weekly/aa101700a.htm. Accessed June 24, 2012.
21. Gladwell, Malcolm. (2004) "The ketchup conundrum." *The New Yorker*. September 6, 2004. http://www.gladwell.com/2004/2004_09_06_a_ketchup. html. Accessed June 24, 2012.
22. "What Exactly Is Umami?" (2011) Umami Information Center. http://www. umamiinfo.com/2011/02/What-exactly-is-umami.php. June 24, 2012.
23. Hamilton, Adam. (2008) Sermon at United Methodist Church of the Resurrection. Leawood, Kansas.
24. Destro, Lisa and Holguin-Veras, Jose. (n.d.) "Estimating Material Convergence: Flow of Donations for Hurricane Katrina." Rennsselaer Polytechnic Institute. http://transp.rpi.edu/~HUM-LOG/Doc/donations.pdf. Accessed June 25, 2012.
25. "What Is a Meme?" (2012) The Daily Meme. http://thedailymeme.com/ what-is-a-meme/. Accessed June 25, 2012.
26. Van Grove, Jennifer. (2010) "Red Cross Raises $5 Million for Haiti Through Text Messages." Mashable. http://mashable.com/2010/01/13/haiti-red-cross-donations/. Accessed June 28, 2012.
27. Show, Shane. (2010) "The Rise of Text Messaging." Mashable. http://mashable. com/2010/08/17/text-messaging-infographic/. Accessed June 28, 2012.
28. Parr, Ben. (2010) "The Average Teenager Sends 3,339 Text Messages Per Month." Mashable. http://mashable.com/2010/10/14/nielsen-texting-stats/. Accessed June 28, 2012.
29. Perez, Marin. (2010) "Pew: 72% of Adults Use Text Messaging." IntoMobile Blog. http://www.intomobile.com/2010/09/02/pew-text-messaging-adult/. Accessed June 28, 2012.
30. Smith, Aaron. (2011) "Americans and Text Messaging." Pew Internet. http://www.pewinternet.org/Reports/2011/Cell-Phone-Texting-2011/ Main-Report/How-Americans-Use-Text-Messaging.aspx. Accessed June 28, 2012.
31. Gahran, Amy. (2012) Donating to charity via text message: Lessons from Haiti. *CNN*. http://articles.cnn.com/2012-01-12/tech/tech_mobile_charity-donations-text-messages_1_text-donations-text-message-haitian-earthquake-relief?_s=PM:TECH. Accessed June 29, 2012.
32. Qualman, Erik. (2012) "Social Gaming Infographic: 81 Million Play Each Day + More Stats." Socialnomics. http://www.socialnomics.net/2012/01/20/ social-gaming-infographic-81-million-play-each-day-more-stats/. Accessed June 29, 2012.
33. MacMillian, Douglas. (2012) "Zynga Tops Sales Estimate on 'Hidden Chronicles' Lure." Bloomberg. http://www.bloomberg.com/news/2012-02-14/zynga-sales-profit-exceed-estimates-as-hidden-chronicles-lures-gamers. html. Accessed June 29, 2012.
34. "Zynga Provides In-Game Donation to Aid Japanese Relief." (2011) M91Game Blog. http://www.91mgame.com/2011/12/14/zynga-provides-in-game-donation-aid-japanese-disaster/. Accessed June 29, 2012.

35. "Social Media for Social Good." (2011) TriplePundit. http://www. triplepundit.com/2011/11/social-media-social-good/. Accessed June 29, 2012.
36. Baron, Frank. (2011) Researchers are skeptical that DOD can use social media to predict future conflict. *Stars and Stripes.* http://www.stripes.com/ blogs/stripes-central/stripes-central-1.8040/researchers-skeptical-dod-can- use-social-media-to-predict-future-conflict-1.155296. Accessed June 30, 2012.
37. "Wikipedia: Wikipedians." (n.d.) Wikipedia. http://en.wikipedia.org/wiki/ Wikipedia:Wikipedians. Accessed July 1, 2012.
38. Kash, Wiley. (2011) "Feds@Work: FEMA's Craig Fugate Gets Ahead of the Storm." AOL Government. http://gov.aol.com/2011/08/26/feds-work- femas-craig-fugate-gets-ahead-of-the-storm/. Accessed July 1, 2012.
39. Ehrlich, Brenna. (2011) "Vancouver Rioters Exposed on Crowdsourced Tumblr." Mashable. http://mashable.com/2011/06/16/vancouver-2011- tumblr/. July 1, 2012.
40. "Riot2011." (2012) VancouverPoliceBlog. http://vancouver.ca/police/2011riot/ riot-updates.html. Accessed July 2, 2012.
41. Uscher-Pines, Lori, et al. (2012) "Why Aren't Americans Listening to Disaster Preparedness Messaging?" Rand Corporation Study. http://www.rand.org/ blog/2012/06/why-arent-americans-listening-to-disaster-preparedness. html. Accessed July 3, 2012.
42. Daigle, Dave. (2012) "Zombie Preparedness." Presentation to Midwest Disasters 2.0 Social Media Workshop." February.
43. Marsh, Wendell. (2011) "CDC 'Zombie Apocalypse' Disaster Campaign Crashes Website." http://www.reuters.com/article/2011/05/19/us-usa- zombies-idUSTRE74I7W620110519 accessed on September 17, 2012.
44. "McKaylaisNotImpressed." (2012) KnowYourMeme. http://knowyourmeme. com/memes/mckayla-is-not-impressed. Accessed September 17, 2012.
45. "McKayla Maroney Is Not Impressed with Meme Inspired by Her." The Inquisitr. http://www.inquisitr.com/297160/mckayla-maroney-is- not-impressed-with-meme-inspired-by-her/. Accessed September 17, 2012.

7

Collaboration

Collaborative production where people have to coordinate with one another to get anything done is considerably harder than simply sharing, but the results can be more profound. New tools allow large groups to collaborate, by taking advantage of non-financial motivations and by allowing for wildly differing levels of contribution.

Clay Shirky[1]

INTRODUCTION

As has been established numerous times in the earlier chapters of this book, social media and emerging technologies are highly dependent on community and conversation. Much as with the physical relationship between individuals, friends, family, co-workers, neighbors, or acquaintances, there is often a genuine and real value created between the parties involved. This same experience can often occur with an individual, organization, business, or community. This type of relationship connectivity is what creates the sense of patriotism, religious fervor, community pride, team spirit, and brand loyalty within various groups or communities. The concept is also mirrored within social media outlets including blogs, microblogs, social networks, and photo and video sharing where networks are joined, messages are redistributed, and photos and videos are viewed in the thousands (or millions).

179

Within social media environments, these activities are both individual and community-centered as they are shared and discussed thoroughly.

Because of the uniquely passionate engagement that is created through conversations and the subsequent relationships, there is an inherent capability to create and support opportunities for partnership and collaboration, especially within a social environment. Unlike efficiency and magnification that were discussed in Chapters 5 and 6, respectively, the capability and potential benefit of collaboration shifts from secondary and indirect measures to formal and direct actions that reflect those natural relationships discussed earlier.

The importance of collaboration has and will continue to be important to professional emergency managers. The need for collaboration within the field of emergency management is twofold. First, the inherent function of emergency management is to help coordinate resources and responses to major events affecting a local community. Second, emergency managers are often overlooked in communities that have not recently had major emergencies and consequently are often underequipped and understaffed. These two characteristics make collaboration unavoidable, which is why there are government-, legal-, and community-based collaborations that are standard practice for emergency managers. These collaborations often include relationships with state and regional governments as well as nongovernmental organizations such as the American Red Cross and Salvation Army. See Figure 7.1.

Unfortunately, the average emergency manager does not yet see using social media in this same vein. In contrast, most emergency managers are limiting their use of social media to infrequent communication systems where preparedness and response messages can be posted. As has been laid out in the first six chapters, the complexity of social media and how they should be integrated into the operational, planning, and response protocol is far greater. Consequently, this adaptation of social media as a collaborative tool is another characteristic of this new leadership paradigm in emergency management.

CHARACTERISTICS OF COLLABORATION

The first step to adopting expanded collaboration as a major component of the modern emergency management model is to understand the various sociological and psychological characteristics of collaboration. This includes how organizations are formed within a community, sustained

180

Figure 7.1 Collaborating with nonprofit organizations such as the American Red Cross is a fundamental component of emergency management. (From FEMA/ Charles Powell. With permission.)

as a social benefit, create products, and leverage outputs. This process is also analyzed in the context of how it is emulated and replicated within social technologies, and therefore how it can be applied within the new paradigm of leadership that is being addressed throughout this book.

The first component to consider is the structure of collaboration. Although there are many variations and types of individuals who collectively come together to collaborate on various projects, they must have like-mindedness and similar perspectives to create the synergy necessary for true and effective collaboration. Certainly there are far more technical names for this collection, but Seth Godin refers to it as a "tribe." His terminology harkens back to Native American tribes and other civilizations that were inherently built around community and culture. Godin is, however, right in that many of these same characteristics have been rediscovered via social media networks and other social media outlets due to the fact that previously geographically dispersed individuals sharing common interests are now reunited throughout the globe utilizing these channels. Consequently, even tribes built around the smallest and seemingly most insignificant factors or details now have strength in numbers.

It is interesting that this dispersed connectivity creates a new form of culture with a novel set of rules (see Figure 7.2). For example, there

Figure 7.2 Social media and emerging technologies are allowing community collaboration to be diversified with no geographic limitations. (From FEMA/ Michael Rieger. With permission.)

no longer necessarily needs to be inherent connectivity between these individuals based on culture, ethnicity, gender, or (as already established) geography. Instead, this new model of culture is built on nongeographic specific components such as interests, passions, opinions, advocacy, hobbies, and professional associations as a few examples. Regardless of the foundation, cultural connectivity is important because it leads to greater loyalty and allegiance within the community as well as "supercharged communication," which in turn encourages and facilitates collaboration.[2]

These social tribes most often develop organically without the influence or intervention of external agencies. It is important for emergency managers and first-responders to consider how this process should be facilitated. First and foremost, it is important to create a community around ideas that have "stickiness" and are beneficial to the organization or community. From a traditional perspective, emergency managers have pushed messages about topics such as personal preparedness, volunteerism, and certain other community readiness and safety messages (e.g., "stop, drop, and roll"). Although these messages are important, they are not inherently sticky in a traditional culture of community as they lack the conventional connectors that were established earlier. However, as social media and other emerging technologies have created alternative senses of culture, the ability for those passionately and technologically connected to emergency preparedness to come together and create longstanding and sustainable concepts has increased as well. This concept is discussed later in this chapter.

The greater challenge for emergency managers is to allow these tribes to grow and expand around issues that have previously been under the sole control and purview of professional emergency management and response organizations. Under this new culture creation, preparedness and response messages are often created and distributed outside of formal systems and thus may or may not be consistent with official sources such as the local or state emergency management organizations. For example, the emergency volunteer and donations management group known as Toomers for Tuscaloosa that spontaneously arose after the 2011 outbreak of tornadoes across Alabama actively distributed and received information during response and recovery that had no measure of review, approval, or even consideration by the Alabama Emergency Management Agency. In this particular case, Toomers for Tuscaloosa repeatedly attempted to engage local and state agencies as well as voluntary organizations active in disasters that might otherwise be deeply involved in the distribution of messages. Instead, thousands of affected residents as well as interested parties throughout the United States went to Toomers for Tuscaloosa for information perceived as genuine rather than official.[3]

BENEFIT OF INDEPENDENT TRIBES[5]

1. Improved centralized passion within the culture of the group
2. Tightened communication within the group
3. Growth in membership of group

Although it has yet to happen in a widespread fashion within the emergency management community, Godin states that "granting independence to a rising tribe . . . is harder to swallow but it generally leads to quick and beneficial relationships between the [formal and informal] groups."[4] These beneficial connections are divided into three parts. First, the rise of tribes helps improve the centralized passion shared within the culture of the group. If the passion is declared or forced, it can ironically dissipate the energy and effectiveness. Second, embraced tribes help tighten communications as the group is more interested in the accurate and effective dissemination of cultural messages.

Last, organic tribes—particularly in social media environments—help grow and maintain membership on their own. Those passionate and interested in the topic are the most likely to advocate and spread the needed messages.[5]

SIMULTANEOUS PRODUCTION

Collaboration also affects the style and structure of production. For example, an individual or formal emergency management organization engages in the creation of plans and other products most often in a sequential or independent structure. Under this structure, a plan is developed only after a sequential list of items is completed one after another in a building block format. In many ways, this process is repeated within each discipline and organization at all levels of the given community, which creates individualized and separated sequential production. This separation is often referred to as a siloed approach (see Figure 7.3). There is a concerted effort within the emergency management and first-responder communities to avoid these so-called silos; however, it has become increasingly challenging with reduction in personnel and resources due to budget cutbacks and restraints in many organizations truly to cross and move beyond these production boundaries.

Figure 7.3 Sequential and independent operations within emergency management often create functional connection components that are ultimately disconnected such as commercial storage silos. (From Public Domain/Llano Estacado. With permission.)

In contrast to the sequential and often siloed approach of traditional emergency management leadership and organization, collaboration through social media systems allows for simultaneous production. As a nontraditional example, the crowdsourcing capability of Wikipedia leverages simultaneous production to create an efficient output. For example, an article written utilizing traditional methodology would have one person write content, a second person edit, and either repeat the cycle or have an additional person make the revisions. In contrast, Wikipedia utilizes multiple writers and multiple editors simultaneously to write not just an assigned section, but potentially overlapping sections as well. Moreover, because of the simultaneous writing and editing functions that exist through simultaneous editing, the need for singular (and final) approval is also eliminated.

Unfortunately, emulating a simultaneous production process is extraordinarily challenging for emergency managers. Not only is the average emergency manager already juggling responsibilities in multiple areas (all in sequential mode), there is typically limited trust of individuals outside the organization. Volunteers—both affiliated and spontaneous—are important to emergency management and response organizations, but they are typically limited to response support (e.g., mass care and social services) and restricted preparedness duties. Because liability still falls to the professional or designated emergency manager, there often is concern at deferring this to individuals outside the organization and thus leveraging the possibilities of simultaneous production (see Figure 7.4).

However, there are forward-leaning and ground-breaking examples where emergency management leaders are looking beyond this limitation and seeing the potential benefit of simultaneous product development. For example, in 2011 the Shadow Lake region of Oregon was being challenged by an uncontrolled wildfire and emergency management personnel were struggling with managing and distributing social media information. The incident response teams from the National Incident Management Organization (NIMO) contacted Jeff Phillips of Los Ranchos, New Mexico, to help set up a Virtual Operations Support Team (VOST) to support NIMO's handling of information related to the wildfire (note: Jeff Phillips is highlighted in the "Leaders in the Open" section of Chapter 4). The VOST quickly identified three different people from three different parts of the country (Washington, DC, Seattle, Washington, and New Mexico) to simultaneously to set up a blog, Twitter, e-mail, DropBox, Facebook, and Keepstream accounts

Figure 7.4 Emergency managers often only leverage sequential production rather than the simultaneous production that occurs frequently in social media systems. (From FEMA/Leif Skoogfors. With permission.)

to share, manage, and monitor information via those streams. They assigned tasks and divided the work among the three identified VOST support personnel to ensure each of those functional areas could be managed separately, but with independent authority and directive while not losing sight of the collective purpose and direction.[6] This contrasts greatly with traditional incident command system and national incident management system models that would have suggested each of these ultimately needed to have the same review and control (e.g., public information officer or incident commander).

WHAT IS . . . A VIRTUAL OPERATIONS SUPPORT TEAM (VOST)?

A Virtual Operations Support Team (VOST) is a group of trusted agents who support emergency management and disaster recovery efforts through the use of new communication technologies and social media tools via the Internet to those on-site at a response who may otherwise be overwhelmed or unwilling to handle the volume of data generated during the emergent event.[6]

COLLABORATION CREATES ART

This is perhaps one of the more abstract concepts included in this book, but is important for leaders in the field of emergency management to consider when adapting their leadership strategies to current issues surrounding the use and impact of social media. The creation of art being described is not necessarily the type of art that comes to most people's minds. Emergency managers involved in collaborative activities are not concerned about paintings, sculpture, or other interpretive media. Rather, art is the production of what Seth Godin calls "emotional labor." His definition (and the ultimate application to emergency managers) is significantly greater than Arlie Hochschild's sociological standard of emotional labor that referred to it as "the process by which workers are expected to manage their feelings in accordance with organizationally defined rules and guidelines."[7] Godin changes this paradigm by simply describing the process of creation that includes the input of emotional investment and prideful engagement. Under Godin's description, emotional labor inherently requires groups of individuals to work together and ultimately engage in collaboration.[8]

Godin defines art by three characteristics. Specifically, art is made by humans (via emotional labor), is created to have an impact, and is a gift. The final two components are worth further consideration by emergency management leaders. For instance, for actions to become art they must have an impact, which therefore means they change someone else after they are applied. Likewise, for actions to become more than simply the movement and collection of individual parts, the created art must be inherently free, which thus makes generosity a critical part of the making of art.[9] Given this definition, all three characteristics are supported by the act and process of collaboration, particularly when applied with emergency management. As has been established throughout the book, emergency management is inherently designed to have an impact on its community, but often struggles to utilize a process that is efficient and effective considering the limited resources available. Consequently, when social-based collaboration is utilized, this process is improved thus allowing for the process to be truly released. Moreover, social collaboration is also most often facilitated through volunteerism, which is built around giving and generosity (see Figure 7.5).

One of the best examples of the creation of art in association with emergency management is the creation of Mission 4636 to support disaster response and recovery during the Haiti earthquake in 2010.

Figure 7.5 Collaborative art is based on being effective and on emotional labor most commonly visualized by the use of volunteers before, during, and after disasters. (From FEMA/Leo "Jace" Anderson. With permission.)

Specifically, a group of volunteers established a free phone number (4636) to which locally affected Haitians could text specific requests for medical care, food, water, security, and shelter. The challenge was that most of the messages were posted in Haitian Creole and needed translations. Volunteers from throughout the world across seven time zones and six languages translated and geolocated more than 80,000 messages and sent them to Crisis Commons which was leveraging Ushahidi to map issues during the disasters. Due to the success of immediate life safety support, additional disaster information was gathered including basic resource needs, the location of unaccompanied children, and extended medical care needs (e.g., pregnancy or diabetes).[10,11] Clearly, the Mission 4636 project involved emotional labor, meaningful to the Haitian community, and was an extraordinarily generous gift of the combination of volunteer translators from around the globe.

DEMOGRAPHIC CUES TO UNDERSTANDING COLLABORATION

Collaboration is a dynamic and complex process that clearly has a role in professional emergency management (please see Figure 7.6). Although there are traditional components of collaboration long vested in various

Figure 7.6 Mission 4636 was a form of collaborative art that was instituted and supported by volunteers throughout the world to support basic needs requests by Haitians affected by the 2010 earthquake. (From USAF/Master Sgt. Jeremy Lock. With permission.)

emergency management roles, the public expectations driven by social technologies such as Facebook and Twitter are forcing changing models and adaptation of collaboration before, during, and after emergencies and disasters. Therefore, it is important for leaders seeking out modern methods for emergency management to understand the demographic characteristics that will amplify or hinder efforts to apply social strategies for collaboration.

According to Jason Ryan Dorsey, author of *Y-Size Your Business*, generations are defined by the year they were born and the context of living for the particular individual.[12] This adds a dimension to common (not technical) views of demographics that often are limited simply to the time of a person's birth. The problem with this common perspective (and the reason for Dorsey's adaptation) is that it eliminates the cultural and community impacts on an individual. For example, two women born in 1965 may both have some characteristics of the revolutionary culture that may have risen during that time period including a heightened awareness of feminism, racial equality, and post-modernism. However, if one woman was born on a farm in rural Oregon and the other was born in New York City there will most likely be significant differences in work ethic, perceived worldviews, ethnic connectivity, and social relevance.

Likewise, understanding how people will react and potentially collaborate is dependent on when major life-defining moments occur.

For example, surviving an emergency or disaster as a pre-teen would be significantly different than as a thirty-year-old. According to Dorsey, an individual must be "old enough to emotionally and logically process the significance of an event for it to shape [the person] from the moment it occurs."[13] This is part of the reason why it is extremely difficult for emergency managers to convince an average citizen that personal preparedness for an emergency or disaster is so important. Specifically, if they have not experienced a disaster or were not emotionally or logically mature enough to understand it, they will be unconvinced of its importance. However, with the rise of social media systems that share and disseminate information at near instantaneous speeds (see Chapter 3), people are seeing, feeling, and virtually experiencing disasters from their community, region, nation, or throughout the world even if it did not directly affect them.

This disaster empathy via social media systems is most profound in the so-called Millennial or Y-generation. This generational cohort is commonly defined by those born between 1977 and 1995 and by having personally experienced a range of events from the Challenger Shuttle explosion in 1986 to the terrorist attacks of September 11, 2001. The generational empathy of this cohort is most likely due to the fact that most individuals within these generational boundaries are digital natives and are thus quicker and more passionate about digital interaction and collaboration.[13] It is interesting that Gen Y individuals define loyalty (and ultimately success) based on the level of contributions by others into the greater community system. Consequently, they have higher expectations about what is and can be done via collaboration with other high-effort individuals, particularly during challenging times such as emergencies and disasters.[13]

Clearly, Gen Y individuals are not the only people who can embrace the possibilities of social media or its facilitation of collaboration. Many individuals of all ages and cultures have embraced technologies and social media, both individually and professionally, and understand the distinctive effects that are occurring. However, because the age and generalized demographic of the average emergency manager trends older (approximately 46 to 50 years old), there is a dichotomy between those emergency managers with years of traditional experience and limited comprehension of social media, and those emergency managers who are comfortable and passionate about social media, but lack the experience of real-world disasters.[14] This creates a significant divide in many communities as multiple generations of emergency managers (and their supporting functional staff) begin to work together to move their professional organizations and the communities they represent toward a process that embraces public expectations from social technologies.

PUBLIC EXPECTATIONS FOR COLLABORATION

In 2010, Facebook co-founder Mark Zuckerberg publicly stated that privacy is no longer the social norm (see Figure 7.7). Rather, Zuckerberg proposed that within the decade of explosive growth in social media systems people have accepted and embraced the idea and functionality that personal information (including photos, videos, and geographic locations) is shared openly.[15] Although Facebook posts, tweets, YouTube videos, and various other social postings have become ubiquitous and commonly integrated into traditional and social media outlets, the full openness projected by Zuckerberg is not yet a reality. However, as the public moves toward full social integration, the expectations of how social media should and will affect their lives is changing.

This contrasts with traditional emergency management leadership that is built around concepts—both internally and externally—that aim to speak loudly and with the greatest amount of authority possible. This so-called "megaphone effect" is grounded in civil defense and military foundations built around hierarchical and command authority decision making. From an operational perspective, this structure is often required

Figure 7.7 Mark Zuckerberg, co-founder of Facebook, meets with President Barack Obama. (From U.S. White House/Pete Souza. With permission.)

191

Figure 7.8 Traditional government campaigns such as the Uncle Sam military recruitment posters often talk down to citizens, which is no longer appreciated or accepted by the general public. (From U.S. Department of Defense/Public Domain. With permission.)

due to the high risk and quick response necessary to facilitate effective life-safety responses. However, when it comes to public engagement and response, this type of approach is outdated and ineffective. Famous examples of this model include the Smokey the Bear education model and the Uncle Sam recruiting campaign. In both cases, the formal government response is to create the perspective that the official government authority figure is unilaterally knowledgeable and provides direction and command about what to do to achieve perceived success. The challenge is that most citizens do not like being talked down to when it comes to choices they have to make. Much as with the social media systems they have so fully embraced, they want to engage in conversations with their authority figures who are often seen as empowered or appointed by the general public (see Figure 7.8).

CROWDSOURCING FOR COLLABORATION

The public desire to engage in conversation, especially in emergency management functions, ultimately leads to greater understanding of the issues and challenges. Because the public feels empowered through social systems that engage through the inherent social and physical communities, they often become driven to help address these challenges through facilitated collaboration. As was discussed in Chapter 6, this process most often occurs via crowdsourcing processes. Previous examples showed how crowdsourcing can lead to the magnification of emergency management efforts, but there are many more examples of crowdsourcing leading to efficient and effective collaboration possibilities between those embracing social technologies and local, regional, and state-level emergency management organizations.

In his book, *Crowdsourcing: Why the Power of Crowds Is Driving the Future of Business*, Jeff Howe defines collaborative crowdsourcing as the process when a "company or institution takes a job traditionally performed by a designated agent (usually an employee) and outsources it to an undefined, generally large group of people over the Internet."[16] As perhaps the most extreme example, some organizations have given complete control of their organizational Twitter accounts to citizens or community representatives. For example, in late 2011, the government of Sweden created a campaign that would allow individual Swedish citizens to fully control the official @Sweden Twitter account for up to one week. Over the course of the next year, numerous individuals ranging from age 18 to 60 controlled the account and talked about a wide variety of issues including personal holiday pictures, private activities, and personal and religious beliefs. In this particular case, the Swedish government wanted the uniqueness of Swedish culture to be presented genuinely and organically, which was considered more effective, interesting, and believable than a polished marketing campaign released by formal government sources.[17]

Unlike the @Sweden crowdsourcing project, most examples within emergency management organically arise in response to an individual or community group's desire to provide altruistic support to affected individuals. This happened numerous times during the recovery process from the 2011 outbreak of tornadoes that hit the state of Alabama. As numerous communities were affected due to the more than 60 confirmed tornadoes, people throughout the state were dealing with collection and removal of debris that had been scattered over their yards, neighborhoods, and in some cases communities. A woman named Patty Bullion, who was herself dealing with debris collection, noticed that there were many pictures among the debris, most of which did not belong to her or her family. Instead, Ms. Bullion created a Facebook page ("Pictures and Documents found after the April 27, 2011 Tornadoes") and posted scanned copies of the first hundred tattered photos that she had recovered in her area with the hope that they could be reconnected with their original owners. As the Facebook page grew in size, more and more people added photos that were discovered and were uploaded by followers of the site. Ultimately, more than 2,000 photos and documents were returned to their owners within the first year and more than 97,000 people have liked the Facebook page (see Figure 7.9).[21]

Likewise, the same series of tornadoes that struck Alabama were also causing cascading problems for other components of the community. For

Figure 7.9 Noteworthy family pictures such as this one were discovered after the 2011 Alabama tornadoes and returned to their original owners through collaborative crowdsourcing during the recovery process. (From FEMA/Greig[v1] Powers. With permission.)

example, weddings throughout the state scheduled for the summer of 2011 were significantly affected as locations were destroyed, supplies lost or damaged, and wedding dresses unable to be delivered due to storms or being damaged or lost during the tornadoes. Consequently, a local woman named Mariesa Stokes created a Facebook page called "Wedding Dresses for Tornado Victims." Through this page, Ms. Stokes encouraged people to donate their wedding gowns, services, and other support items to help local brides who had been affected by the storm. Within two weeks of the event 40 people donated their (used) wedding dresses to the cause of helping those brides in need. Likewise, dozens of other people offered or donated wedding shoes, mother-of-the-bride dresses, and many other services.[22] These donations continued to be received through the first anniversary of the tornadoes with donaters and receivers providing positive feedback using the Facebook page.

As for formal emergency preparedness and response, crowdsourcing is still a relatively new and wholly underutilized component. As has been repeatedly discussed, most of the positive examples of crowdsourcing and collaborative processes in reaction to disasters have been organically generated by community members (individually or collectively) and not formal emergency management professionals. Only after the fact did these groups attempt to discover ways to integrate their collaboration into the traditional emergency management processes. This type of process must be reversed by emergency management leaders embracing changing public expectations. By leveraging collaborative crowdsourcing and the related potential tools available to them, emergency management leaders will shift the scope and impact of emergency preparedness, response, and recovery.

OPENING THE BOX: CROWDSOURCING FOR CANCER

Cancer is one of the most far-reaching health conditions. It comes in many forms and can touch individuals of all ages, races, demographics, cultures, and geographic locations. Billions of dollars have been spent by commercial and academic researchers to understand transmission, spread, and exposure rates from both genetic and environmental factors. Although significant strides have been made over the years, treatments are often limited to expensive and intensive options such as chemotherapy and radiation that leave the patient with significant and often painful side effects.

However, over the last few years with the growing use of social media and both the intentional and unintentional uses of crowdsourcing to solve grandiose problems, cancer researchers and oncologists have come to embrace a new model of discovery called open-source medical research. For example, Jay Bradner, a researcher at Harvard University, and his team identified a new molecule with particular anticancer properties. Instead of patenting the molecule to preserve traditional business practices, Bradner published the findings and mailed samples to more than 40 other laboratories to continue research on the molecule with the perspective that the collected wisdom, experience, time, and personnel would vastly increase the odds that this molecule (or a derivative) might be an easier and more effective treatment (if not cure) for cancer.[19] Likewise, GE launched its Healthymagination Challenge in September 2011 in an attempt to identify and accelerate ideas that advanced breast cancer early detection and diagnostics. Through a series of challenges, GE welcomed researchers, businesses, students, and other innovators to submit breakthrough ideas for consideration, with the top five splitting $100 million in seed money for innovation and product delivery. During the first phase (which closed in late 2012), almost 4,000 people engaged in the challenge by submitting more than 500 ideas and nearly 200 comments on suggested treatment pathways.[20] This kind of creative, silo-breaking process of crowdsourcing solutions to major problems is phenomenal. Emergency managers and first-responder communities should consider some of these same approaches to the routine and challenging problems of emergency preparedness, response, and recovery to address longstanding challenges.

EMERGENCY MANAGEMENT AND COLLABORATION

Most emergency managers understand the need for collaboration to help augment and support response and recovery efforts within their community. This need is particularly important in light of the limited resources available to most emergency management organizations. Unfortunately, this collaboration is not in a mode or model conducive to public expectations generated from social media use.

Emergency management and first-responder leaders are most comfortable with controlled collaboration. For example, Community Emergency Response Teams (CERT) are highly embraced by most communities as valued assets, but are often assigned limited tasks and collaboration activities. Rather, the controlling organization directs activities through the megaphone approach as described earlier. Likewise, many communities have identified the need for increased public–private partnerships, but are often unsure of how to collaborate and engage with these organizations due to concerns about privacy, bias, organizational regulations, and ethical behaviors. Consequently, much as with the CERT volunteer groups, emergency managers will profess the desire for strong collaboration, but provide only minimal engagement and collaboration opportunities.

Likewise, true collaboration with the public is often an afterthought. Some emergency managers, motivated by legal, ethical, or traditional strictures, profess to want public engagement in planning and preparedness processes, but rarely provide anything more than artificial engagement. For example, public gatherings or town hall meetings are often scheduled in communities attempting to seek public feedback, but without significant public outcry related to emergency management (e.g., Hurricane Katrina response and recovery) the general public almost never engages. Moreover, when engagement does occur it often slips toward a more authoritative approach rather than a mutually binding process of collaboration and engagement. It is this type of dualistic approach that leads to failed attempts at collaboration for the average emergency manager. Having a public gathering with a handful of people when contrasted to the hundreds (if not thousands) who can be engaged through social systems is in many ways a ridiculous artifact of traditional pre-social approaches. In other words, as one public administrator stated, "Traditional government hierarchical organizations . . . still remain relevant, but their ability to achieve their mission is being tested as they must find ways to achieve their goals in the shadow of [collaborative] networks" (see Figure 7.10).[18]

COLLABORATIVE TOOLS: PUBLIC ADOPTION

There are few systematic examples where formalized emergency management agencies have fully and organically embraced collaboration based on the social expectations of the public. However, there are

Figure 7.10 The effectiveness of traditional town hall gatherings is being undermined by the effectiveness of social technologies where people can easily and quickly engage in collaborative discussions. (From FEMA/Cheryl Reyes. With permission.)

a growing number of emergent and sometimes traditionally organized volunteer groups that are providing extremely valuable support for disaster response and recovery. These applications include crisis mapping, virtual volunteerism, gamification, and crowdsourcing. These emergent examples represent phenomenal possibilities for emulation of modeling and collaborative processes.

One of the most interesting examples of positive and integrated collaboration between municipal emergency response organizations and an active and engaged community is the Adopt-a-Hydrant program that was first implemented in Boston, Massachusetts. With more than 13,000 fire hydrants throughout the city of Boston, the Boston Fire Department has had a significant challenge in maintaining the functionality of these devices, particularly during winter when snow piles up around the hydrants making them difficult if not impossible to use. Consequently, Boston, in partnership with Code for America, created an Adopt-a-Hydrant program to allow local citizens, businesses, or community organizations to volunteer to clear the areas around the hydrants during storm events and ensure their availability for use.[23] The Adopt-a-Hydrant model program is being utilized in other communities (for various reasons) including Buenos Aires,

Figure 7.11 Innovative community collaboration programs such as "Adopt-a-Hydrant" allow community members to be engaged in emergency response by supplementing the needs of formal emergency response organizations. (From FEMA/Andrea Booher. With permission.)

Honolulu, and Chicago just to name a few.[24] This is a powerful example of ensuring community resiliency during emergencies and disasters and to supplement emergency response capabilities within the community. This is a quintessential example of communities leveraging the capabilities of social and community collaboration (see Figure 7.11).

COLLABORATIVE TOOLS: OPEN SOURCE TECHNOLOGIES

In addition to the public adoption of certain support mechanisms such as the fire hydrants, some communities are beginning to leverage open source technologies as a form of social collaboration. Open source technologies are those that are developed in collaboration with external partners by using government controlled or generated data with no direct benefit or compensation necessary. For example, the National Weather Service provides weather data (including advisory information) to the general public. External organizations and businesses (e.g., Weather Channel and AccuWeather) use these data streams to generate third-party applications, software, and web access to the data in repackaged formats that may be graphically focused or overlaid onto other types of information (e.g., geography).

WHAT IS . . . OPEN SOURCE TECHNOLOGY?

Open source technologies are those that are developed by using government controlled or generated data in collaboration with external partners with no direct benefit or compensation necessary. Positive examples include Ushahidi, Sahana, and various crime-reporting mobile applications.

The most common first-responder and emergency management example of open source technologies is crime mapping. Most municipal law enforcement agencies make significant amounts of their crime data available online for public review and consideration. This includes parties involved in crime, locations of events, timing, and various other personal, geographical, and legal characteristics. In most cases, the information that is shared and open is not part of an adjudication process or a component of witness protection. This is a significant step toward open government (as discussed in Chapter 1) and contributes strongly to open-source development.

For example, San Francisco has initiated open data programming including information available from law enforcement. However, simply making the information available is insufficient to allow public engagement as there are millions of pieces of information that are indigestible to the general public in raw form. However, because of open source technologies and development, application developers have leveraged San Francisco's open law enforcement data to produce seven different applications that are available on various mobile platforms. These apps have a diversity of purpose as well, with some being focused on educating the public about risk and others (in partnership with the city) identifying high crime rate areas. Likewise, each has its own set of unique interfaces (including augmented reality) that allows users to select when, where, and how they want to interact with the data.

It is interesting that these kinds of unorganized nonspecific partnerships are profoundly social. Without any additional costs, formal emergency management and first-response organizations are able to provide data and education to their constituency about various issues that could be affecting their community. This type of more-with-less mentality is not only efficient (see Chapter 5), but is also entrepreneurial at its core (see Chapter 4). Organizations can add value by embracing social collaboration strategies such as open source technologies to maximize the benefit to the community and ultimately reduce risk, creating a positive "profit" within the world of emergency management.

Ushahidi represents another excellent collaborative tool that is open source. Specifically, Ushahidi is an open source crowd (or crisis) mapping suite of software products that was originally developed in 2008 to help Kenyan journalists monitor results in a politically (and often violently) contentious area. After 45,000 Kenyans contributed to the monitoring site, it quickly became clear that Ushahidi was a phenomenal tool not just for election monitoring, but for any emergent event in need of accountability and tracking such as an emergency or disaster.[25] Since that time it has routinely been used in partnership with student groups, professional media outlets, nonprofit organizations, and (occasionally) professional emergency management organizations.

As an organization, Ushahidi says that it is built for "democratizing information, increasing transparency, and lowering the barriers for individuals to share their stories."[25] The last phrase is what is most important to emergency managers. Social collaboration is when a group or technology creates a mechanism for people with compelling needs or issues to present a perspective that is unfiltered and easily submitted. Unfortunately, this type of collaboration is particularly challenging to traditional emergency managers because the open perspective, need, or issue may or may not be in line with official disaster response protocols.

For example, Toomers for Tuscaloosa routinely connected people with needs (e.g., diapers) with those who could provide the need without integration into local donations management systems or official recognition from the local or state volunteer organizations active in disasters. This circumvention leads some emergency managers to worry whether the items were reaching those truly in need or whether emergent groups like Toomers for Tuscaloosa were legally, ethically, and financially legitimate enough to be trusted. Although these are certainly valid concerns (particularly with emergent groups), there are a growing number of emergent examples where a highly effective process has been utilized to help those in need by others (not in need) only through connection via a social collaboration tool.

LEADERS IN THE OPEN: SCOTT REUTER

Scott Reuter is a disaster response professional who is a leader among Oregon's community service and faith-based organizations that provide assistance to those affected by disasters during their long-term recovery.

In addition, he is a strong advocate for the creation and sustainment of volunteer organizations active in disasters throughout the Pacific Northwest and much of the United States. Likewise, he is well versed in social media and the growth of the Virtual Operations Support Teams movement. In the following essay written for this book, Scott Reuter discusses the collaborative capabilities of social media.

Forced Collaborative Investment Leads to Relationships and Trust

Scott Reuter

Like it or not, emergency management is in a time of rapid evolution. I feel that whereas previous generations enchanted by modernism embraced paradigm-shifting technologies such as the telegraph, telephone, and radio, there's resistance to the latest big technological and social innovation, which is social media. Most people that I speak to about social media realize that they are affecting all of our lives in many ways. This shift has come fast. When Hurricane Katrina hit New Orleans in 2005, Twitter did not yet exist and Facebook was one and a half years old. So it's understandable that in a profession like crisis communications and emergency management, those who've worked and known pre-social media methods of operation are cautious and hesitant to embrace it, and are in some cases outright resistant to this inevitable yet necessary change.

I recently observed (through social media) a government official who went out in front of the media at a press conference and confidently announced that there was no "official" social media account. Moreover, he stated that the public should ignore all postings about the emergency that were to be found there. That made me curious, so I searched Facebook on the name of that disaster. I found 11 new Facebook accounts that were set up specifically to discuss this one relatively minor emergency! Just think how much better it would have been for this person to offer an "official" Facebook account and make positive use of all of that energy that was being expended by many people, most of whom were probably well-intentioned.

Over the past couple of years many of us "SMEMers" who enjoy working together via social media have banded together to help each other on a variety of disaster efforts and training exercises. We've experimented with tools, apps, and ways to monitor disaster events on social media, learning how to help those affected. We often work with an emergency manager or volunteer leader. We're a diverse mix of professionals and volunteers, and we're very open to sharing what we've learned. We all talk about our projects on Twitter, Facebook, and Google+, and several of us also blog about our experiences.

From what I've seen, there are as many ways to approach these issues as there are people. Some approach from an institutional point of view, doing their best to work from within their organization or agency, seeking approval to move forward cautiously, taking baby steps as they go. Others dive in head first without checking the depth, or asking permission, and there are those who fall somewhere in between. All should be praised and encouraged for making the effort to pioneer in a difficult and fast-changing field.

The hard part is no longer finding lots of volunteers; the difficulty is the time that you must invest to build relationships and trust, and maintain the skills of your team of new technical volunteers. (These volunteers are numerous and dedicated enough and have proven their worth in enough disasters to warrant a new acronym: the VTC, or Volunteer Technical Community). I say this not to overwhelm, but to point out that this is in fact nothing new. You've trained and incorporated volunteer firefighters, volunteer ham radio operators, CERTs, and search and rescue teams. All required specialized training, policies, and time to incorporate them in the way your organization operates in disasters. You've done this before, and you'll do it again because they bring value and resources to your organization and community.

Collaboration is in the DNA of social media. Why ask a question of one person or a small group when you can ask everyone on social media? Just imagine how many more answers and possible solutions if you share a problem on social media instead of just asking one colleague. Also remember that you're not in this alone; you'll be collaborating with people in your profession who are already on social media, people who are looking forward to your joining them (e.g., follow hashtags including #SMEM, #HSEM, #VOST, and #SMEMChat).

You'll see people gathered on social media having great conversations on subjects that will interest you, and they don't talk only about social media. Just as conferences are about building relationships and making contacts, so are social media.

ENDNOTES

1. Shirky, Clay. (2009) *Here Comes Everybody: The Power of Organizing without Organizations.* New York: Penguin Books, p. 109.
2. The power of tribes. (2012) *The Economist.* http://www.economist.com/node/21543487. Accessed July 6, 2012.
3. Hart, Holly. (2012) "Toomers for Tuscaloosa." Speech at Midwest Disasters 2.0 Social Media Workshop". February 22, 2012.
4. Godin, Seth. (2011) "Independence and Subjugation." Seth Godin's Blog. http://sethgodin.typepad.com/seths_blog/2011/11/13/index.html. Accessed July 7, 2012.
5. Godin, Seth. (2008) *Tribes: We Need You to Lead Us.* New York: Portfolio.
6. Stephens, Kim. (2012) "What is the Virtual Operations Support Team?" iDisaster Blog. http://idisaster.wordpress.com/2012/02/13/what-is-a-virtual-operations-support-team/. Accessed July 8, 2012.
7. Wharton, Amy S. (2009) The sociology of emotional labor. *Annual Review of Sociology.* http://www.annualreviews.org/doi/abs/10.1146/annurev-soc-070308-115944?journalCode=soc. Accessed July 9, 2012.
8. Godin, Seth. (2011) *Linchpin: Are You Dispensable?*" New York: Portfolio.
9. Godin, Seth. (2010) "Making Art." Seth Godin's Blog. http://sethgodin.typepad.com/seths_blog/2010/01/making-art.html/. Accessed July 9, 2012.
10. Garrett, Francesca. (2010) "We Are the Volunteers of Mission 4636." Ushahidi Blog. http://blog.ushahidi.com/index.php/2010/01/27/mission-4636/. Accessed July 9, 2012.
11. "Mission 4636." (n.d.) Mission 4636 Blog. http://www.mission4636.org/. Accessed July 9, 2012.
12. Dorsey, Jason Ryan. (2011) "Gen Y: The Impacts of Demographics." Speech at International Association of Emergency Managers (IAEM) Annual Conference. November 1, 2011.
13. Dorsey, Jason Ryan. (2009) *Y-Size Your Business: How Gen Y Employees Can Save You Money and Grow Your Business.* Hackensack, NJ: Wiley Press. p. 17.
14. Crowe, Adam. (2012) *Disasters 2.0: The Application of Social Media in Modern Emergency Management.* Boca Raton, FL: CRC Press.
15. Barnett, Emma. (2010) Facebook's Mark Zuckerberg says privacy is no longer the 'social norm.' *The Telegraph.* http://www.telegraph.co.uk/technology/facebook/6966628/Facebooks-Mark-Zuckerberg-says-privacy-is-no-longer-a-social-norm.html. Accessed July 11, 2012.
16. Howe, Jeff. (2008) *Crowdsourcing: Why the Power of the Crowd Is Driving Business.* New York: Crown Business.
17. Lyall, Sarah. (2012) "Swedes' Twitter Voice: Anyone Saying (Blush) Almost Anything." *New York Times.* http://www.nytimes.com/2012/06/11/world/europe/many-voices-of-sweden-via-twitter.html?_r=3. Accessed July 12, 2012.

18. Posner, Paul. (2009) A public administration education for the third party governance era: reclaiming leadership in the field. In *The Collaborative Public Manager: New Ideas for the Twenty-First Century*. Washington, DC: Georgetown University Press.
19. "Open Source Cancer Research." (n.d.) Know Cancer. http://www.knowcancer.com/blog/open-source-cancer-research-ted-talk/. Accessed July 13, 2012.
20. "Emerging Health Innovators Selected." (2012) GE's Healthymagination Challenge Blog. http://challenge.healthymagination.com/health. Accessed July 14, 2012.
21. Bonvillian, Crystal. (2012) "Facebook Page That Reunited Victims with Photos, Documents Shutting Down." Al.com. http://blog.al.com/breaking/2012/04/facebook_page_that_reunited_vi.html. Accessed July 14, 2012.
22. Temple, Chanda. (2011) "To Have and To Help: What People Are Doing to Help Alabama Brides Affected by the April 27 Tornadoes." Al.com. http://blog.al.com/living-news/2011/05/to_have_and_to_help_what_peopl.html. Accessed July 14, 2012.
23. Fox, Jeremy C. (2012) "City Introduces Adopt a Hydrant Program." Boston.com. http://www.boston.com/yourtown/news/downtown/2012/01/city_introduces_adopt-a-hydran.html. Accessed July 14, 2012.
24. "Adopt a Hydrant." (n.d) Code for America Blog. http://codeforamerica.org/?cfa_project=adopt-a-hydrant. Accessed July 14, 2012.
25. "About Us." (2012) Ushahidi.com. http://ushahidi.com/about-us. Accessed July 16, 2012.

Section III

Attitude and Engagement

True humility . . . makes us modest by reminding us how far we
have come short of what we can be.

Ralph Stockmen[1]

The first section of this book focused on identifying the characteristics of
social media that are fundamental to its growth and utilization in the general population. This utilization has become so widespread, universally
integrated, and ubiquitous in both traditional and popular culture that
the general public has significantly altered its expectations for organizations, businesses, and perhaps most important, its governmental representation. Consequently, governmental operations, including professional
emergency managers, have had to identify what new characteristics need
to exist to lead their communities into this new paradigm. These characteristics were identified as transparency, instantaneous speed, and
entrepreneurism in Chapters 2, 3, and 4, respectively.

The second section focused on the capability of the general public
to embrace social media technologies to improve efficiency (Chapter 5),
magnification (Chapter 6), and collaboration (Chapter 7) of organizational
goals and strategies. This process is particularly important to emergency
managers who have struggled for the last decade with changing national
priorities and funding limitations, as well as additional personnel and
resource challenges unique to local and regional emergency preparedness
efforts. Leadership and organizational examples were shared to create the
foundation of what social media can do considering the altered expectations of the general public.

The third section of this book focuses on the final steps for emergency managers to embrace social media and public expectations about its use. This section focuses on the attitude and approach of emergency managers seeking ways to embrace social media to lead their organizations into a more social future. Specifically, humility, ethics, and the need for creativity are discussed in the next three chapters. Considerations of each are discussed as well as real-life scenarios and examples of when, where, and how they can be implemented.

ENDNOTE

1. Marcum, David and Smith, Steven. (2008) *Egonomics: What Makes Ego Our Greatest Asset (or Most Expensive Liability)*. New York: Touchstone.

8

Humility

Do nothing out of selfish ambition or vain conceit, but in humility consider others better than yourselves. Each of you should look not only to your own interests, but also to the interest of others.

Philippians 2:3–4 (NIV)

FRAGMENTED RESPONSE

Disasters are some of the most humbling experiences for those affected and the communities that surround them. Individuals or their families are often physically and emotionally forced to alter their lifestyles for short to long periods of time depending on the severity of the event. These personal alterations inherently force those in need to seek out and receive support from external sources ranging from friends and family to formalized response organizations such as the American Red Cross, Salvation Army, or emergency management agency. Regardless of the source of the support, these individuals and their families are by default humbled due to their inability to facilitate basic needs such as food, water, shelter, clothing, and financial support (see Figure 8.1).

Likewise, disaster survivors who are displaced are often completely dependent on government emergency response agencies to provide restoration and recovery to their community (including home and personal property). Safety processes including evacuation, curfews, and barricades limiting access are controlled by law enforcement and often are maintained for reasons unknown or unseen by the affected community. Similarly, individuals who need and seek out financial assistance from governmental

Figure 8.1 People who are affected by emergencies and disasters are inherently humbled by the experience due to their difficulties in facilitating basic needs such as food, water, sheltering, and clothing. (From FEMA/Christopher Mardorf. With permission.)

agencies such as FEMA or the Small Business Administration are often limited by the processing and procedural time required to apply, review, and be granted funds to restore affected personal property such as homes, vehicles, and businesses. This process can be further limited and delayed by local and state building codes, especially as community leaders grapple with applying mitigation strategies during recovery. Disaster survivors are humbled at every stage of the recovery process due to their nearly full dependency on other individuals and community organizations to facilitate the process.

The challenge for emergency managers is that community-based disaster recovery is often fragmented, with duties and responsibilities being shared among various disciplines at all levels of government. Inherently, local governments are overwhelmed beyond their capability and must interact with and depend on state or federal agencies to restore basic services to local citizens. Similarly, large-scale events including hurricanes or tornado outbreaks affect multiple localities and often overwhelm state resources, further fragmenting efficiency and effectiveness. Lastly, even small disasters have political undertones that must invariably be remembered for both the positive and negative impacts they have on the pace of community recovery after a disaster. Even though the disaster survivors are the impetus for all the action and complexity described, the needs and unique challenges they face during the process can often be overlooked by the various parties fixated on the individual components for which they are responsible.

EMPOWERING DISASTER SURVIVORS

These same disaster survivors heavily utilize social media before the emergency or disaster to communicate with supportive friends and family as well as trusted organizations and businesses. Information is routinely shared through text, photos, and video on multiple individual and connected social networks such as Facebook, Twitter, YouTube, Pinterest, and Instagram, and can range from simple sharing to more complex technological altruism and advocacy. For example, on average, more than 300 million photos were uploaded to Facebook per day in 2012. Likewise, during that same period of time there were more than 42 million pages with 10 or more "likes."[2] Citizens expect to utilize social media as a primary method of receiving information.

This expectation does not stop during disaster response and recovery. For example, immediately following the theater shooting in Aurora, Colorado, individuals flocked to social media systems such as Reddit and Storify for information about the shooting and the immediate response and recovery activities (see Figure 8.2). Both of these sources not only

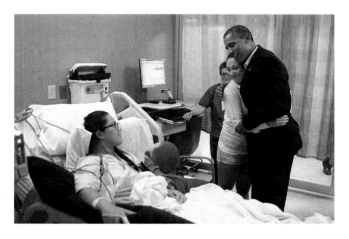

Figure 8.2 President Barack Obama visits with victims of the Aurora shooting. Victims and witnesses all flocked to social media to exchange information immediately following the event. (From White House/Pete Souza. With permission.)

contained republished information from traditional media outlets, but messages from eyewitnesses and actual victims of the event. These collaborative efforts created a continuously updated timeline including links and dynamic documentation. Moreover, because people from inside the theater were engaged in the community, people were able to get unique and invaluable information that was not available via any other media format. Specifically, one of the Reddit commentators stated, "How cool is it [that] we can ask a guy a question over the Internet about an event that happened less than 8 hours ago first hand . . . Reporters couldn't get on a plane and find someone that quickly . . . the future is now."[18]

As evidence that the Aurora Theater shooting was not an isolated event, this phenomenon was documented in 2010 and again 2011 when the American Red Cross conducted a survey of more than 1,000 Internet users (see Figure 8.3). The survey found that nearly 20% of those surveyed

Figure 8.3 The American Red Cross surveys have routinely validated that social media users expect emergency response agencies to monitor and utilize social media during disasters. (From FEMA/Cynthia Hunter. With permission.)

would utilize Facebook to gather information about emergencies and disasters. Likewise, nearly 25% of the general population and more than 30% of the online population would utilize a social media system to notify friends and family of their status during the event. Moreover, the most profound findings were related to the public expectations of their formal governmental response agencies. Approximately 80% of those surveyed indicated they believed that emergency response organizations should regularly monitor social media sites in order to promptly respond. In addition, more than 39% indicated they would expect emergency management organizations to respond within one hour of posting a message to a social media system during an emergency or disaster.[3]

These findings have a profound impact on this new leadership paradigm. They strongly indicate that public expectations are already incorporating their day-to-day usage of social media into when, where, and how they seek out and receive information during emergencies and disasters. A prime example of this phenomenon was after the oil spill that occurred following the explosion of the Deepwater Horizon oil rig in 2010. Citizens immediately took to Twitter, Facebook, and other social systems to express their interest and concern about the event. However, as the event progressed and BP struggled to control the underwater leak and greater threats were identified to the environment, citizens ramped up efforts not only to publicly complain and heap fault on BP, Halliburton, and the U.S. federal government, but also provide accountability and correct action to issues that were developing. One of the most profound examples of this was the Louisiana Bucket Brigade which was a group of environmental activists and students who were utilizing Ushahidi to leverage crowdsourcing to identify evidence of spill issues including environmental and health concerns.[4] Ultimately, the Louisiana Bucket Brigade generated more than 4,000 public reports related to the events and provided significant community accountability for the public and private response and governmental intervention.[5]

At the same time, governmental organizations and BP were fighting both publicly and privately about who was to blame and just how significant (or insignificant) the spill really was to the communities along the Gulf Coast. Each entity sought to push blame onto the other for lack of regulation or lack of safety oversight and control. Unfortunately, at the same time more than 40% of the Gulf Coast waters were closed to commercial and recreational fishing, which had a cascading effect on a variety of local and national industries with some individual businesses projecting

213

multimillion dollar losses over the next decade as a consequence of this event.[6] It is this type of dichotomy that is at the crux of modern emergency management. The division and fragmentation of response creates a culture of preparedness and response that often forgets or neglects recognition of the need for humility.

It is interesting that this is not the case at the individual level. There are thousands of disaster response volunteers who understand the need for humility and serve their communities in their time of need for no greater purpose than to help those individuals who have been affected by these disasters (see Figure 8.4). In many ways this type of one-on-one recognition is magnified via social media where individuals are able to engage through online social communities and networks with individuals they may or may not ordinarily engage with via their traditional (and physical) relationships. This is most common immediately after an emergency or disaster where emergent Facebook groups, organic hashtags, and third-party applications (e.g., Crowd Maps) get developed. For example, after the 2011 EF5 tornado that affected Joplin,

Figure 8.4 An individual volunteer is much more likely than a traditional emergency manager to understand the inherent humility that exists during disaster response and recovery. (From FEMA/Marilee Caliendo. With permission.)

Missouri, multiple Facebook pages (e.g., "Joplin, MO Tornado Recovery," "Joplin Tornado Citizen Checks," and "Animals Lost and Found in Joplin, MO Tornado"), numerous twitter hashtags (#joplin, #prayersforjoplin, and #joplintornado), and a crowd map were all generated and heavily used by local and regional citizens to connect with those in need and provide a humble and respectful response to the community.[7-9]

WHAT IS HUMILITY?

If humility is an expectation of the general public due to the possibilities and purpose of social technologies, emergency managers must find a way to better understand humility in ways that are being integrated into modern leadership strategies. Although there are various components that are evaluated and explained later in this chapter, the one critical element of humility is the concept of its communal nature. According to John Dickson, author of the book *Humilitas: A Lost Key to Life, Love, and Leadership*, "Unless a leader is trusted by the team, she will not get the best out of them . . . because all organizations, even hugely hierarchical ones like the military are still communities of people in relationships."[10] Much as with all components of social media discussed throughout this book, the foundations and impact of humility are all based on the natural (and now technologically driven) connectivity between individuals. It also shows why emergency management leaders must understand, acknowledge, and adopt a humble outlook within their community.

Unfortunately, humility is not often seen as an admirable trait, especially in command-and-control organizations. Rather, individuals expect generals, chiefs, and other emergency response leaders to make bold, confident, quick, and timely decisions based on granted authority and without consideration of humility (see Figure 8.5). This expectation is based on a faulty assumption of what humility is all about. For example, most people perceive humility to be a lowering of a person's status to a level subordinate to those in a shared community or collective. Although it is accurate to believe that humility is when an individual is focused on the needs or importance of another person (or group of persons), it does not exist inherently to be subordinate, different, or countercultural. Rather, this subordination fulfills a purpose that is targeted at the broader community to achieve a greater good.

Figure 8.5 Cultural expectations often state that individuals in leadership positions within highly hierarchical organizations (e.g., fire chief) must make command decisions without humility, but effective leaders—particularly in light of growing expectations—can often do both. (From FEMA/Hazard J. Bentley III. With permission.)

DEVOTION TO PROGRESS

In *Egonomics: What Makes Our Ego Our Greatest Asset (or Most Expensive Liability)* David Marcum and Steven Smith identify three components of humility. The first component of humility is an overall devotion to progress or what they refer to as a "We, then me" mentality.[11] In other words, community welfare is an extremely strong motivator. As discussed in Chapter 7, the connectivity and creation of community is now strongly diversified due to the capabilities of social media (e.g., geography is no longer required for connectivity). Moreover, social media systems and various emerging technologies such as Wikipedia and other crowd-sourcing systems have built an expectation around the idea of shared awareness where an individual's purpose is driven more by the collective importance than individual means. It is this drive that pushes the "core ambition of humility" to be "a remarkable devotion to progress."[11] This is what drives most of the volunteerism and donations generation after emergencies and disasters.

The question is whether emergency managers can adopt this same principle on the formal side of disaster response. This is extraordinarily challenging as managers and organizational leaders become isolated from direct community engagement the farther up the organizational hierarchy they are. This isolation often creates an extreme fear of failure, which in turn limits the application of innovative approaches that may help bridge a gap in the community and create efficiency, magnification, and collaboration (as described in Section II). One method for emergency managers to employ to overcome this challenge is to embrace failure at every turn.

This is one of the most challenging components to emergency management. As was established in Chapter 4 when entrepreneurism was discussed, failure is an inevitability in disaster response. The impact to lives and property can be reduced or mitigated, but cannot be fully eliminated. Consequently, it is an interesting paradox that emergency managers struggle so much to maintain humility during emergency response and recovery, especially during major events. For example, the coordination of emergency management with Hurricane Katrina and the Deepwater Horizon oil spill was complex and required the cooperation and collaboration of local, state, federal, and private assets. Unfortunately, the leaders of these communities, and in some cases emergency managers, spent significant time denying failures and attempting to spin public perceptions about fault and responsibility (see Figure 8.6). These denials and the associated political and public relations challenges were present for

Figure 8.6 Business and government leaders simultaneously tried to deflect blame during the Deepwater Horizon oil spill even though there was a growing suspicion that multiple failures had occurred across all the involved organizations. (From White House/Pete Souza. With permission.)

Figure 8.7 Distinguished leaders such as former Secretary of State Colin Powell have noted the value and need of failure to help teach humility and improve future processes. (From Secretary of State/Unknown. With permission.)

extended periods of time, even in the face of significant and widespread evidence of the inefficiencies of response, recovery, and collaboration.

Embracing failure is initially counterintuitive, however, it is critical to emergency managers on a variety of levels. Distinguished leaders including Colin Powell have noted that they leverage each failure as an opportunity to engage in the practice of humility and to learn from the experience (see Figure 8.7).[12] When leaders are reminded that they can fail, they are far more willing and open to ask for help and engage those around them. In the traditional sense, this has occurred only within a trusted group of individuals (often emergency management personnel or trusted volunteers). However, as organizations have become extremely limited in budgetary and personnel resources, this invariably must expand to the broader community, most often through social media. In some areas this occurs in complex collaborative environments (e.g., crowdsourcing), but most simply can occur through common conversations via Facebook and Twitter. For example, acknowledging mistakes on Twitter and Facebook not only is a humble approach, but also creates community engagement and allows for public accountability.

DUALITY

The second major component of humility is the inherent duality of its nature. Simultaneously, humility requires recognition of both the particular positive and negative leadership and personality traits. For example, a humble person can concurrently acknowledge his own brilliance and his lack thereof. As Dickson states in *Humilitas*, even the greatest experts in a given field can acknowledge logically that there is that much more knowledge in every other specialty that they do not know.[10] This realization alone should be humbling. If they do not acknowledge this duality, they are engaging in competency extrapolation by trying to project their own expertise on other areas. It is this very duality that an individual or group of individuals can simultaneously be incredibly knowledgeable and yet still be ignorant in so many ways that is critical to emergency managers throughout the world.

WHAT IS . . . COMPETENCY EXTRAPOLATION?

Competency extrapolation is when an expert in a given area maintains a belief that her expertise is equally high in all (or most) connected areas. This type of approach typically ignores the fact that the sheer amount of knowledge required to achieve expertise in one area cannot be mastered by one person.[10] The presence of competency extrapolation inherently challenges humility.

This duality occurs frequently in disaster response and recovery, but is most clearly evident during damage assessment processes. Traditionally, emergency managers utilize small teams of individuals and volunteers to drive and walk through affected areas to note damaged buildings and critical infrastructure (e.g., downed electrical lines). This information is supplemented by reports from first-response and infrastructure workers who notice damaged conditions. The challenge with this approach is that it is limited to the number of workers utilized and the quantity of reports generated. Although those reports are generated by eyewitnesses who are localized experts, there is vast terrain—both geographically and socially—that has yet to be reviewed and considered after the disaster. As such, it can leave large swaths of the affected community with continued needs that are unidentified and unaddressed.

In contrast, social media systems have significantly changed this paradigm by allowing reporting from anyone within the community (see Figure 8.8). This is one of the most profound possibilities of

Figure 8.8 Localized infrastructure damage such as this washed out road can be reported and addressed far more quickly when crowdsourcing tools like Ushahidi are used to support and supplement traditional damage assessment teams. (From FEMA/Marvin Nauman. With permission.)

crowdsourcing tools such as Ushahidi. As has been discussed several times in earlier chapters, Ushahidi is a visualization tool that allows for the collection and gathering of information from the general public via various technological platforms including text messages, Twitter, and web submissions.[13] The Ushahidi platform has been utilized numerous times in international emergencies and disasters, including flooding in Thailand (2011), Hurricane Irene (2011), an earthquake in Nepal (2011), the Fukushima earthquake (2011), and the Haiti earthquake (2010) just to name a few.[14] Instead of a limited number of first-responders, there were literally hundreds if not thousands of reports from the general public. This was particularly important during the Deepwater Horizon oil spill where public concerns were primarily focused on the spread and locations of oil along the Gulf Coast. Unfortunately, traditional responders were spread thin across the very wide area of potential impact along the coasts of Florida, Alabama, Mississippi, and Louisiana. Emergency management leaders must quickly accept the possibility that traditional mechanisms are limited and can be better leveraged when used in parallel with those utilized by and expected through social systems such as Ushahidi.

CONSTRUCTIVE DISCONTENT

The third component of humility that is identified in *Egonomics* is the presence of constructive discontent. Constructive discontent is the drive and expectation that the status quo is never sufficient and that additional considerations and direction should be implemented. It is similar in nature to the entrepreneurial drive and innovative spirit that was discussed in Chapter 4. This constructive discontent is not to say that every practice, particularly in emergency management, is inherently flawed. However, emergency managers need to acknowledge that new political, cultural, social, ethical, or technological applications arise that must be considered and addressed within the framework established in that given community. With this acknowledged, it is clear that emergency managers must therefore constantly seek to evaluate new ways or methods to achieve emergency preparedness within their community.

For example, the profession of emergency management is traditionally focused on doing the greatest good for the greatest number of people. Although this vision and purpose has never wavered, the last 20 years have shown an increasingly important need to consider those who do not naturally fall in the "greatest number of people." These unique and "special" populations have always been a component of a given community, but were particularly highlighted in the aftermath of Hurricane Katrina's impact on the city of New Orleans. Thousands of displaced and affected citizens felt their needs and interests were overlooked during the event. Since that time there have been progressively more complex considerations to address these kinds of issues.

Some of the early planning considerations simply sought to identify what populations within their given community had special considerations when it came to emergency preparedness, response, and recovery (see Figure 8.9). For example, emergency managers in the Greater Kansas City area broke down special needs populations into five categories: economically challenged, language proficiency issues, handicapped (physically or emotionally), age vulnerable (under 5 or over 65), and geographically or culturally isolated (e.g., Amish communities).[15] However, this type of collective description under the banner of "special needs" was quickly rebuffed by community leaders who indicated that this type of labeling could be discriminatory or condescending. The next several years continued to be challenging for emergency managers to address this need, as terms such as "vulnerable needs" or "functional needs" were tossed around in an attempt to meet the needs, concerns, and issues of all constituents.

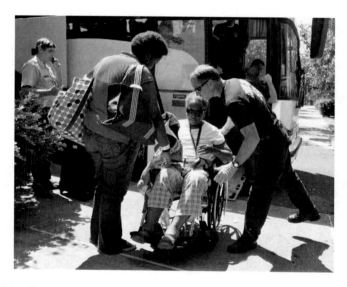

Figure 8.9 Community sectors with unique vulnerabilities and needs have traditionally been very challenging to emergency managers. (From FEMA/Patsy Lynch. With permission.)

In the end, under the leadership of FEMA administrator Craig Fugate (see Chapter 1), FEMA began a process of pushing for local communities to plan for the "Whole Community." This strategy changed the focus from separation and division to one of unification and consensus building, and was truly a sign from leaders in the field that this issue had no easy solution. The need for humility was significant and prudent to incorporate into disaster response planning.

Some emergency management professionals were frustrated by these challenges and changes, but those who approached the problem humbly and empathetically realized that this was a genuine opportunity to address major challenges during disaster response and minimize the chance of repeating the failures of response that occurred after Hurricane Katrina.

This same concept is present in how emergency management professionals of every type have engaged in social media systems. With few exceptions, average emergency managers are not social media experts. They may have led their organizations to active engagement, but social media utilization and application in disaster response fields is almost always behind the curve as compared to businesses, marketing agencies, and other more progressive organizations. This creates a situation (much like the duality mentioned above) where emergency managers are inherently not application experts in social media, but are specialists in coordinating disaster response and recovery. Consequently, there must be a constant evaluation of whether social media conversations being conducted by emergency management professionals are taking place in the most appropriate spaces. For example, at one point in time MySpace was the largest and most influential social networking site. Consequently, some of the early adopters within the first-responder community leveraged this tool for information exchange and recruitment possibilities. However, as Facebook grew exponentially in the late 2000s and MySpace shrunk in a corresponding fashion, many agencies had to acknowledge (publicly or subconsciously) that they were no longer engaging in areas that worked. Only by humbly acknowledging these types of change were these agencies able to continue to engage and grow within the field.

OPENING THE BOX: HUMILITY ON HIGH

Mt. Everest lies between Tibet and Nepal, with its summit reaching higher than 29,000 feet. Between 1920 and 1952, seven major climbing expeditions attempted and ultimately failed to reach the summit. The famous mountain climber George Leigh-Mallory even died in 1924 during an attempted climb. After joining two Mt. Everest reconnaissance expeditions in 1951 and 1952, Edmund Hillary joined a climbing expedition in 1953 and managed to reach the summit with Tenzing Norgay, a Nepalese native who had climbed with the last five expeditions. These two men were the only two to make it to the top. At 11:30 in the morning, these two men stood at 29,028 feet above sea level at the highest spot on earth. Upon completion, Edmund Hillary returned to Great Britain and was knighted by Queen Elizabeth II. As the years passed, Hillary expanded his explorations to the Antarctic, but ultimately returned to Nepal in the 1960s to aid the local people by helping to build clinics, hospitals, and 17 different schools. He later worked with the Nepalese government to declare the area around Mt. Everest a national park to ensure its preservation and protection. Ultimately, Sir Edmund Hillary died in 1988 in his native New Zealand.[16] Clearly, this man was a hero, expert, and humanitarian recognized and respected throughout the world. It would be very easy for Sir Edmund Hillary to have more ego than humility; however, there is one classic example of where his humility existed in the presence of others (see Figure 8.10). Specifically, upon one of his trips back to the Himalayas a group of climbers recognized him and asked for a picture. To complete the scene, someone in the group thrust an ice pick into his hand to "look the part." Meanwhile, another climber (who did not recognize Hillary) walked by the group and stopped the photo to correct Sir Edmund Hillary's grip on the pick. Hillary thanked the man and returned to the photo without any objection or irritation.[10] A simple humble act was a profound reflection of how those with knowledge, power, ability, or awareness can achieve greater purpose, power, and fulfillment through humble responses.

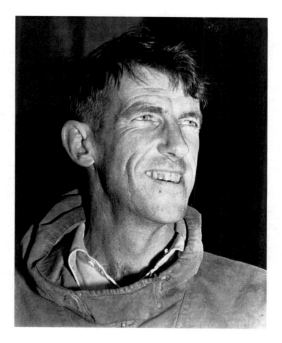

Figure 8.10 A portrait of Sir Edmund Hillary who was known for his skill and humility. (From Public Domain/Unknown.)

PUBLIC EXPECTATIONS OF SOCIAL KNOWLEDGE

If anecdotal evidence is insufficient to establish the need for humility within this new leadership paradigm, public expectations are clear about the control and distribution of information. Although citizens still acknowledge government as a source of information, they no longer see it as the sole or primary (or often even trustworthy) source. Rather, citizens leverage multiple streams of information, including social media systems, to collect information about an event and frame it in a way that is understandable to the individual and in sync with their respective worldviews. It is this organic aggregation that is so empowering to these citizens and ultimately to emergency managers.

This creates a scenario where members of the constituency know as much or more than the average emergency manager. This is primarily because citizens only have one focus, the self preservation of knowledge and information. In contrast, emergency managers have duties and obligations to coordinate functions and supervise response and recovery functions while also trying to collect and disseminate public information. This dichotomy often leads to situations where emergency managers are responding to incident-related issues far before planning and preparedness have developed enough to address these needs.

Consequently, the tendency of emergency managers and other professional first-responders is to deny this possibility by assuming that information collected or shared from social media sources is inherently erroneous or misguided simply because it has not been confirmed by traditional sources. This approach is flawed and devoid of humility and often leads to distasteful and sometimes offensive community engagement. This type of overreaction is occasionally seen when an individual speaks to another in a language that is not his or her primary tongue. Specifically, rather than focusing on the language connection, people often speak the primary language louder, implying auditory issues or a lack of mental capacity rather than simply a linguistics challenge.

CROWD SPEED

Much as with the concept of superior knowledge established earlier, the crowd collects, analyzes, and redistributes information at amazing speeds. As discussed in Chapter 3, social media information is routinely

225

exchanged at a nearly instantaneous rate. Although difficult to fathom, this speed of information exchange is increased during disasters and other large-scale events due to the dynamic nature of the activities and involvement of the respective communities. It is this crowd speed that not only must be accepted by emergency managers, but also inherently leads to humility regarding the control or management of social media information.

As people who utilize social media have become more comfortable with the connectedness of these systems and the speed of information exchange, they have become increasingly willing and interested in asking the online community for feedback, engagement, and ultimately greater knowledge. This type of action is inherently humbling in nature. By asking for the assistance of the crowd, these individuals have acknowledged that they can more quickly and efficiently address issues than they could as individuals. It is this behavior that establishes the public's expectations of how government responders, particularly during emergencies, should engage social systems such as Facebook, Twitter, and YouTube.

Some emergency management organizations have acknowledged this concept and begun to humbly engage social technologies during an event to improve situational awareness. For example, in 2010, FEMA administrator Fugate publicly acknowledged his own use of Twitter on his phone to identify issues related to an explosion in California and a fire in Florida more quickly. At the same time Fugate acknowledged that the collected information from Twitter regarding these two disasters was in advance of official word from local, state, or federal emergency management officials (see Figure 8.11).[17] Considering the bureaucracy established earlier and the public embrace of social media, this reality would be clear to the average citizen. Unfortunately, the vast majority of emergency management community leaders still deny the possibility of not only using social media tools but the public knowledge and speed of delivery that supports and utilizes these systems.

WHY EMERGENCY MANAGERS STRUGGLE WITH HUMILITY

The professional field of emergency management has experienced several dynamic changes over the past 60 years. Although noteworthy disasters are scattered throughout history, formalized attempts to manage disasters

Figure 8.11 FEMA Administrator Craig Fugate is a strong proponent of the use of social media systems to gather and aggregate social media information. (From FEMA/Patsy Lynch. With permission.)

did not really occur until the mid-twentieth century with the rise of the Cold War. At that point, many local communities dedicated personnel and resources (e.g., fallout shelters, radios, etc.) to the management of possible nuclear fallout. Given that this period of time immediately followed World War II and coincided (at certain points) with the Korean conflict and Vietnam War, many of those individuals assigned these early civil defense and emergency management responsibilities were military veterans.

As the concept of civil defense eventually modified into a more generalized emergency preparedness approach, the use of ex-military to serve in these roles did not diminish. Consequently, the stylistic approach for planning and response was often based on militaristic formats and heavily based on command-and-control formats of management. Even though the profession of emergency management began to become more formalized in the early 1990s with a concerted effort to create formalized education programs and utilize an all-hazard planning approach, the influence of military and paramilitary organizations is still heavily felt in many communities.

Likewise, after the terrorist attacks of September 11th, President George W. Bush passed Homeland Security Presidential Directive 5 (HSPD-5) which called for the establishment of a national response system. To fulfill this directive, the National Incident Management System (NIMS) was created, implemented, and mandated for all levels of governments. Part of the management system of NIMS was based on the Incident Command System (ICS), which was a longstanding best practice in California wildfire response. Much like the militaristic basis discussed earlier, ICS established the need for a clear command-and-control structure where all information and action would be managed through appropriate span of control as well as review and approval (see Figure 8.12).

These systematic and structural components of traditional emergency management make the profession heavily authoritative and ego-driven. Clearly there are many successes within the emergency preparedness and response community that have been achieved through

Figure 8.12 After the terrorist attacks of September 11, 2001, President George W. Bush issued Homeland Security Presidential Directive 5 (HSPD-5) that ultimately established the National Incident Management System (NIMS), which was heavily based on command and control. (From White House/Unknown. With permission.)

these foundations. However, the growth of social media and the public expectations related to those systems is extremely significant and should push the emergency management community and its strongest leaders to reconsider these models. If not, John Dickson says in *Humilitas*, "People who imagine that they know most of what is important to know are hermetically sealed from learning new things and receiving constructive criticism."[10]

Ego-Driven Assumptions

Because the field of emergency management is often challenged by strong egos and an inherent difficulty in embracing humility, there is a collection of assumptions that often influence emergency preparedness, response, and recovery activities. Max Bazerman and Michael Watkins address these assumptions in their book, *Predictable Surprises: The Disasters You Should Have Seen Coming and How to Prevent Them*. Specifically, they identify five common assumptions: positive illusions, egocentric manner, discounting the future, maintaining the status quo, and inability to personally engage.[19]

The first illusion presented in *Predictable Surprises* is the tendency to maintain positive illusions in the face of significant challenges. While maintaining this assumption, emergency managers tend to conclude that either a problem does not exist or is simply not severe enough to merit significant attention. In some ways components of the community planning issues that ultimately have led to the whole community concept discussed earlier have fallen into this category. Many emergency managers, particularly those in resource- and personnel-limited communities, have simply long chosen to ignore the challenge of functional and access needs communities, considering the issue of unimportance within the greater framework of emergency management. Likewise, social media have been treated in a similar fashion. Even with strong evidence that social media are becoming ubiquitous among the general population and heavily used before, during, and after disasters, many emergency managers have chosen to consider social media simply as a fad and a fleeting function that will eventually simply go away. In case of both whole community planning and the criticality of social media, the lack of humility through the exercise of the positive illusion is an extreme detriment to successful emergency management.

The second assumption established by Bazerman and Watkins is the tendency for emergency managers and disaster response officials to discount the impact of future events such as emergencies, disasters, and large-scale catastrophes. The foundations of this assumption are systematic for standard emergency management practices. For example, industry practices are for emergency managers as leaders to conduct a hazard analysis within their communities to identify what risks and hazards may affect the quality of life in the area. In most cases, hazard analysis creates a risk score by evaluating probability and vulnerability to the given risk. For example, emergency management in so-called "Tornado Alley" would consider the vulnerability and probability of a tornado to occur to both be high. On the other hand, local communities in these same areas would consider the probability and vulnerability of a tsunami to both be extremely low. This type of process is continued for all local hazards and ultimately creates a priority regarding those events that are more likely to occur and occasion greater vulnerability in the given community. Conversely, those hazards with low probability and low vulnerability are often given minimal attention if not completely ignored.

This secondary impact is what can lead to the assumption of discounting future possibilities. Catastrophic events often fall into this consideration, as most communities consider them so unlikely or improbable that they are unwilling to plan or dedicate resources to address these issues. Although FEMA and some larger localities have begun to try to address catastrophic planning, the standard is not uniform and is unrealistic to most emergency management organizations. However, real-life events such as Hurricane Katrina, the Fukushima Daiichi meltdown, and the Joplin tornado fell into this category and were never really considered during the emergency preparedness planning process. It is extremely challenging to address these issues in light of accurate hazard analysis, and there are difficult challenges both systematically and personally to change; however, there needs to be significant consideration of when, where, and how to more accurately address the potential of future events (see Figure 8.13).

Likewise, before the terrorist attacks of September 11, 2001, many citizens and homeland security professionals felt that the United States homeland was safe from bombings, suicide attacks, and other acts of terrorism. These attacks and subsequent threats were extremely humbling as American citizens and leaders simply refused to believe that the future could be filled with such atrocities. It is interesting that as time has passed and these events move further into history, many citizens, elected officials, and emergency response personnel have slowly shifted back to

Figure 8.13 Catastrophic events such as the EF5 tornado that struck Joplin, Missouri, are extremely difficult to plan for and ultimately are an example of a fundamental flaw of ignoring the possibility of future events. (From FEMA/Leo "Jace" Anderson. With permission.)

a comfort zone and a feeling that risk in the future is small and much less significant than traditional threats and hazards that affect their communities every year.

The last set of assumptions identified in *Predictable Surprises* is the egocentric nature of humans, but particularly emergency managers and disaster response personnel. This concept is divided into two parts. First, emergency managers tend to defer to their own knowledge, skills, and abilities when faced with challenges. Although these characteristics also comprise the foundations of confidence, it is the fine line where the outlook shifts to an egocentric focus and loses sight of best practices that can grossly affect how well communities are prepared for disasters. This is particularly complicated when emergency managers and local community leaders lack personal experience with disasters, particularly large-scale events. This lack of personal experience is also paramount as communities adopt social media and consider public expectations related to social technologies. Consequently, many leaders simply do not see social media as a valuable tool or something with longevity and therefore underestimate the need to consider it in community planning. In both cases, these approaches lack humility and can otherwise undermine successful emergency preparedness and response.

SERVANT LEADERSHIP

Converting from an egocentric model of leadership and operations to one based on humility will be extremely difficult for a significant portion of the emergency management community. It will truly be a fundamental shift in organizational and personal philosophies through the cycle of emergency preparedness, response, recovery, and mitigation. Communities certainly would like their emergency management and disaster response personnel to be bold and confident, however, the general public clearly has shifted their expectations to one of community influence and control. This component of the new leadership paradigm discussed throughout the book shifts away from command and control toward one of service.

This concept of servant leadership was first coined by Robert K. Greenleaf in his 1970 essay called, "The Servant as Leader."[20] Greenleaf described this model as beginning "with the natural feeling that one wants to . . serve first . . . [bringing] one to aspire to lead."[21] This process is manifest when the leader's priority mind-set is related to the need of others. Although all emergency managers and disaster responders are ostensibly public servants, the focus on the citizen is sometimes overlooked, forgotten, or disregarded due to some of the reasons mentioned earlier. As a test of the degree of servant leadership present, those served should be assessed to determine if they become "healthier, wiser, freer, more autonomous [and] more likely themselves to become servants."[21] These characteristics of servant leadership are almost universally present within online social communities. As has been discussed throughout this book, individuals actively engaged in systems such as Twitter, Facebook, and other social systems have a collective knowledge, wisdom, and perceived autonomy that has never been seen at this level. Consequently, engaging in servant leadership is one method to help emergency managers maintain true and engaging humility.

RULE OF THREE

In addition to the attitude necessary to become a servant leader, emergency managers must adopt practical approaches to engage in personal and organizational behaviors that encourage and facilitate humility. This is particularly challenging when organizations are attempting to utilize social media on a day-to-day basis to monitor and distribute information before, during, and after an event. The general public will engage at various levels and with an assortment of responses that may be good or bad. This latter issue is what is most often challenging to the emergency management community that (as already established) is often egocentric. Because the professional practices of emergency management are often not easily understood by the general public, there is inherently a tension between the misunderstanding and criticism of the public and professional practices intended to prevent loss of life and impact on property.

WHAT IS . . . THE RULE OF THREE?

The Rule of Three is an approach in social media to divide messaging into three focus areas that help contribute to efforts of humility. These three focus areas are brand related, areas of expertise, and answering questions from the general public.[22]

Consequently, one day-to-day strategy to maintain humility within the community is to apply the Rule of Three. This Rule of Three is a process that divides the amount of time spent by an organization into three types of focus. The first third of an organization's social media focus should talk about the purpose and focus of the organization. Based on the need for an entrepreneurial outlook (see Chapter 4), this should also include a marketable presence or brand component for the organization (e.g., logo) to establish credibility and connection with the community. The second third of the social media postings should contain interesting information about emergency management or disaster response that helps the community understand what happens before and after disasters. Likewise, this would be the opportunity for organizations to promote personal and family preparedness.[22] The third component of messaging for emergency management organizations using social media is to interact with followers and to answer questions that are presented. Clearly these three components are not separate, but rather are intertwined and overlapping at all times and should provide a practical methodology for emergency managers to employ to help manage their transition from an egocentric model to one of humility and true servitude.

LEADERS IN THE OPEN: HAL GRIEB

Hal Grieb is a professional emergency manager and social media expert. He has served in an emergency management capacity for the Florida National Guard, City of Plano (TX), Previstar, and the University of Florida.

Mr. Grieb is extremely active in social media and was awarded the 2011 Statesman Texas Social Media Award for Government. In the following essay written for this book, he shares his views of how social media mandate a high sense of humility within emergency management.

Steps toward Greater Humility

Hal Grieb

You. Will. Die. According to all my research, the human species mortality rate has consistently hovered at approximately 100%. This means that even as someone reads this book others that have read the pages before may no longer be here. Sit back for a moment and reflect on this. What are the first thoughts that come to you? All your past accomplishments, your present work, and your future are merely fleeting specs in cosmic time. When I reflect on this, I personally feel a humbling cloud of reality cover my core being. Thoughts of selfish moments spent ignoring family and friends, and my earthly aspirations of career goals and legacy become focused and prioritized.

Humility is a constant work in progress. Be wary of those who pride themselves on their own humility. I wanted to write this chapter not to give you the secrets of being humble, but I personally needed it due to a confessed selfish pride in seeing my work be touted as great to my peers. As I become older I see the short-term memory of civilization's thoughts of grandeur being replaced with thoughts of how to help those wanting to learn to utilize social media and more broadly become better stewards of those they are charged with protecting, whether through first response or in more strategic planning and coordination levels of emergency management and homeland security.

The first step is to proclaim your weakness and learn from those who are a few steps ahead. Humility is no more than a way to remind yourself constantly of your core priorities whether family, profession, or in volunteering. There are even best practices from people like Agnes Gonxha Bojaxhiu (Mother Teresa) and her rules of humility.

I. Speak as Little as Possible about Yourself

When using today's i-Generation of technology with devices and platforms focused on the individual (i.e., iPhone, iPad, and the good old original *MY*Space) begin by omitting words such as "I" and "Me" from your posts. Heck, for fun go to your favorite posting platform and do a self-check on how self-focused your posts are. By understanding how you speak about yourself versus helping empower others, you will be starting down the transformative journey of humility.

2. Keep Busy with Your Own Affairs and Not Those of Others

Why are you using social media and other community-driven technologies? Really look at how you engage your colleagues using these tools. Is it really constructive criticism to help someone off-target, or an easy quip to help feel good about the projects on which you are working?

3. Avoid Curiosity

You may know this as the "shiny toy syndrome." Yes it has all the latest blinkies and flashies. Its user interface is slick and intuitive. Now, with all the flash and appeal, by utilizing it, does it serve your community effectively? Is it easily augmented into your existing plans and programs? If not, by getting overextended you will never be able to complete your current goals and provide a quality social media or technology interface to help those you are truly trying to reach. This does not mean you cannot check out new technologies, just ensure that the time spent exploring does not eat away at the time needed for doing.

4. Do Not Interfere in the Affairs of Others

Rather than interfere, do support, help, and empower others. We are all trying to help our people help each other. Petty interference only hinders the whole community approach.

5. Accept Small Irritations with Good Humor

In everything we do, we must realize we are only human. Finding humor in how we can get caught up in the smallest irritation brings levity to our career path and state of sanity. We all get irritated when technology or people hit our "pet peeves." By knowing what these pet peeves are, we can work to maintain compassion on those things that can drive us to the brink of insanity, then laugh for letting the little things bog us down.

6. Do Not Dwell on the Faults of Others

How many times have you been blissfully engaged in a technology and then out of nowhere, the developers release a new user interface? How many people complain about new upgrades or how something needs to be changed to make it easier for them? One must try to pause and reflect inwardly on whether the need to point faults outward is based on a fault inward. Another technique is to try to understand more fully what the intent of a technology really is. User interfaces may change (or not change) due to compliance, new future feature rollouts, and so on.

7. ACCEPT CENSURES EVEN IF UNMERITED

Many have and will continually disapprove of new technologies and social media use in emergency management. Some of the criticism has some merit; some of it does not. It is not your job to win over people's opinions with words. Accept that others are in this world who will not approve of your work in social media and emergency management and instead prove the worth of your work through silent action.

8. GIVE IN TO THE WILL OF OTHERS

I don't have all the answers, which is a tough nut to crack personally. Years ago I scored very strongly as a D in the DiSC personality test my employer administered. The administrator compared me to a bull in a glass factory based on my scores. Although humorous, I know that professionally, I will get nowhere breaking everything near or around me due to not harnessing my will to support others.

9. ACCEPT INSULTS AND INJURIES

Why? Because not accepting them will only lead you to a destructive path of bitterness and self-doubt and could derail your projects from ever being implemented successfully.

10. ACCEPT CONTEMPT, BEING FORGOTTEN, AND DISREGARDED

Working in social media and any web technology is not about the individual. It's about providing something to help those in need. If you begin to get caught up in the acclaim you receive from doing good work (on a given project) instead of from the good work itself, your intentions will become self-destructive and apparent to all.

11. BE COURTEOUS AND DELICATE EVEN WHEN PROVOKED BY SOMEONE

Take a breath, calm down, and kill them with kindness. Nothing wise has been spoken when filled with provoked anger.

12. DO NOT SEEK TO BE ADMIRED AND LOVED

Yes, your Klout score can be used as a nice quantitative analysis for your program's social media reach. It is not meant to showcase the adoration of the Internet for you. This can be hard because humans are social beings. We thrive on admiration and love. The key point is if that is all you are seeking you can quickly become prey to shortcuts intended only to meet this, thereby sabotaging your core work.

13. Do Not Protect Yourself Behind Your Own Dignity

Your true intentions, passions, and your project performance will help shield you from those who wish to harm you.

14. Give in, in Discussions, Even When You Are Right

There are times in our lives where we must willingly walk into a discussion that we know will be tense, heated, and possibly unwinnable. Many discussions are not had to be won or lost. They are there to facilitate the development of a shared path that can be followed and agreed upon as meeting the needs of an entire organization. I often remind myself of a quote I heard from author Andy Stanley at a leadership summit regarding heated discussions, "You have to understand the upside of their side, and the downside of yours." Keeping this in mind brings a more outside perspective that can at worst lead the discussion to be left at simply agreeing to disagree rather than an embittered debate or argument.

15. Always Choose the More Difficult Task

Growth can only come to those who work for it. When hard work and difficult tasks are accomplished, the feeling that comes with that is great. Without those willing to sacrifice themselves for the difficult tasks that lie ahead, greater good would never be realized. Society needs leaders to blaze trails into those areas that scare many. By taking on difficult things in your area of influence you forge a path for those following you toward a new, more exciting horizon.

Note: The views expressed by Hal Grieb are his own personal views and do not represent his employer or any organization with which he is affiliated.

ENDNOTES

1. Marcum, David and Smith, Steven. (2008) *Egonomics: What Makes Ego Our Greatest Asset (or Most Expensive Liability)*. New York: Touchstone.

2. "Key Facts." (2012) Facebook Newsroom. http://newsroom.fb.com/content/default.aspx?NewsAreaId=22. Accessed July 19, 2012.
3. "More Americans Using Social Media and Technology in Emergencies." (2012) American Red Cross Press Release. http://www.redcross.org/portal/site/en/menuitem.94aae335470e233f6cf911df43181aa0/?vgnextoid=7a82d1efe68f1310VgnVCM10000089f0870aRCRD. Accessed July 19, 2012.
4. Crowe, Adam. (2012) *Disasters 2.0: The Application of Social Media on Modern Emergency Management*. Boca Raton, FL: CRC Press.
5. "The Lousiana Bucket Brigade Honored for Oil Spill Response Work." (2012) Lousiana Bucket Brigade Blog. http://www.labucketbrigade.org/article.php?id=744. Accessed July 20, 2012.
6. Johnson, Allen Jr., Calkins, Lauren, Fisk, Margaret Cronin. (2012) "BP Spill Victims Face Economic Fallout Two Years Later." Bloomberg. http://www.bloomberg.com/news/2012-02-23/bp-oil-spill-haunts-gulf-business-owners-almost-two-years-after-disaster.html. Accessed July 21, 2012.
7. "Joplin Tornado." (2011) Joplin Tornado Crowd Map. https://joplintornado.crowdmap.com/. Accessed July 22, 2012.
8. Stephens, Kim. (2011) "Joplin Tornado Demonstrates Social Media's 5 Key Roles in Disaster Response and Recovery." iDisaster Blog. http://idisaster.wordpress.com/2011/05/23/joplin-tornado-demonstrates-social-medias-5-key-roles-in-disaster-response-and-recovery/. Accessed July 22, 2012.
9. Rempel, Michelle. (2011) "Hashing out Hashtags on Twitter." Simplifying Social Media Blog. http://www.mediavinemarketing.com/simplify-social-media/hashing-out-hashtags-on-twitter/. July 22, 2012.
10. Dickson, John. (2011) *Humilitas: The Lost Key to Life, Love, and Leadership*. New York: Zondervan.
11. Marcum, David and Smith Stephen. (2008) *Egonomics: What Makes Ego Our Greatest Asset (or Most Expensive Liability)*. New York: Touchstone.
12. Asmus, Mary Jo. (2012) "The Value in Failing a Little Everyday." SmartBlog on Leadership. http://smartblogs.com/leadership/2012/06/20/the-value-in-failing-a-little-every-day/. Accessed July 23, 2012.
13. "About Us." (2012) Ushahidi Blog. http://www.ushahidi.com/about-us. Accessed July 24, 2012.
14. "Tracking Disaster Reports on Ushahidi." (2012) Institute of Hazard, Risk, and Resilience Blog. http://ihrrblog.org/2012/01/15/tracking-disaster-reports-with-ushahidi/. Accessed July 24, 2012.
15. Crowe, Adam. (2012) *Disasters 2.0: The Application of Social Media in Modern Emergency Management*. Boca Raton, FL: CRC Press.
16. "From Beekeeper to World Explorer." (2008) Academy of Achievement. http://www.achievement.org/autodoc/page/hil0bio-1/. Accessed July 26, 2012.
17. Trocki, Liz. (2010) "FEMA Head Uses Social Media for Situational Awareness." AWARE: Alerts, Warnings, and Response to Emergencies. http://www.awareforum.org/2010/10/fema-head-uses-twitter-for-situational-awareness/. July 28, 2012.

18. Ingram, Matthew. (2012) "The Colorado Shooting and the Crowdsourced Future of News." Gigaom. http://gigaom.com/2012/07/20/the-colorado-shooting-and-the-crowdsourced-future-of-news/. Accessed July 29, 2012.
19. Bazerman, Max and Watkins, Michael. (2008) *Predictable Surprises: The Disasters You Should Have Seen Coming and How to Prevent Them.* Boston: Harvard Business School Press.
20. "About Us." (2011) Greenleaf Center for Servant Leadership. http://www.greenleaf.org/aboutus/history.html. Accessed July 31, 2012.
21. "What is Servant Leadership?" (2011) Greenleaf Center for Servant Leadership. http://www.greenleaf.org/whatissl/. Accessed July 31, 2012.
22. Guth, Amy. (2012) The rule of thirds in social media. *Chicago Tribune.* http://articles.chicagotribune.com/2012-07-05/features/ct-tribu-social-media-thirds-20120705_1_social-media-media-tips-column-amyguth-and-scottkleinberg. August 2, 2012.

9

Creativity and Design

We stand at a seminal moment—at a crossroads as it were—between what we might call the new age of disclosure and that new era of inattention.

Jim Carroll[1]

FORM OR FUNCTION

Seth Godin often writes about the need for creativity and function within traditional operations. For example, in one of his blog posts he talks about the necessity of significant safety signage that he noted in a recent trip to a well-known national amusement park. He notes that the signs were all presented differently using various colors, sizes, shapes, and fonts. These variations ultimately challenged the effectiveness of the signs because they were hard to read and inconsistent from ride to ride and place to place. The lack of design is inefficient, ineffective, and ultimately unnecessary. Specifically, Godin states that "The cost of making each sign attractive is precisely zero . . . same amount of ink, same amount of wood . . . yet if more people read the signs, injuries would decrease, lines would move faster and . . . [the park] would make more money."[2] It is this very divide that defines much of the operations within professional emergency management. Function should lead design, but that isn't always the case (please see Figure 9.1).

Creativity and design are not often associated (if ever) with professional emergency managers. As discussed in the first eight chapters,

Figure 9.1 Emergency preparedness and safety signage often utilize mixed colors, fonts, sizes, and shapes that can ultimately lead to confusing and ineffective messaging. (From FEMA/Adam Dubrowa. With permission.)

emergency management within all disciplines and functions is often built around a command and control structure that functions to perform traditional disaster roles ranging across preparedness, response, recovery, and mitigation activities. Consequently, the dominant focus (as it should be) is on how to facilitate operational considerations so that the represented organization, community, or constituency is prepared to address physical, community, and cultural needs that may arise during emergencies or disasters.

However, this type of approach often tends to generate a myopic focus by emergency managers, who in many ways simply forget to incorporate the community they represent. Although this seems counterintuitive, as the sole function of emergency management is to protect the community, it can easily occur when emergency managers only utilize traditional public engagement strategies such as town hall meetings and unilateral public education. Much as with the earlier-discussed elements of this new leadership paradigm, social media strongly support and facilitate the delivery of creativity and design in emergency management in such a way that helps support rather than contradict the priorities of community preparedness for emergencies and disasters.

CREATIVITY IMPROVES FUNCTIONALITY

Before understanding why creativity must be incorporated into new leadership models, the components of creativity must first be examined. There are several major components that are evaluated later in this chapter, however, the first fundamental component of creativity is that it improves functionality. This is perhaps most famously stated by Apple co-founder Steve Jobs who said, "Design is not just what it looks like, [but also] . . . design is how it works."[3] Under the leadership and vision of Steve Jobs, Apple revolutionized the technology sector with its introduction of the iPod and iTunes in 2001. These new "i" devices ultimately provided the same functionality (music player, playlists, etc.) as other available components, but they were fundamentally more simply designed, easier to operate, and ultimately integrated with other Apple products and technologies. Apple sold more than 1 million units within 18 months of their initial release and more than 275 million devices within 10 years.[4] See Figure 9.2.

Figure 9.2 The iPhone and iPod are two of the most profound examples of design serving an item's looks and functions. (From Adam Crowe. With permission.)

Clearly emergency managers do not sell or produce technology products as Apple does at the individual, organizational, or profession levels. However, as was discussed in Chapter 4 regarding the importance of incorporating entrepreneurial methodologies, there are many things that emergency managers can learn from successful businesses and their leaders. For example, emergency managers have long struggled with their served community or constituency understanding the purpose, mission, and impact of their respective organizations. As mentioned in *Predictable Surprises* (see Chapter 8), individuals are more likely to understand and appreciate emergency preparedness (both individually and at the corporate level) when they have experienced emergencies or disasters.[5] As most communities have not experienced disasters, particularly large-scale events, this creates a significant challenge for emergency management leaders to create a compelling and convincing argument for when, where, and how emergency preparedness should be conducted within a community.

The most common approach to address this problem is for emergency managers to convince the general public analytically. Statistics, numbers, and data are often presented to convince the public; however, this is often unconvincing and uninteresting. Specifically, if the general public is ignoring the possibilities and consequences of potential disasters due to lack of experience, they are unengaged and therefore not listening to these statistics. In addition, according to Clay Shirky, people do not consume data, but rather stories.[6] These two issues strongly combine to indicate a need for emergency managers to shift away from data-driven community engagement to one of storytelling.

The most obvious and cost-effective strategy for this change is the integration of social media. Although many emergency management organizations (albeit far from all) have begun to utilize social media for information dissemination and collection, they still are primarily pushing data. However, these data need to be packaged, much like stories, in ways that are interesting, relevant, and emotionally provocative to initiate change in behavior and ultimately improve the functionality of emergency management within a given community. For example, in 2011, the U.S. Centers for Disease Control and Prevention (CDC) released a preparedness campaign based around zombies, as described in Chapter 6. Although not applicable to all community partners, there is a significant cross-section of the general public that is engaged and intrigued by zombie-related content and storytelling. By utilizing this interest, the CDC created a compelling storytelling mechanism that greatly exceeded traditional functional approaches. Please see Figure 9.3.

Figure 9.3 The CDC released a zombie preparedness campaign in 2011 that began to leverage fresh and creative storytelling to make preparedness interesting and relevant. (From CDC/Unknown. With Permission.)

THE DESIGN COMPONENT OF CREATIVITY

In addition to the functional components of applied creativity, it is also defined through design. In many ways, design is an offshoot of function. If creativity improves function it is often done through designing an orderly, inclusive, and innovative approach to planning, preparedness, and operational considerations. This clearly delineates the intentions and goals of the leader and ultimately the represented organization.

Although many emergency managers would consider themselves organized and, fundamentally, planners, few of them have design instincts on when, where, and how planning and operational components should fit together. Most emergency management organizations have limited staff and resources with far too many projects, priorities, and conflicting interests to truly lay out well-organized plans of operation. Much as with the simultaneous production discussed as part of the magnification possibilities in Chapter 6, emergency managers struggle with processes that are not sequential in nature. Under typical circumstances, this overwhelmed state of management only allows projects to be prioritized based on the most pressing social, cultural, or political issues.

The incorporation of design can help bring this issue full circle for modern emergency managers. Maintaining a high level of design and order can help bring clarity to the priorities and structure of an emergency management organization. This occurs because all projects are viewed concurrently and co-mingled such that efficiencies and alignment can occur within the professional and volunteer components. The tie between design and creativity is both organic and prudent in modern times. Emergency managers must proactively and creatively look beyond traditional approaches to find those ways to achieve simultaneous production. At this time, and most likely in the near future, this

245

process is not necessarily uniform across the emergency management disciplines, but rather occurs jurisdiction by jurisdiction and community by community.

TYPES OF DESIGN INTELLIGENCE

In *Unleashing the Power of Design Thinking,* Kevin Clark and Ron Smith establish the concept that there is a type of approach called "design intelligence." They divide this so-called design intelligence into three subcategories: emotional intelligence, integral intelligence, and experimental intelligence.[7] Each of these subcomponents addresses core capabilities that need to exist for leaders to effectively apply creativity and the related design into operational and functional components of their organization. These characteristics are particularly important to facilitating this new leadership paradigm within the field of emergency management.

The first element of design intelligence is the emotional connection necessary to facilitate creativity. Emotional intelligence is the ability to understand and embrace those cultural elements that within the context of a given community create attachment, commitment, conviction, and ultimately action.[7] These contextual reactions are what marketers and advertisers heavily rely on to drive potential customers toward engaging with or purchasing their products. Although emergency management products are difficult to articulate and therefore put into emotional context prior to an event, the aftermath and subsequent recovery after a disaster are filled with emotional context (see Figure 9.4). This is why emergency managers struggle with the surge of volunteers and donations after a disaster. Individuals from the area (and now throughout the world thanks to social media) are emotionally affected and feel compelled to respond.

The challenge is that most emergency management organizations struggle to leverage these opportunities. Nongovernmental organizations (e.g., American Red Cross, The Salvation Army, etc.) of various types and sizes typically handle volunteer management and donations management on behalf of the affected community. The challenge is that the process is reactionary and simply tries to keep up with managing the emotional impact rather than leveraging it for the benefit of the community recovering from the disaster. These organizations do tremendous work and ultimately provide significant resources, but they contrast greatly with the rise of emergent volunteerism groups. For example, the often-cited Toomers for Tuscaloosa organization that

Figure 9.4 Emotional connectivity is critical to appropriate creativity and design, but is often extremely difficult for emergency managers to achieve. (From FEMA/Jocelyn Augustino. With permission.)

arose after the 2011 tornadoes that tore through the state of Alabama was significantly successful because it created a design to present and channel the emotional drive of the event to create more attention and energy than traditional organizations.

The second component of design intelligence is what Clark and Smith called integral intelligence. Integral intelligence is the ability to bring together separate and often divergent priorities and capabilities into one unified ecosystem or community.[7] Most organizations tend to subdivide endlessly to help manage and control these divergent components regardless of whether each can be optimized and ultimately added back together as a collection of parts. However, a design mindset looks for creative opportunities to find synergies and similarities among the pieces to create a structure that is greater than the sum of the individual units. This is why many organizations undergo significant and well-designed branding campaigns that tie multiple products, locations, or technologies together even though they may have few initial connections.

According to the American Marketing Association, a brand is a name, term, sign, symbol, or design that helps create uniform identification of goods and services with a particular provider. A well-leveraged

Figure 9.5 Although well-organized branding is extremely important to emergency management organizations, it is uncommon within the emergency management community outside FEMA and several large jurisdictions. (From FEMA/Bill Koplitz. With permission.)

brand helps improve messaging, credibility, emotional connectivity, and loyalty.[8] With the exception of FEMA and some of the emergency management agencies in the largest cities and jurisdictions, most emergency management organizations lack branding (see Figure 9.5). Instead, each component of the organization's activities is prepared and dealt with separately and without effective integration.

However, social media and emerging technologies can help new leaders in emergency management find ways to begin to efficiently and effectively create a well-designed brand. Although there are certainly images, pictures, and content that are utilized in social media that help create the branding pattern described above, the possibilities of social media far exceed this concept. Specifically, the tone, content, and transparency of the messaging will create a social brand that—if facilitated correctly—will increase loyalty, trustworthiness, and ultimately the effectiveness of public communications and engagement. For example, the American Red Cross does a fantastic job of leveraging multiple social media channels not only to spread the message and purpose of the American Red Cross, but present this information through the individual personalities, quirks, and passions of their leaders and workers.

Ryan found two more 4 bottle
packs of Dogfish Head's Midas
Touch beer.... when we drink we
do it right #gettngslizzerd

HootSuite · 2/15/11 11:24 PM

Figure 9.6 A screenshot of the unintentional Tweet sent on the official American Red Cross Twitter page by an employee who thought it was a personal account. (From Screenshot. With permission.)

These personalities (and ultimately humility) were evident even when mistakes happened. For example, in 2010, an American Red Cross social media expert named Gloria Huang accidentally posted a personal message containing the hashtag #gettngslizzard to the formal American Red Cross Twitter account (see Figure 9.6). Instead of trying to hide the mistake, the social media team at the American Red Cross simply removed the tweet and addressed the mistake in an open and honest way.[9] Ironically, the reputation of the American Red Cross got a boost because they stuck to the social media brand they had worked to create and build within their broader community.

In addition to the emotional and integrated design, the third component of intelligent design is experiential. Experiential intelligence is the ability to understand and incorporate all five human senses to create a design that is tangible and vibrant.[7] This type of design helps the end-user improve the interaction with the products. Much as with the emotional engagement described earlier, when customers can see, smell, hear, taste, and feel something they are far more likely to perceive the product as having increased quality or personal value. This personalization and perceived quality is extraordinarily important to emergency management. If the public values the functions and purpose of professional emergency management organizations, they are much more likely to comply with preparedness, prevention, and protective action statements and engage in the processes of response and recovery when needed.

Clearly social media do not allow the general public to see, smell, hear, taste, or feel the products of emergency management in a traditional physical sense. However, public engagement and collaboration via social media channels do allow the general public to experiment and get a sensory experience into the emergency management process. This process most often occurs via crowdsourcing, crisis mapping, and other collective experiences where individuals can ask questions, clarify information, and contribute knowledge and experiences. This experiential involvement can also occur during open source development and so-called "hacking" events. These types of events are primarily occurring in the emergent volunteerism sector by organizations using Ushahidi, Sahana, and various other sources.

COLLABORATIVE AND INTERACTIVE CREATIVITY

Most people associate creativity with art and perceive the process to be solitary in nature with little or no outside engagement, the only engagement being the acceptance of the products created or perhaps the art produced. However, creativity can also be inherently interactive and collaborative. Much as with the crowdsourcing and crowd wisdom that has been discussed throughout this book and is widely utilized by various emergent disaster response groups, creativity can be funneled through this process as well. Because creativity is as much about design and structure as it is the creation of art (although neither is present without the other), multiple parties can work together to create form and function that exceed the individual pieces and improve the efficiency and effectiveness of the process.

Ultimately, collaborative creativity leads to innovation. Because of the shifting public expectations that are being driven by the presence of social technologies, the process of innovation is also shifting away from traditional physical product generation to one of ideas and behaviors. Thomas Kouloulos, a "Fast Company" blogger, stated, "The greatest shift in the way we view innovation will be that the innovation surrounding behavior will need to be as continuous a process as the innovation of products has been over the last [one] hundred years."[10] Kouloulos addresses how various innovations from Apple, eBay, OnStar, and Google not only improve efficiency, but changed how people engage in the given market. Specifically, he talks about the alterations of the "very nature of the relationship between music and people" (iTunes) and the "experience of shopping and how community plays a role in the experience." (eBay)[10]

This type of behavior-altering innovation through creative design and development is critical to emergency management. It is ironic in many ways, as emergency managers and disaster responders have long sought out innovative products to communicate more clearly, farther, faster, or be more resistant to physical hazards, but have rarely (if ever) sought to leverage innovation to change behavior. Moreover, when emergency management leaders do attempt to leverage innovation to lead behavior change it is often unsuccessful and occasionally controversial because it lacks transparency and saleable benefit to the general public. This will be one of the most difficult hurdles for leaders within emergency management to adopt and use. As discussed in Chapter 4, innovation is not a term or a process often adopted by emergency managers who are highly driven by structure, hierarchy, and best practice.

OPENING THE BOX: COMMERCIALS BY THE CROWD

The climax of the National Football League (NFL) season is the Super Bowl where the league's top two teams compete in a final game to determine a league champion. This game has been held annually since 1967 in hosted locations throughout the United States.[13] Between the growing popularity of the sport and the celebratory nature of the event, it has long been a well-attended and highly watched event. Because of the public spectacle associated with this event and the high publicity involved, the commercial advertising slots in between game play on the televised broadcasts have always come at a premium. During Super Bowl I in 1967, a 30-second advertisement cost approximately $40,000.[14] This compares to the 2012 Super Bowl where advertisers paid $4 million for the same amount of airtime.[14] These costs do not go up in a linear fashion, but rather go up and down as a reflection of current economic trends such as recessions or bull markets. During the down times, businesses have often simply not engaged in Super Bowl marketing due to the high cost of production and ad purchasing. However, this concept was upended by the impact of crowdsourced creativity.

Since 2007, Doritos brand flavored tortilla chips has held its "Crash the Super Bowl" campaign, which is intended to allow the

Doritos consumer, "To turn its Super Bowl airtime into one of the most memorable ads of the evening."[12] Specifically, the creative consumers of Doritos were given an opportunity to create a video about the product that, if selected, would be one of the advertisements utilized by Doritos during the Super Bowl and possibly win the original creator $1 million. This past year Doritos received more than 6,200 video entries and selected five finalists. Of those five, two peaked at number one based on *USAToday* and Facebook AdMeters. Moreover, the Doritos crowdsourced video called, "Man's Best Friend," was created for just $20 by a freelance graphic designer and musician named Jonathan Friedman who utilized equipment he already owned and had readily available.[12]

This type of creativity crowdsourcing is not just a temporary move by Doritos. They have publicly stated that the "core mission [of the company] is to challenge the status quo and hand the power over to its consumer."[12] Clearly, innovation, creativity, and incentivizing the process in a seamless way helps magnify the image, brand, and ultimately consumer response to the Doritos product. Consequently, it is a prime example of how status quo and standard operations are not always the most efficient or effective solution.

CREATIVITY DRIVES EPIDEMICS

All forms of creativity ultimately create an attraction between the creator and the user. Whether the creativity or closely related design is intended to drive innovation, art, behavior, or product generation, they ultimately need to draw people from where they are and toward an intended ideal, behavior, action, or program. This element is critical for emergency managers to understand and apply, because limited budgets make behavior change and product acceptance extremely difficult. Fortunately, applying creativity to the emergency management process can not only help in the direct disaster readiness process, but also in the magnification of its results within a given community.

Specifically, creativity and design drive epidemics. Much akin to what was established in Chapter 6 when discussing magnification, the drive toward epidemics is a clear and consistent consideration necessary to adapt and leverage modern public expectations. Videos, messages, moving tributes, public gaffs, and errors go "viral" within minutes via the various social media channels such as Facebook, Twitter, and YouTube. This type of nonlinear response is uncharacteristic in day-to-day life. Moreover, these changes or events that generate epidemics are often insignificant, but simply provide enough virtual push to tip the event from slow moving or static to exponential in its growth and expansion.[15] Therefore, when epidemics occur with social technology systems they leverage the available tools to create results that are not only faster, but often more efficient and cost effective at the same time. According to Malcolm Gladwell, "Epidemics are, at their root, about . . . transformation . . . to make an idea or attitude or product tip, we're trying to change our audience in some small, yet critical response . . . to infect them, sweep them up in [an] epidemic [to] convert them from hostility to acceptance."[17] See Figure 9.7.

This type of social epidemic was present in 2011 during the so-called Arab Spring. Pro-democracy activists in the Middle East had long advocated for revolutions in the countries where dictators and oppressive regimes actively suppress both individual freedoms and open political discourse, but had never been able to identify methodologies that would sustain any revolution. However, starting in 2011, activists in Tunisia, Egypt, Libya, and Bahrain began to utilize social media systems such

Figure 9.7 Creativity and design have to drive epidemics that convert the general public and constituency from hostility to acceptance. (From FEMA/Patsy Lynch. With permission.)

as Facebook to improve the speed, efficiency, and anonymous nature of critical information exchange.[16] Although this seems straightforward, it occurred despite the fact that the Egyptian State Security Intelligence Service ordered the blocking of Twitter, Facebook, SMS texting, and other Internet sites within the country.[17] Quickly various allies of the movement initiated creatively designed systems and countersystems (e.g., old 56K modems) that helped facilitate the information exchange despite the attempted governmental limitations. The importance of the epidemic spread of information through social media was aptly summarized by graffiti that appeared on an historic street in Tunis the day after the Tunisian government was overturned and that simply said, "Facebook thanks!"[16]

Emergency managers must consider this impact when attempting to apply new leadership techniques to address public changes in government response tactics. First and foremost, emergency managers must have an awareness of the likelihood that disaster victims will leverage social applications in creative ways during an emergency or disaster to help address their needs with or without government interaction. Second, emergency managers must themselves consider leveraging creativity and design before, during, and after emergencies to improve the epidemic response of their community, as well as to encourage the behavior necessary for community readiness and to employ the tools necessary to be ready for all types of community challenges.

HINDRANCES TO CREATIVITY

The biggest challenge to understanding, applying, and leveraging the potential of creativity and design lies with its epidemic potential. As stated earlier, there is significant potential for how epidemics can help spread information and products, which can in turn help innovative processes and change behaviors. Unfortunately for emergency managers, positive epidemics struggle against other epidemics, both physical and information-based. For example, one study noted that an average American is now exposed to 254 different commercial messages in a day, which is an increase of 25% since the mid-1970s (see Figure 9.8).[18] This creates a muddled stream of information during normal times, which becomes even more complicated during disasters when upwards of 5,000 tweets can be posted per second about a particular emergent event.[11]

Figure 9.8 Epidemics created by emergency managers often struggle to gain traction in the community due to the overwhelming pace of the more than 250 commercial messages (such as this one) that individuals see each day. (From Public Domain/British Government.)

This overabundance of information has led to what Malcolm Gladwell calls a stickiness problem. Ideas—no matter how great or important—must stick within the affected community to be useful.[18] When it is "sticky" it latches on and grows exponentially faster than would ordinarily be expected. Chip and Dan Heath expand Gladwell's stickiness concept in their book, *Made to Stick: Why Some Ideas Survive and Others Die*. Specifically, they suggest that truly sticky concepts need to be simple, unexpected, concrete, credible, emotional, and storylike. These characteristics are extremely important for emergency managers to understand. First, traditional public education and outreach in the emergency management field is often presented in a stale and repetitive fashion that lacks the emotional, unexpected, and personalized components that contribute to stickiness. This type of outreach is compounded by the fact that social media systems are moving ideas, behavior, and products at faster rates and with greater viral value. If emergency managers can begin to modernize their approaches with a particular focus on creative storytelling they may significantly improve their outreach and public education effectiveness. See Table 9.1.

Table 9.1 Characteristics of Sticky Ideas

1. Simple
2. Unexpected
3. Concrete
4. Credible
5. Emotional
6. Storylike

Source: Made to Stick: Why Some Ideas Survive and Others Die by Chip and Dan Heath.[19]

The secondary challenge for emergency managers is dealing with viral creativity that is occurring within their community or during their respective emergency or disaster. Given the pace of information exchange on social media during disasters most emergency management organizations are simply overwhelmed and choose to ignore this process. However, it is prudent to try to find ways to filter this viral response to glean critical information that can either be utilized to benefit the mission and purpose of emergency preparedness or to correct misinformation and misdirection. One way to facilitate this is to try to establish monitored hashtags before events occur. Communities such as Houston have prelisted hashtags related to events that may occur within the community. This type of methodology does not always work, but does increase the chances of emergency management organizations successfully being a part of the viral activity.

FACILITATORS OF CREATIVITY AND CONNECTIVITY

As has been routinely established throughout this book and in much of the professional and anecdotal literature on social media, the actual social media systems including Facebook, Twitter, and YouTube are not what is important for emergency managers to consider and utilize to prepare their communities for emergencies and disasters. Instead, emergency managers must understand the fundamentals of how social media work and why information is quickly shared during emergent events such as a disaster. Perhaps the most important of these fundamental elements is the importance of the people behind the social media systems. It is their personal passion, relationships, and drive that are not only changing how emergency management must be conducted, but also may provide primary solutions as well.

For example, Malcolm Gladwell identifies three different types of community members: connectors, mavens, and salesmen (see Figure 9.9).[21] The first of these community types are the connectors who, as the name suggests, have an inherent ability to connect people around ideas, concepts, and products. They are often defined as having an abundance of acquaintances and social power. The second community type are the mavens who accumulate knowledge and information on seemingly unimportant items, products, prices, or places. This collective knowledge helps bridge gaps between issues, products, and community characteristics that might otherwise be divergent. The third and final characteristic is that of the salesmen. As expected, this group of people possesses the skills and the personality to convince others of the need to engage in (or buy) something they otherwise may not have wanted.[21] Each of these individuals naturally and organically maintains certain characteristics

Figure 9.9 Emergency managers must begin to leverage the skills and abilities of connectors, mavens, and salespeople within their community to help drive epidemics and creative behavior. (From FEMA/Jocelyn Augustino. With permission.)

and drive that may or may not be present within those individuals working in emergency management and response within a given community. Individually they are influential, but much as with social media,
they often combine to have exponentially greater results, particularly
when carried over to emerging systems such as Facebook, Twitter, and
Pinterest.

The impact and influence of these types of personalities are often
profound, as these three personality types (and the variations that surround them) help provide clarity and purpose to information that otherwise might appear muddled or disjointed. For example, the authors of
Predictable Surprises state that "Vividness of information affects many of
our most important decisions about life."[5] Consequently, it is critical to
acknowledge that these individuals provide clarity and dramatic character to affected communities. Therefore, emergency managers must not
only understand these types of personalities (both inside and outside
the social media realm), but also consider how to leverage them within
a given community to meet organizational needs before, during, and
after a disaster strikes. Within social media, this may include the identification and cultivation of those personalities within a given community
who might serve these roles and ultimately help the community. These
communities may be geographic or within social constructions such as
hashtags or social groups.

BECOMING DESIGN-MINDED

The last section of this chapter concentrates on specific considerations
for emergency managers to become focused and active in the process
of being creative and design oriented. There are certainly leaders
across all sectors who have experience and knowledge about creativity
and design, but the challenge is integrating them into a professional
sector such as emergency management and disaster response. This
is particularly true when it is perhaps the antithesis of what most
emergency response professionals expect and desire professionally.
However, as this book has consistently identified, the general public
has grown to accept and expect that its governmental representatives
(before, during, and after disasters) would act in the same ways they
act on a day-to-day basis. It is this expectation that justifies emergency
management understanding and engaging in these creative and design
characteristics.

In *Design Thinking: Integrating Innovation, Customer Experience, and Brand Value*, Thomas Lockwood established 10 principles to aid in the acceptance and adaptation of creativity and design. Although not all 10 principles directly apply to emergency managers, there are some overarching concepts that can be immediately gleaned for those in such positions. For example, several of the principles focus around cultural changes within the organization that build connectivity inside and outside the organization. A secondary pattern presented by Lockwood is the concept of becoming customer-centric in all activities. As described earlier, emergency management and disaster response organizations would consider themselves customer-focused, but this perspective is flawed due to the power of community choice. Unlike government, which takes years to change in democratic environments, customers who purchase items at commercial enterprises such as Walmart and Target can immediately shift their purchasing power and loyalty to another store if they feel their customer experience is poor. This is not possible in governmental emergency management, and therefore affects the perspective of customer focus.

TEN PRINCIPLES TO BECOMING DESIGN-MINDED[22]

1. Develop empathy for the customer.
2. Engage unique design processes.
3. Connect with corporate culture.
4. Set design strategy and policy.
5. Align and define business strategy and design strategy.
6. Design for innovation and transformation.
7. Design for relevance for each priority.
8. Focus on the customer experience.
9. Empower creativity.
10. Be a design leader.

Unfortunately, the concept of customer-centric government can quickly become like clichéd campaign promises that lack the substance and gravitas necessary to be truly successful. Moreover, as was established in Chapter 4, it is difficult for emergency managers and other government operators to fully appreciate and quantify the idea that the products generated by government have the same weight and nature as traditional physical goods. When emergency managers successfully understand this concept it is easier to begin to creatively design a framework to maintain customer focus at all times.

One methodology for emergency managers to facilitate and maintain a customer-centric focus is to become a customer advocate. Advocacy is a delicate subject for government operations as the default assumption is that government is a representative of the community—the whole community—without specific allegiances or interests. Most government organizations actively or passively choose to defer advocacy to community groups and nongovernmental organizations. Unfortunately, this is contrary to many of the public expectations related to social media. Many individuals use personal or grouping mechanisms to generate advocacy for a variety of issues with a range of importance and criticality. The various tools such as Facebook and Twitter become amplification tools that allow anyone from anywhere to advocate. As discussed in every chapter, there is a growing expectation that government will follow suit.

Government may not ever fully advocate for particular actions, however, this type of public expectation can be facilitated through a different type of advocacy. Specifically, government advocacy in a world driven by social technologies revolves around the facilitation of government customers. This means setting up systems that protect and encourage the local community to advocate. Although there are numerous creative ways to build this framework, emergency management agencies must meet whatever expectations exist within their given communities, acknowledge complaints, empower and involve the community, and eliminate difficult questions that are seen as the purview of government.[23] Clearly these are very broad guidelines, but customers (like disasters) are unique and have specific characteristics depending on geographic, social, cultural, and political foundations. Designing a system that creatively creates an area, physically or virtually, where this can occur is critical to the future of emergency management.

For example, San Francisco attempts to create an open and transparent system of citizen engagement within the city. Governmental data are open and the general public is encouraged to utilize them for any means they see as necessary or needed.[11] This has typically come in the form of crime and environmental mapping, but it is certainly not limited to these uses. In many ways these types of documents ultimately are created because someone from the public desired to advocate for safer or more environmentally friendly communities. These types of programs are relatively common in more progressive communities such as San Francisco and Seattle, but have grown as more communities have seen the need and benefit of being open to customers and building a system that not only allows but promotes public customers to advocate for any number of things about which they are passionate.

DEVELOPING WHOLE PRODUCTS

As discussed at the very beginning of this chapter, Steve Jobs and his leadership at Apple serve as one of the most significant examples of integrating creativity and design into the operational core of an organization and letting it seep through the ethos of the entire operation. Steve Jobs managed to create "whole products" that were connected through form and fashion to facilitate better products and a superior user experience.[24] For example, the iPod, iPhone, and iPad all basically function from the same simple design and leverage the same core support systems (e.g., power chargers, applications, and iTunes).[24] Moreover, Apple vertically controlled all manufacturing processes expecting higher quality raw material and a willingness to spend more money for a greater product. In both cases, this type of "whole product" would be a revolutionary application for most emergency management offices.

In contrast, emergency managers are notorious for working within so-called silos that divide disciplines such as fire and police as well as levels of government during emergency response and recovery. This type of separation was one of the major findings of the 9/11 Commission, as organizations from different jurisdictions, disciplines, and intelligence agencies often passively or aggressively refused to work together before, during, or after the event.[25] This longstanding tendency to separate has unfortunately bled over to the relationship sustained with the constituency in each community. Specifically, emergency managers perform the range of functions necessary to prepare their community and citizens to engage in their day-to-day lives. Likewise, even though many emergency management organizations do try to engage the public through traditional outreach mechanisms, it is often disjointed and intermittent as funding and resource availability are usually sporadic at best. This leads to an environment where the general public rarely understands its role in preparedness, much less the complexity of community response, recovery, and mitigation.

The challenge with this approach is that the public expects open connectivity. Silos and separation are the antithesis of what social media and other technologies are driving toward. The fact that social media are fundamentally open and free naturally creates networks of like-minded people who share common priorities. It is against this backdrop that emergency managers must work to design products, systems, services, and ultimately branding that will facilitate a "whole product" concept. Certainly the budgetary and resource restrictions have not changed for emergency managers, however, the opportunity to engage in online and social media systems is easy and cost effective. Designing and implementing a creative outreach that leverages a consistent attitude and outlook is free. Leveraging social media systems to translate that design in a genuine and straightforward manner will ingratiate an emergency management organization to their community and create a bridge between professional activities and the personal interest that will help create not only an organization, but a concept of community preparedness in which they want to engage and believe.

OPENING THE BOX: THE GREAT SALESPEOPLE

There are salesmen and saleswomen throughout the world selling products of all types and sizes. There are many stereotypes of certain types of sellers (e.g., car salespeople) that define how people not only approach the buying process, but the product as well. This type of seller–buyer relationship is no more present than among pitchmen for products that are advertised and sold in long information-based commercials commonly referred to as infomercials. The first and arguably most successful infomercial pitchman was a man named Ron Popeil who helped usher in new kitchen products such as the Dial-O-Matic, Chop-O-Matic, and Veg-O-Matic through many late-night television commercials that lasted an entire 30 minutes. Mr. Popeil's crowning achievement was the development and pitch of an at-home rotisserie cooker called the Showtime Rotisserie that within three years of its release had such a positive response that nearly $3 billion in sales were generated. It is interesting that Mr. Popeil did not use a single focus group, marketer, public relations team, advertising company, consultant, or outside researcher to make and sell his product. He simply "dreamed up something new in his kitchen and went out and pitched it himself."[26] Although Mr. Popeil was an amazing salesman, the success of his products was ultimately the products themselves. For example, Mr. Popeil insisted that the door on the Showtime Rotisserie be a clear pane of glass with a slight slant to let the maximum amount of light in the machine so that the chicken would be visible at all times.[26] Like Popeil, Billy Mays also had a well-known infomercial. He too had best-selling products, such as OrangeGlo and OxiClean, utilizing various commercials and product placements.[27] In addition to Popeil's focus on letting the quality product speak for itself, Mays strove to highlight how the products he was pitching could help make consumers' lives better. He also included a call-to-action to not only engage the audience through incentives, but also drive them to immediate action. Lastly, Mays watched his competitors closely to understand his market share and to adjust his plan quickly to recover any losses.[28] In the end, Popeil and Mays are fantastic examples of how creativity and design do not have to be complex, but rather can be simple and straightforward.

BRANDING IN EMERGENCY MANAGEMENT

At the beginning of this chapter, branding was defined as the process an organization undertakes to create uniform identification of goods and services through the use of a name, term, sign, symbol, product, design, or other overarching component.[8] Private organizations, large nonprofits, and many educational entities utilize branding to increase new customer generation while also improving customer retention. Branding is successful when it resonates on an emotional level with potential customers, clients, and prospects because this is where change and commitment occur. In other words, "Your brand resides within the hearts and minds of customers, clients, and prospects . . . [as] the sum total of their experiences and perceptions, some of which you can influence and some that you cannot."[8]

WHAT IS . . . BRANDING?

Branding is the process an organization undertakes to create uniform identification of goods and services through the use of a name, term, sign, symbol, product, design, or other component. Emergency management organizations are often poorly branded, which affects how the community responds to their proposed mission.[8]

This visceral and emotional response to branding is a complicated physical and biological response. People move throughout the world based on expected actions and reactions. In simpler terms, if something looks, smells, and feels like a known item (e.g., a duck) then it is probably what was expected. Not questioning expected behaviors allows the world to function quickly and within minimal interference from constant questions and thought-provoking considerations. This process is particularly important during emergencies and disasters as humans must react according to preconceived notions and expectations of what will happen and encourage survival.

Although some of these reactions are inherent, much of this response to expected actions is influenced by outside factors.[29] Building a framework, or brand, that is not only more appealing, but alters the perceived reality alters expectations. For example, from 1966 to 2011 Joe Paterno was the head football coach for Penn State University. During that time, Paterno won hundreds of games and actively promoted messages about playing with honor, respect, and sportsmanship. Quotes such as "Success without honor is an unseasoned dish; it will satisfy your hunger, but it won't taste good," were routinely attributed to him.[30] He was renowned inside and outside sports for living correctly off the field and finding success on it. Paterno never set out to create this brand, but this is exactly what he did (see Figure 9.10). Unfortunately, by 2011, Paterno was embroiled in the Jerry Sandusky scandal that involved the molestation of dozens of young boys. After investigations and criminal actions, it quickly became evident that Paterno knew about the activities and hid parts of it to protect the football program.[31] This type of action was the complete opposite of the image and brand he had long supported. Unfortunately, by the time of his death, the concept of Paterno had been forever changed.

Brands fail when they become inconsistent or components become incompatible with each other. In the Paterno example, it was not a judgment of his actions that was important (see Chapter 10), but rather the juxtaposition of the cover-up against years of public profession of high moral value. This same type of duality appeared after Hurricane Katrina when the public had long perceived (rightfully or wrongly) that government, particularly emergency management and response organizations, would come to the quick and efficient aid of affected populations after a disaster. Instead, the public perceived a lack of response and a clear presence of infighting among the local, state, and federal emergency response agencies. Clearly, consistent behavior and appearance (both in presented and response form) is critical for emergency management.

Figure 9.10 Noteworthy figures, such as Joe Paterno, whether intentionally or not, often create brands surrounding philosophy or purpose that can easily be derailed if mistakes or misdirection occur related to that brand. (From Public Domain/Unknown.)

Traditional branding campaigns initiated by major corporations are costly and employ traditional media (e.g., television); however, this will never be a realistic possibility for emergency management organizations. Alternatively, the utilization of social media is a powerful tool for emergency managers attempting to build a brand around their services and appearance. First, social media users are highly likely to share and redistribute information. For example, market research firm AYTM released a study showing that 42% of consumers have mentioned a brand on their Facebook page, 41% have shared a video or link about a brand, and 39% have retweeted about a brand.[32] This type of action has powerful amplification possibilities and will ultimately help promote successful branding activities and undermine inconsistent ones.

Second, social media are a good method for emergency management organizations to distribute messages before, during, and after a disaster that accurately and transparently reflect the actual actions that are occurring. As was discussed in Chapter 2, this type of open approach is effective at increasing the likelihood that the general public will engage and ultimately increase the productivity of the emergency management organization. Likewise, because social media systems are often linked, branding strategies in social media also include systematic nomenclature, consistent imagery, and reliable engagement. For example, these include consistent Twitter handles and Facebook URLs, as well as steady postings and responses to comments and questions.

LEADERS IN THE OPEN: ETHAN RILEY

Ethan Riley has served in the emergency management and public information sector for much of the last decade. He has overseen statewide development of emergency networks, including the integration of social media technologies. He has also led efforts that have been recognized as statewide and national models of how to leverage social media in creative and thoughtful ways to increase community participation and engagement. In the following passage written for this book, Mr. Riley discusses how creativity is a necessary component of leveraging social media in emergency management.

Simple Creativity Is the Ultimate Sophistication

Ethan Riley

Preparedness doesn't pique the same interest as the latest smartphone or turbocharged luxury automobile. It's safe to assume that no one ever bivouacked outside a big-box store for the chance to buy a NOAA weather radio or a manual can opener. And it's likely that no one ever will. Shocking!

Still, it falls to the greater emergency management community—that's you and me—to send a message of personal preparedness to a sometimes dubious public, the majority of whom cannot, due to no fault of their own, identify with survivors of a natural disaster or other calamity. People are tremendously charitable and empathetic toward survivors of an emergency, but few can "sympathize" with the emotional and financial fallout of the experience. Clarence Day may have put it best, "Information is pretty thin stuff unless mixed with experience."

So, communicating preparedness becomes a challenge of application and of concretizing an experience that is as *real* to most people as hitting the lotto. One way to get people to experience preparedness is to get them to perform simple preparedness acts broken down into tasks performed with (or even against) others. A number of public outreach campaigns are making strides in this area, recognizing that simplicity is often the best option.

Simple doesn't have to mean boring or antiquated. Certain inspirational brands have, in fact, earned a fan base for their projects by selling simplicity. Simple simply means usable, viable, and replicable.

In the case of the Arizona Division of Emergency Management (ADEM), simple experiences have resulted in a reinvestment in a *vernacular* approach to raising public awareness. By "vernacular" I mean a do-it-yourself method of participatory outreach that leverages local partnership(s) and encourages sharing in a congregational activity such as voting in an online survey.

ADEM partnered with Le Cordon Bleu College of Culinary Arts in Scottsdale in Summer 2011 to launch the Emergency Kit Cook-Off, http://emergencykitcookoff.blogspot.com, an open National Preparedness Month activity inspired by the customizable contents of a 72-hour emergency kit. The cook-off (#KitCookoff) was a reboot of the fusty preparedness message—plan, pack, inquire, and inspire—designed to involve people in preparedness, not just talk about it. ADEM and Le Cordon Bleu worked with the public to pick the nonperishables that our chef cooked with on live television. Home cooks were also called to post a recipe to the website incorporating those same ingredients.

The Great ShakeOut is another standout example of what we're talking about. These earthquake drills are arguably the most successful public outreach programs today. Millions of people across the globe participate in the drills every year. Sure, the program's success can be attributed to many things, but the one–two punch of (1) a group performance of (2) a simple behavior (the drop, cover, and hold on) increases the self-efficacy of participants; they feel competent in their ability to perform a simple task with others.

Speaking of keeping it simple, the Clark Regional Emergency Services Agency (CRESA), in Clark County, Washington, engages the world community with its 30 Days, 30 Ways (#30days30ways) campaign (http://www.30days30ways.com). The 30 Days, 30 Ways campaign presents players with a daily preparedness challenge, nothing too taxing, to post proof of completion of to the website. Simple, participatory, and (dare I say it) verging on fun, this campaign communicates what some might consider an "alarmist" message with a coolness and in a manner that plays like an interactive Advent calendar; never mind that you can win chocolate.

In each of the abovementioned cases, the public, whether they be players or voters or test cooks, participates in simple tasks that can be effective beyond the rhetorical situation by priming them for follow-up information that will have been contextualized with experience. Therein lies the lesson: involve your public in experiential and cost-effective ways that empower them to become change agents through testimonial and example. Let's take the preparedness message beyond the poster contest and squarely into the lives of our citizens.

Note: The views expressed by Ethan Riley are his own personal views and do not represent his employer or any organization he is affiliated with.

ENDNOTES

1. Carroll, Jim. (2009) "Accountancy in the Twitter Era." Jim Carroll Blog. http://www.jimcarroll.com/2009/06/accountancy-in-the-twitter-era/. Accessed August 2, 2012.
2. Godin, Seth. (2002) "How Much Does Style Cost?" Seth Godin's Blog. http://sethgodin.typepad.com/seths_blog/2002/08/index.html. Accessed August 4, 2012.
3. Peters, Meghan. (2011) "15 Inspirational Quotes by Steve Jobs." Mashable. http://mashable.com/2011/10/05/steve-jobs-quotes/#28597-6. Accessed August 5, 2012.
4. "iPod + iTunes Timeline." (2012) Apple Press Room. http://www.apple.com/pr/products/ipodhistory/. Accessed August 5, 2012.
5. Bazerman, Max and Watkins, Michael. (2008) *Predictable Surprises: The Disasters You Should Have Seen Coming and How to Prevent Them.* Boston: Harvard Business School Press.
6. Shirky, Clay. (2012) Clay Shirky on digital journalism: "Journalists are addicted to secrets" – video. *The Guardian.* http://www.guardian.co.uk/technology/video/2012/apr/04/clay-shirky-data-video?CMP=twt_gu. Accessed August 5, 2012.
7. Clark, Kevin and Smith, Ron. (2008) "Unleashing the Power of Design Thinking." Design Management Institute. http://www.dmi.org/dmi/html/publications/news/ebulletin/08193CLA08.pdf. Accessed August 7, 2012.

8. Lake, Laura. (n.d.) "What is Branding and How Important Is It to Your Marketing Strategy?" About.com. http://marketing.about.com/cs/brandmktg/a/whatisbranding.htm. Accessed August 7, 2012.

9. Wasserman, Todd. (2011) "Red Cross Does PR Disaster Recovery on Rogue Tweet." Mashable. http://mashable.com/2011/02/16/red-cross-tweet/. Accessed August 8, 2012.

10. Koulopoulos, Thomas. (2012) "Innovation Isn't About New Products, It's About Changing Behaviors." Fast Company Blog. http://www.fastcompany.com/1844177/innovation-isnt-about-new-products-its-about-changing-behavior. Accessed August 11, 2012.

11. Crowe, Adam. (2012) *Disasters 2.0: The Application of Social Media on Modern Emergency Management.* Boca Raton, FL: CRC Press.

12. Erickson, Christine. (2012) "Crowd Powered: Why Doritos Lets Fans Make Its Superbowl Ads." Mashable. http://mashable.com/2012/04/05/doritos-crash-super-bowl/. Accessed August 11, 2012.

13. "Super Bowl XLVI." (n.d.) National Football League. http://www.nfl.com/superbowl/history. Accessed August 12, 2012.

14. Edwards, Jim and Terbush, Jon. (2012) CHART: The incredible inflation of Super Bowl ads since 1967. *Business Insider.* http://articles.businessinsider.com/2012-01-26/news/30665762_1_business-insider-super-bowl-ad-prices-advertising. Accessed August 12, 2012.

15. Gladwell, Malcolm. (n.d) "What is the Tipping Point?" Gladwell Blog. http://www.gladwell.com/tippingpoint/. Accessed August 12, 2012.

16. Elezz, Mostafa Abou. (2012) "Social Networks; Catalyzers of Arab Spring." Middle East Online. http://www.middle-east-online.com/english/?id=50404. Accessed August 12, 2012.

17. Woodcock, Bill. (2012) "Overview of the Egyptian Internet Shutdown." DHS Packet Clearning House. http://www.pch.net/resources/misc/Egypt-PCH-Overview.pdf. Accessed August 12, 2012.

18. Gladwell, Malcolm. (2002) *The Tipping Point: How Little Things Can Make a Big Difference.* New York: Back Bay Books, pp. 98, 117.

19. Kiviat, Barbara. (2006) Change agents: Are you sticky? *Time Magazine.* http://www.time.com/time/magazine/article/0,9171,1552029,00.html. Accessed August 13, 2012.

20. "Report Severe Weather Impacts to @HoustonOEM Using Your Twitter Account." (2012) City of Houston. http://www.houstonoem.net/go/doc/4027/1265527/Report-severe-weather-impacts-to-HoustonOEM-using-your-Twitter-account-. Accessed August 13, 2012.

21. Gladwell, Malcolm. (n.d) "Reading Guide: The Power of the Few." Malcolm Gladwell's Blog. http://www.gladwell.com/tippingpoint/guide/chapter2.html. Accessed August 13, 2012.

22. Lockwood, Thomas. (2009) *Design Thinking: Integrating Innovation, Customer Experience, and Brand Value.* New York: Allworth Press.

23. "Satisfying the Customer." (2005) TechRepublic. http://www.techrepublic.com/article/satisfying-the-customer/5745976. Accessed August 14, 2012.

24. Ellett, John. (2011) Steve Jobs' legacy for marketers. *Forbes.* http://www. forbes.com/sites/johnellett/2011/10/07/steve-jobs-legacy-for-marketers/. Accessed August 14, 2012.
25. "The 9/11 Commission Report." (2002) 9/11 Commission. http://www.9-11commission.gov/report/911Report.pdf. Accessed August 14, 2012.
26. Gladwell, Malcolm. (2000) The pitchman. Gladwell: Articles from the *New Yorker.* http://www.gladwell.com/2000/2000_10_30_a_pitchman.html. Accessed August 14, 2012.
27. Billy Mays biography. (2012) *A&E Biography.* http://www.biography.com/ people/billy-mays-481592. Accessed August 15, 2012.
28. Johnson, Nathania. (2009) "7 Lessons From the Late, Great Pitchman Billy Mays." Search Engine Watch. http://searchenginewatch.com/ article/2052140/7-Marketing-Lessons-from-the-Late-Great-Pitchman-Billy-Mays. Accessed August 15, 2012.
29. Koch, Christopher. (2010) Looks can deceive: Why perception and reality don't always match up. *Scientific American.* http://www.scientificamerican. com/article.cfm?id=looks-can-deceive&page=2. Accessed August 15, 2012.
30. "Joe Paterno Quotes." (n.d.) Good Reads. http://www.goodreads.com/ author/quotes/591907.Joe_Paterno. Accessed August 15, 2012.
31. Joe Paterno bio. (2012) *A&E Biography.* http://www.biography.com/people/ joe-paterno-9434584. Accessed August 15, 2012.
32. Michalik, Martin. (2011) "How Branding Works in the Age of Social Media." VirtualBlog. http://www.viralblog.com/social-media/how-branding-works-in-the-social-media-age/. Accessed August 15, 2012.

10

Ethics and Character

Don't say things. What you are stands over you the while, and
thunders so that I cannot hear what you say to the contrary.

Ralph Waldo Emerson[1]

INTRODUCTION

As much as the last two chapters were about leadership characteristics
that are not common in the field of emergency management, this chapter
focuses on the value of ethics that are routinely touted as critical elements
for government leaders such as emergency managers and first-responders.
However, there are two challenges that exist. First, many emergency managers lack the comprehension of just what it means to be ethical. Second,
governmental organizations and the leaders that represent them continue
to become embroiled in scandals. This is not to say that every emergency
management leader or governmental administrator is inherently unethical, but it does strongly imply that the current environment is unsuitable
to encourage, promote, and facilitate ethical behavior.

This is further complicated by a fully perceived and partially real
increase in the public's role and responsibility for demanding accountability from its government representatives. Some of this has increased
from the 24/7 nature of traditional journalism, which not only provides
images and information in a timely manner, but also often inflames the
extremes of a given situation. This is particularly applicable during emergencies and disasters where basic life functions, critical infrastructure,

and community balance are often pushed to extremes such that balance and perspective are skewed.

Likewise, this public expectation has exponentially more impact with the rise of social media. With more than 950 million Facebook user accounts (as of June 2012) and more than 500 million Twitter accounts (not to mention nearly complete YouTube integration into traditional websites and social media sites), the influence and power of social media are evident.[2,4] Via these sites and the range of other social systems (e.g., Wiki sites) available to the average citizen, the awareness of government actions (including emergency response) is extremely heightened.

For example, in 2010, an online information aggregation site called WikiLeaks released nearly 500,000 classified U.S. military documents detailing American government decisions about the wars in Afghanistan and Iraq that had been underway for much of the previous decade.[3] Ultimately, American military investigators at the Pentagon determined that a 22-year-old army intelligence analyst who had been based near Baghdad with high-level security clearance downloaded the majority of these documents and shared them with WikiLeaks.[5] Ultimately, the documents revealed some politically sensitive internal commentary from American leaders such as former Secretary of State Hillary Clinton which created an impression that American governmental leaders were saying one thing and doing something else (see Figure 10.1).

Much as in the discussion of transparency in Chapter 2, it is critical to understand that ethical behavior is often presented as a totalitarian option, or in colloquial terms, black and white. The struggle is that people (as defined by their cultural, political, and community connections) do not have a universal definition of ethics and all related behavior. There are literally thousands of articles, books, essays, and general commentary written that attempt to limit the perspective and direction of ethical behavior. However, it is important to understand that ethical behavior is a spectrum of behaviors that have natural and intended results when applied appropriately, particularly in light of the transparent and available information exchanged via social media systems.

TRENDS IN ETHICAL BEHAVIOR

As has been established several times throughout this book, the general public already has poor expectations of the ethical standards of governmental leaders. Trust in current leaders of all major parties and

Figure 10.1 More than 500,000 classified U.S. military documents were released by the online site WikiLeaks, which ultimately led to the exposure of embarrassing internal and classified commentary from American leaders including former Secretary of State Hillary Clinton. (From U.S. Senate/Unknown. With permission.)

all branches of government is at an all-time low. Likewise, public ethics scandals have affected major businesses and private entities as well. For example, trusted individuals or corporate entities including Bernie Madoff and Enron ultimately swindled billions of dollars from subordinate individuals or groups of individuals through various manipulated accounting and financial schemes.

A National Business Ethics Survey of Fortune 500 employees found that there was significant identification of unethical behavior in the workforce. Specifically, between 45 and 52% (depending on the size of the company) observed ethical misconduct over the 12 months prior to the study. Of those who identified unethical behavior, 65 to 74% ultimately reported it to upper management.[9] In contrast, according to the Ethics Resource Center, approximately 60% of surveyed government workers acknowledged observing ethical misconduct over the same period of time. It is interesting that the level of observed unethical behavior was highest in local government (63%) and lowest at the federal level (52%), with previous surveys showing an uptick in the number and rate of observed incidences.[10] In both surveys, it was projected that those reporting the observed unethical behavior would be higher except for a sense (real or perceived) that reported misconduct (or whistleblowing) would bring internal organization retaliation.

The so-called "Fast and Furious" scandal that broke in 2011 and was further reviewed by the U.S. Congress through much of 2012 was a classic example of an ethical violation for both real and perceived breakdowns in trust. Specifically, Operation Fast and Furious was launched in 2009 by high-ranking U.S. Department of Justice officials in conjunction with the Federal Bureau of Investigation (FBI), Drug Enforcement Agency (DEA), and the Bureau of Alcohol, Tobacco, and Firearms (ATF) as part of an overarching strategy to reduce (or eliminate) gun trafficking networks between the United States and Mexico. Specific field agents allowed more than 2,000 weapons to move back across the border (rather than actively prosecute the gun-runners) in an attempt to track the movement of weapons and identify the top bosses of the weapon and drug cartels in Mexico. Unfortunately, more than 1,700 of these weapons were lost with more than 100 found at bloody crime scenes on both sides of the border, including the murder of a U.S. border patrol agent. As this information became public, accusations were made by American political party members (led by Republican Congressman Darrell Issa) about potential cover-ups and failures of government.[23] Sitting Attorney General Eric Holder was even charged with contempt by congressional oversight committees (see Figure 10.2). Whether one person or organization was right or wrong is irrelevant in these kinds of cases. It is merely the real and certainly perceived violation of various community ethical standards that undermines the effectiveness and public trustworthiness of these agencies.

When unethical behavior occurs—in governmental or critical business sectors—it leads to an erosion of public trust. Individual leaders and organizational character can be highly at risk when this type of behavior is conducted. Although it is clear that unethical behavior already exists in the workforce, it is important to understand that the rates of misconduct are amplified by certain environmental considerations. These include a lack of awareness of internal management and organizational leaders, as well as internal organizational systems that lack the accountability and cross-checking necessary to curb this type of behavior.[11] These two

Figure 10.2 Perceived and real public violations of trust often lead to questions of ethical behavior similar to those faced by Attorney General Eric Holder during the Fast and Furious scandal investigation. (From U.S. Department of Justice/Unknown. With permission.)

environmental conditions are common in the emergency management community due to the limited staff and specialized nature of the operation. Most organizational leaders defer control and oversight to the management of the small agency that is either overlooked or buried within the organization's hierarchy until a disaster strikes.

BEYOND EMOTIONS, RELIGION, OR LAW

The general public most often defines ethical behavior based on emotional, religious, or legal standards. Each of these can vary significantly from community to community. Individual cultural groupings and associations often create these standards over many years of engagement and activities. These observed standards can change over time as communities adapt to changing public expectations from the integration of technology, science, and experiential developments. For example, the Hippocratic oath (the foundation for the ethical behavior of medical physicians) originally called for not performing abortions, maintaining patient confidentiality, and only performing tasks on patients that will benefit their medical condition. However, modern interpretations of these ethical standards have been modified with abortions being legal (in most countries), patient confidentiality becoming loosened for the integration of collective studies and specialty practices, and the modification of direct patient benefit to accept group improvements or application (e.g., clinical trials).[6]

Beyond the medical field, there are additional perceived ethical standards that have changed over time. Community concepts and standards regarding sexuality (including homosexuality), gender roles, personal credit and savings, role of government, racial equality, military service, and the recreational use of tobacco, drugs, and alcohol are among those that have changed. For example, in the United States, cultural standards have become less accepting of public smoking and alcohol use and more accepting of recreational (and illicit) drug use. The challenge is that these types of changes are not consistent or clear from community to community within a broader culture (e.g., country or region). They are not even clear within larger government bodies such as countries, states, or even cities. This is especially true when there are common political and religious divisions within a community. Some communities are deeply divided by these issues with both sides referring to standards of ethical behavior that are being disregarded in the given area. This is particularly present during political campaigning when divergent parties are in close competition.

Likewise, legal elements of ethical standards are also extraordinarily challenging. Inherently, laws are written with the intention of strict interpretation. For example, if a community establishes a law stating that murder is illegal (and thus unethical), a person who kills someone else should be considered guilty of that crime. However, in most cultures there are shades of interpretation and mitigating circumstances that create division and discussion about legal standards of ethics. Legal standards of ethics are the most overwhelming as they are nearly impossible to abide by from community to community. As a result, disappointment and conflict often closely follow which can quickly interfere with progress and success.

SOCIETAL STANDARDS

In addition to the ethical associations with religious, legal, and emotional standards, there is also a misperception that ethical behaviors are simply those activities, attitudes, and actions that are generally accepted by society. However, "whatever society accepts" is not sufficient to define ethical behavior due to the fact that collective standards of ethics can become corrupted. For example, Nazi Germany is an example of a morally corrupt society. Within a matter of years, a blended community of various cultures was led astray to create an ethical standard that was ultimately accepted by a majority of the country which called for the open and active persecution of certain religious and cultural groups.[7]

Likewise, simply sampling a community to determine ethical standards is also insufficient. When considering the legal considerations related to ethical standards, it is extraordinarily difficult to establish a collective ethical behavior by asking one person after another and adding up the results. This type of survey process will simply establish the two (or more) divisive components of the particular issue. For example, surveying the general public about the ethics of abortion would simply confirm that some people accept abortion as an ethical behavior and others do not.[7] This process needs to institute a method to establish "well-founded standards of right and wrong that prescribe what humans ought to do, usually in terms of rights, obligations, benefits to society, fairness, or specific virtues."[7]

WHAT IS . . . ETHICAL BEHAVIOR?

Ethical behavior is defined as established standards of right and wrong that prescribe human activities in terms of individual and collective rights, community obligations, cultural benefits, fairness, and equality.[7]

Social media are fast affecting how ethical behavior is defined within the community. Unlike a standard survey, social media allow a congregation of ideas to be generated, shared, clarified, and advocated for in a very short period of time by those most affected by the standard. The component of advocacy is the most important in the creation and development of social standards. The online communities create ethical standards through an inherent focus on community-centric issues that are focused on fundamental rights and privileges of others, which ultimately creates a common-good approach for virtues and ethical standards.[8]

THE INSPIRATION OF ETHICAL BEHAVIOR

As stated earlier, ethical behavior is not simply a collection of behaviors and actions that are compared to a standard. Each community (and subcommunity) has its own set of standards, however, there are characteristics of ethical behavior that do transcend various standards. For example,

277

ethical behavior by leaders can inspire the organizations and communities they serve. Inspirational ethics are built around behavioral codes such as honesty, integrity, wisdom, and high character. These types of behaviors help set an example, inspire, and ultimately steer the ethical behavior of others by offering them "a cue or written rule to remind personnel of the right thing to do . . . [or] an 'outside in' process for ethical behavior management" (see Figure 10.3).[12] This inspirational process is particularly important to organizations, as formalized internal policies addressing ethics are often intentionally extremely generic (as again, standards vary based on culture, geography, etc.), which can create a muddled approach for individual workers or members of the community.

It is interesting that social media can provide a similar inspirational process. People who maintain certain "high bar" behaviors such as encouraging ethical conduct, identifying missteps, and sharing information in a transparent fashion often inspire others to do the same thing through the social media systems. For example, individuals who might not otherwise have the confidence or ability to act or speak in a certain way are empowered by inspirational ethics and the freedom available on social media. When this occurs, individuals can simply post or redistribute (e.g., retweet) messages with the confidence that their behavior parallels that of a community leader and is in accordance with a community standard. This concept is part of the component of self-correction and regulation that is common to social media systems such as Facebook

Figure 10.3 Great leaders such as Martin Luther King, Jr., have often used adoption and compliance with community standards of ethics as an inspirational mechanism (From U.S. Library of Congress/Unknown. With permission.)

and Twitter. Based on whatever the community standard or ethos is at that time, specific misinformation or information out of alignment with these standards will be acknowledged, rebuked, and provided with an alternative opinion or action that is more in line with the community standard.

OPENING THE BOX: NEW YORK CITY CRIME

In the early 1990s, several New York City neighborhoods had extremely high crime rates. However, under the leadership of Mayor Rudy Giuliani (and his various assigned community leaders), violent crime dropped by 56% during his eight years as mayor, with murder and robbery both down 67% and aggravated assault down 28% (see Figure 10.4).[13] By the end of his term, the citywide violent crime rate for New York City ranked 136th among American cities which was on par with Boise, Idaho.[14] For example, the homicide rates by the late 1990s were half of what they were a decade earlier and were as low as the rates in the 1970s. According to one observer, "It [was] possible to see signs of everyday life that would have been unthinkable in the early nineties . . . now ordinary people on the streets at dusk, small children riding their bicycles, old people on benches and stoops, [and] people coming out of the subway alone."[14]

Although community leaders across the world have long wanted to find a way to reduce crime rates, their success has often been minimal at best, with increases and decreases often seemingly difficult to correlate with communitywide attempts at curbing violence. Various theories were presented to explain this drop. For instance, the New York City police commissioner who presided over the reduction of crime publicly credited new policing strategies including better coordination between divisions, greater internal accountability, increased arrests for gun possession, and more sophisticated computer-aided analysis. Likewise, many criminologists argued that these changes in crime rates reflected fundamental demographic and sociological trends (e.g., decline and/or stabilization of the crack trade); however, these trend changes were neither specific nor unique to New York City.

These considerations may have partially contributed to the fall in crime in New York City, however, they should be viewed as components that helped influence a change in the overarching behavior and cultural standards in the community. For example,

279

the New York City Transit Authority was particularly challenged before this epidemic shift due to the fact that their subway cars would be tagged with graffiti every night when they were parked at the terminal stations. The tagged subway trains would then run the next day (or days) until the Transit Authority cleaned them up. Because it happened so frequently, the trains became perpetually covered in graffiti and other unkempt markings and the culture of both the transit authority and those integrated into the community became accepting of this criminal activity.[15] This type of acceptance was first described in 1982 as the so-called "broken window" theory which suggests that the "slippery slope to lawlessness" begins when the toleration of these minor violations occurs and that cracking down on these activities discourages more serious crimes.[16]

This held true in New York when Transit Authority leaders began to paint the subway cars every night before they left the terminal stations such that the graffiti tagging (which was still occurring each night) was never seen by the general public. Obviously, repainting the subway cars did not solve the crime problem in New York; however, it is a strong example of how changing an ethical standard within a community can be inspirational and epidemic. The ethical standard of one component can help change the community standard as well.

Figure 10.4 Under Mayor Rudy Giuliani, New York City crime dropped due to ethical and engaged leadership. (From Public Domain/Jason Bedrick.)

Likewise, ethical behavior also contributes to public and community influence, which is critical to both community leaders and the emergency management community. However, influence can create a fine line to walk for government leaders. On the positive side, "using personal influence well and possessing political savvy can aid an organization in gaining visibility and obtaining resources."[17] However, when misapplied, this influence can be seen as disingenuous and unethical.

For example, a man named Cory Booker who currently serves as the mayor of Newark, New Jersey, strikes this balance of ethical influence extremely well. Booker maintains an active Twitter account with nearly 1.2 million followers.[18] To put this in perspective, the entire city of Newark only has approximately 277,000 citizens.[19] Clearly, Booker provides something of value in his Twitter account or people (locally or elsewhere) would not follow him. However, unlike some elected officials (e.g., mayors, governors, etc.) who speak (or in this case tweet) about information that is solely focused on governmental operations or merely spout inspirational quips, Booker professes and acts in compliance with community ethical standards that have been repeatedly acknowledged within his own community and to many others throughout the United States. His ethical standard is perhaps most evident during emergencies and disasters. For example, during the 2010 "Snowmaggedon" event that affected the northeast United States and left five-foot snow drifts, Booker engaged in questions from the general public and addressed specific needs as well as personally delivering diapers to a snowed-in mother and shoveling snow in an older citizen's driveway (see Figure 10.5).[20,21] Booker's local and national success is due to the fact that he presents a certain ethical behavior and delivers it without fail. People are inspired by this type of leadership and seek out ways to emulate this type of behavior.

STRATEGIC RATHER THAN REGULATORY

Ethical behavior is often seen as structured and regulatory in nature. When associated with ethical behavior, rules, regulations, and boundaries are the components or the order and structure of when, where, and how an organization and its leaders will act and engage in the community. However, as has been established throughout this chapter, ethical behavior is less a set of rules and more of a framework of guidelines that is highly dependent on the communities that encompass it. This is particularly true in social media where information and expectations

Figure 10.5 Newark Mayor Cory Booker routinely engages his community via social media to address personal needs that arise during disasters such as the 2010 blizzard. (From FEMA/Michael Rieger. With permission.)

are extremely dynamic. In contrast, social media systems are inherently more open and far less regulatory than traditional approaches to ethical standards.

However, there are opportunities for emergency management and first-responder organizations to strategically adopt ethical behaviors that retain the flexibility and openness that social media communities seek out and expect. For example, Washington, DC Police Chief Cathy Lanier established an organizational policy on how to use social media to engage citizens who are using cell phones to text and transmit information via social media systems during a public safety event (see Figure 10.6). Unlike some law enforcement organizations who try to eliminate public documentation of active scenes, the Washington, DC police established a response ethic built around two rules. First and foremost, law enforcement officials are forbidden from intentionally interfering with the recording of an event by a citizen. Second, after an event has occurred and been recorded, visual materials cannot be seized or deleted by the responding officers. The importance of these rules was clearly laid out by Chief Lanier who said, "A bystander has the same right to take photographs or make recordings as a member of the media" with equal rights to be in "an individual's home or business, common areas of public and

Figure 10.6 Washington, DC Police Chief Cathy Lanier utilized an innovative social media and citizen engagement policy to create a shared community ethical standard related to the documentation of emergency response scenes. (From Public Domain/Unknown.)

private facilities and buildings and any other public or private facility at which the individual has the legal right to be present."[22] Equality between law enforcement and citizens is revolutionary in many ways and is being aided (at least in one community) by the use of social media, emerging technology, and strong leadership.

WHISTLEBLOWER EXPECTATIONS

As discussed earlier in this chapter, observing and maintaining accountability for ethical standards often creates an environment that depends on so-called whistleblowers. According to the Government Accountability Project, a whistleblower is an "employee who discloses information that he reasonably believes is evidence of illegality, gross waste or fraud, mismanagement, abuse of power, general wrongdoing, or a substantial and specific danger to public health and safety . . . [who] speak[s] out to parties that can influence and rectify the situation."[24] Unfortunately, whistleblowing is often looked down upon within organizations—particularly those with strong command and control concepts—as a process that is inappropriate and merely a reflection of the observer's inability to deal with dynamic or changing situations. More important, many organizational leaders will inflict retaliation against the employee in a direct or indirect way to discourage or punish the acts of accountability.

WHAT IS . . . A WHISTLEBLOWER?

A whistleblower is an organizational representative who discloses information to third parties such as the media, upper management, hotlines, and so on that he or she reasonably believes provides evidentiary proof of illegal or fraudulent behavior within the organization with the intention of beginning a process to rectify the witnessed behavior.

To put this retaliatory behavior in perspective, the Ethics Resource Center conducted research in 2011 which shows that 22% of surveyed employees who reported misconduct experienced some form of retaliation in return. This figure compares to the 15% reported in 2009 and the 12% reported in 2007.[25] This type of behavior is extremely detrimental to accountability and the protection of ethical behavior within all organizations. The interesting component is that whistleblowing behavior in social media systems is prevalent, as retaliation is often impossible due to the potential for greater anonymity. For example, the WikiLeaks site already mentioned earlier in this chapter is a leading channel for would-be whistleblowers. Since 2007, millions of documents have been submitted and shared on WikiLeaks by about 1,200 registered (and mostly anonymous) users. These documents led to whistleblowing actions related to questionable policies at the American military prison in Guantanamo Bay, so-called "Climategate" documents revealing possible manipulation of global warming data, and hacked private e-mails from former Republican vice presidential candidate Sarah Palin.[26]

SOCIAL MEDIA IMPACT ON ETHICAL STANDARDS

Although the concept of ethical standards has been around since the early philosophers, the rate of change in community standards usually takes a long time over the slow course of the evolution of given communities. However, social media (as with many of the elements discussed throughout this book) have radically changed the pace and perspective of ethics. Community leaders must now deal with public expectations that exist in traditional sectors as well as those that are being driven by the use and application of social media.

For instance, ethical standards have become far more diverse as social media have splintered communities into more and more divergent parts.

Individuals with niche interests, beliefs, passions, or religious perspectives who were previously separated by geography or culture can now overcome that separation and be unified, as least virtually, through social systems such as Facebook and Twitter. As such, the presence of exponentially more communities means there are an equally significant number of proposed and potential ethical standards, which are as diverse and widespread as the geographic dispersion that used to separate them. This can be both a benefit to broader ethical standards and a drawback. For example, groups of individuals and families affected by rare diseases can utilize social media to help draw attention and interest to their cause. Unfortunately, this same power can also embolden extremist groups who profess hatred and who would otherwise be separated and unlikely to be able to voice their own community standards.

This change in ethical standards has shifted some of the behavioral standards away from egocentric focus to more community-centric. Within many online communities, a movement has risen where functions or responsibilities traditionally performed or controlled by government are being shifted to groups or anonymous individuals. These emergent groups can often perform the function more quickly and efficiently either because of more dedicated resources or because they are not limited by government oversight, accountability, and bureaucracy. This phenomenon has been discussed several times in this book as it relates to emergency volunteer groups that are serving to support disaster response and recovery through digital altruism. From an intelligence perspective, individuals outside the formal military–government complex are also providing positive results. For example, in 2012, an American hacker who calls himself "The Raptor" and claims to be a grandfather took credit for a series of takedowns of online forums utilized by Al Qaeda sympathizers. More interestingly, "The Raptor" also took to Twitter to taunt those operatives associated with the sites that were taken down.[27] Although the anonymity that empowered "The Raptor" to take action could also simply be an online bluff, it clearly creates an environment of perceived (if not real) changes in how ethical standards and community behaviors are established, particularly in an online environment.

CHALLENGES TO LEGAL STANDARDS OF ETHICS

The ethical standards of traditional emergency management communities are significantly different from the changes being driven by current public expectations. As discussed in Chapter 8, emergency management and first-responder communities are often hierarchical with many leaders having military experience and background. Consequently, the emergency management organization is often highly controlled and ordered around traditional ethical standards. In addition, certain biases, legal restrictions, and organizational limitations are significant hindrances to the modification of traditional systems to meet modern community standards of ethics that are heavily influenced by social media and emerging technologies.

In addition to the hierarchical limitations already discussed, there are also some ethical standards that are being strongly challenged by the integration of social media into society. For example, it is a long-standing practice for first-responders such as law enforcement agencies to withhold information related to crimes and particularly the names of related victims until the family (or families) have been notified. This is particularly true with traditional media who often quickly request incident details including information about the victims. However, as social media have become increasingly commonplace among the general public, information has moved so quickly (nearly instantaneously as discussed in Chapter 3) that death notification has, in some cases, preceded official notice from first-responder organizations (see Figure 10.7).[28]

Figure 10.7 Information is exchanged so quickly that law enforcement agents have difficulty maintaining certain traditional ethical standards such as family notification before public release. (From FEMA/Andrea Booher. With permission.)

A similar ethical standard affects emergency medical services (EMS) when they respond to emergencies. Not only do EMS services have the same traditional ethical standard about the notification of victims' families, but they also are limited by certain legal standards related to medical record protection. For example, the Health Insurance Portability and Accountability Act (HIPAA) limits the type of personal and medical information that can be shared (or transmitted) about a patient. But some new leaders have suggested modifications of HIPAA to allow EMS service providers to transmit pictures, scans, or other related information to the responding hospital to allow the doctors and nurses to better prepare for the medical response that will be necessary upon arrival.

Likewise, social media usage (and the expected standards that go with it) presents additional ethical challenges to health and medical providers. For example, in the Fifth Circuit Court of Appeals case Doe v. Green, a paramedic who treated a sexual assault victim posted information about the assault on his MySpace page. The paramedic did not disclose the victim's name, but shared enough information that local news agencies were able to identify the victim and ultimately seek her out at her home. In this particular case, the paramedic's employer was not found negligent, but these types of claims (due to the legal standards present in components such as HIPAA) create significant financial, reputational, and ultimately operational risks to health and medical providers (see Figure 10.8).

Figure 10.8 Ethical standards for emergency medical services providers are also affected by the rise of social media and their impact on the lives of victims and their families. (From FEMA/Jocelyn Augustino. With permission.)

To put this into perspective, health organizations found to be in violation of HIPAA can be penalized anywhere from $100 to $50,000 per violation with additional indirect costs related to public imagery and brand.[29]

CHALLENGES TO INDUSTRIAL STANDARDS OF ETHICS

In addition to some of the limitations already discussed, emergency management has also struggled with the industrial transition from a 1:1 mentality to bulk operations and back to 1:1 operations again. Over the last several hundred years there have been several industrial shifts around the incorporation of new technologies that improved transportation, manufacturing, and information exchange. For example, prior to the adoption of the modern assembly line that was utilized by Henry Ford to make the Model T car, the use of transportation was often a direct correlation between user and equipment. Specifically, individuals worked on their own equipment in their own areas often limited to geography and personalized knowledge. Only after this type of process is fully integrated into the broader community (e.g., gas stations and repair shops) does this one-to-one type relationship change. At that point, a more industrialized process occurs allowing for one component of the process to serve many. This type of shift was also discussed in Chapter 5 within the context of improving efficiency, and it is also has an impact on ethical standards within a given community.

This shift from direct connectivity to a more industrial approach has shifted back, with the rise of web-based information and social media networks, to a more personalized and on-demand expectation. As discussed throughout the book, this new expectation is what is significantly influencing government operations and disaster response. This applies to ethical standards as well. Strategic approaches and ethical behaviors are based on the industrial approach of one serving many. Traditional approaches would establish this as a best practice for emergency management due to the inherent limitations of having to respond to dynamic situations with minimal management and control resources. But the reality is that the general public is beginning to shift their expectations toward more of an on-demand response. Rather than have patience as disaster response plays out and emergency management representatives assess situations and make resource allocations based on most significant needs, individual citizens expect quick and direct responses to their needs no matter how important or rather insignificant the respective issues may be at the given time. As frustrating as this may be to emergency managers, it is the reality of modern public expectations and unfortunately is beginning to be leveraged by traditional media to present disaster response as slow, disorganized, and potentially dysfunctional.

EMERGENCY MANAGEMENT BIASES

Emergency management and disaster responders often struggle with some common sociological biases that interfere with the acceptance of the growing use of social media, its impact on operations, and the potential implications of changes to ethical standards within the served communities. These biases are typically based on faulty assumptions, fear of failure, and misdirected credit (or misappropriated credit). These issues include diagnosis bias, loss aversion, value attribution, and various subcomponents within each of these. Each of these biases interferes with appropriate ethical standards for a given community and changing expectations of the general public.

The first sociological limitation that affects emergency management is what Ori Brafman and Rom Brafman called diagnosis bias in their book, *Sway: The Irresistible Draw of Irrational Behavior*. Diagnosis bias occurs when information about a person or situation is disregarded when it contradicts an understanding, application, or so-called diagnosis about a particular issue.[30] This type of approach can quickly lead to the proverbial "self-fulfilling prophesy", where projected failures fail and projected successes always succeed when in reality the success or failure of the particular consideration may be far greater. Diagnosis bias often also falls along generational lines. In other words, what is acceptable and good for one generation is seen as outdated (or, conversely, immature) by the other. For example, many older generations including baby boomers or the silent generation label younger generations (particularly Gen X and Gen Y) as lazy and unmotivated.

This type of labeling behavior is dangerous to emergency managers as they try to evaluate changing ethical standards that are influenced by social media. As social media usage is higher in younger demographics, the classic bias for emergency managers is to assume social media (and all of its consequences) are simply a fad or only meaningful to younger generations. Similar assumptions exist related to the so-called digital divide, where many emergency managers assume social media are not influential in rural areas or low population centers due to lack of interest, natural networking, or networking infrastructure. However, surveys from Pew Internet consistently show a shrinking divide between those who do and do not use social media. Moreover, international efforts from major technology companies such as Google are pushing to eliminate the divide by making high-speed Internet available to everyone in the community.[31,32] Consequently, assumptions made by emergency managers are quickly being undermined and ultimately may lead to inappropriate engagement in the ethical and community standards being changed because of the actual adoption and use of social media.

OPENING THE BOX: THE PYGMALION EFFECT

The inspiration for this phenomenon was based on several examples of classic and modern literature and media. For example, in classic literature, Pygmalion is a character in Ovid's Metamorphosis who was a sculptor who fell in love with an ivory statue of his own creation. Pygmalion's love for his own creation drives him to beg the gods to give him a wife in the likeness of his sculpture, which they ultimately grant. Likewise, playwright George Bernard Shaw wrote a play called "Pygmalion" that focused on the protagonist's creation of an upper-class woman from a local commoner. This same concept was adapted as the modern musical, "My Fair Lady."

With this inspiration, in 1968, two sociological researchers named Robert Rosenthal and Lenore Jacobson released a study that showed that the expectations of a teacher influence student performance. Specifically, positive expectations from the teacher influenced student performance positively and, conversely, negative views led to negative performance. Or as summarized in a later study by Rosenthal, "When we expect certain behaviors of others, we are likely to act in ways that make the expected behavior more likely to occur."[33] They termed this phenomenon the Pygmalion Effect.

The experiment focused on an elementary school where students were issued intelligence tests prior to enrolling in a particular class. The investigators informed the teachers of names of 20% of the students who showed "unusual potential for intellectual growth" with a strong recommendation that these students would flourish academically within the next year. However, unknown to the teachers the students identified as successful were actually randomly selected with no correlation to the initial intelligence test. Eight months later, the researchers discovered that the randomly selected students who were projected to show "intellectual growth" actually scored significantly higher than other students. This phenomenon was noted again in college algebra, engineering, and various other courses at both the undergraduate and graduate levels. Although it is unclear exactly why the Pygmalion Effect occurs, particularly in education, it has been proposed that teachers often subconsciously or unintentionally give additional teaching, drills, notes, and learning assignments to fulfill the projected results.[34] The question that is unclear is whether the Pygmalion Effect is beneficial or a detriment to the communities in which it occurs. For example, does the prospect of success take away from the possible success of those with projected failure? This is the challenge with certain changes in ethical standards.

LOSS AVERSION, VALUE ATTRIBUTION, AND FUNDAMENTAL ATTRIBUTION ERROR

As was discussed in the context of entrepreneurism in Chapter 4, the average citizen and most emergency managers are very uncomfortable with risk and the potential corresponding loss from any variety of systems. In other words, "Our tendency [is] to go to great lengths to avoid possible losses."[30] This type of approach severely limits an emergency manager's ability to engage the community, as decisions and ultimately ethical consequences are chosen that may have a negative impact on the community or not be in line with current community standards. It is interesting that when loss (and the corresponding risk) is embraced, the various ethical standards of subcultures within a community can often find greater synergy and purpose.

Conversely to loss aversion, a second type of bias can unconsciously overcommit a community leader's interests and resources. This type of bias is called value attribution and has been described as the "inclination to imbue a person or thing with certain qualities based on initial perceived value."[30] This is a natural and organic response that allows people's evaluations to shortcut to predetermined judgments to save time and energy. The problem with this approach is that it assumes so much about a particular resource that limitations, benefits, or secondary applications may be missed. This has a propensity to occur frequently within the emergency management community because the pace and complexity of disasters can often create situations where information exchange is multifaceted and overwhelming. Unfortunately, major disasters have been exacerbated because of value attribution and related assumptions.

The third and final bias that is common within the emergency management community is fundamental attribution error. Clay Shirky describes fundamental attribution error as the interpretation of, "When it comes to other people's behavior human beings invariably make the mistake of overestimating the importance of fundamental character traits and underestimating the importance of situation and context."[35] This is particularly challenging in light of the rising influence of social media. Many government leaders (emergency managers among them) are quick to dismiss social media and all their potential implications simply because they do not use them or generationally they do not see universal application. Rather than openly evaluate the possibilities of their use and how the local community might be changing, they simply ascertain that because good people who have been working in the field for many years do not use it or apply it that social media must not have value. This type of misappropriated value can greatly undermine the ability of emergency managers to blend with the ethical standards that are rising within various communities throughout the world due to the impact and influence of social media.

ETHICAL DECISION MAKING

It is important for emergency management leaders to begin to seek out methodologies that will help bridge the gap from traditional to modern approaches. Unfortunately, in an aggregate sense, the emergency management community is very traditional in its approach to operational considerations and community engagement. Without finding tools and approaches to begin to understand and address these changes, emergency management and disaster response will continue to be clumsy, inefficient, and ultimately detrimental to successful emergency and disaster response in a given community.

One strategy to embrace new expectations about ethical standards is presented by law enforcement veteran and risk manager Gordon Graham who suggests a multistep evaluation process to engage in appropriate ways with community ethical standards. Initially, Graham suggests the identification of community issues that may be ethically divisive and to begin to identify how to engage in a productive and constructive way. Through this identification, an assessment must be made whether the individual organization can address the ethical challenge by itself, or whether a broader community engagement is necessary. Within the assessment of potential successes a timeline must also be considered and may ultimately reflect on the capability to address it fully. Once assessed with a preidentified engagement timeline the process must be implemented and, if successful, shared with colleagues and peers.[36]

Likewise, the application of ethical standards can also be done by creating a culture of ethics within the organization and broader community. Although a "culture of ethics" is often spouted by larger organizations as clichéd mantras, smaller organizations such as emergency management offices truly can create an attitude of openness that is accepting of these ethical changes that have been discussed throughout this chapter. John Mackey, CEO of Whole Foods, refers to this process as making yogurt. What Mackey is referring to is the fact that yogurt is made by the integration of bacteria in milk. The bacteria grows within the milk and changes the status of the entire mixture, creating something that is arguably greater than the sum of its parts. It is created from within and only by the combination of the right ingredients.[37] This type of integration can be possible within an organization as ethics (or another significant leadership quality) can be embedded within and grow in a natural and symbiotic way.

LEADERS IN THE OPEN: BILL BOYD

Bill Boyd has served in the fire service since 1982 and recently retired as fire chief of the Bellingham (Washington) Fire Department. During his tenure as a first-responder, he spent significant time in the roles of incident commander, spokesperson, and often public information officer. Boyd's unique perspective as both chief operator and community voice allowed him to openly and honestly embrace the use of social media in emergencies and disasters. He is a national leader in this area and shares his thoughts in the following essay, written for this book, on how ethics and social media are mixing in the emergency management community. Mr. Boyd maintains the "It's Not My Emergency" blog at www.chiefb2. wordpress.com.

How Fatal Errors Undermine Public Trust

Bill Boyd

The explosion in the use of smartphones and social media tools is exerting tremendous pressure on emergency response organizations to adapt and engage with the public during crises. This new expectation is accompanied by a startling lack of uniform policies and clarity about how to use this new medium. Adding to the confusion is the continuous creation and adaptation of new tools and platforms, creating even more ways to spread information. As a result, there are many examples of "fatal errors" by emergency responders that at the very least undermine public confidence, and in the worst case break the law. Sadly, it is all too easy to make an irretrievable and highly public misstep via social media. Here are three mistakes that public agencies and officials should avoid at all costs.

Repeating incorrect or unsubstantiated information. This happens all too frequently on microblogging sites such as Twitter, where with the click of a button you can repost someone's message to all those who follow you. A highly visible example is the reported death of a celebrity. Often the "dead" celebrity has to go online to refute his or her own death! Fortunately, the "crowd" is quick to correct incorrect information. A nuance to this mistake is repeating outdated information. It is not uncommon to see day-old messages being repeated as if they were current information. This misinformation "echo" causes confusion and inhibits maintaining crisis situational awareness. Like any official release of important emergency information, it should be timely, accurate, and important to the mission at hand.

Disclosing confidential information. Perhaps the most egregious ethical breach an emergency responder can make is to disseminate confidential patient information. Today's sophisticated smartphones with camera/video capabilities make it extremely tempting to take pictures of unique and exciting emergency scenes and immediately post them to the web. In one tragic real-life example, a first-responder took a picture of a young woman who was killed in a traffic accident. He then sent the picture to a friend, who then forwarded it on. Eventually, the woman's family saw the photo. Needless to say, the family was devastated and the responder eventually lost his job. Establishing social media and privacy policies and training on them are critical to protecting patients, employees, and the organization.

Forgetting you are a public official. Even before the evolution of social media sites such as MySpace and Facebook, keeping your personal and professional lives separate was a challenge. Today, these platforms make it too easy to cross the line. Public officials, especially emergency responders, are held to a very high standard, expected to conduct themselves professionally at all times. Sadly there are examples of professional suicide as a result of the posting on their personal social media accounts an inappropriate picture or expression of clearly offensive language or opinions by those holding the public's trust. Hiding behind the veil of First Amendment free speech rights can be a tenuous position for a public official trying to counter a groundswell of negative public opinion.

To avoid making these mistakes, and many others I left off this short list, keep these ethical edicts in mind:

- Accuracy is important. But, sometimes you have to go with the limited information at hand. If the information ends up being wrong, immediately acknowledge it and get the correct information out there as soon as possible, utilizing the same channels used to distribute the original information.
- Never exploit a citizen's misfortune, period.
- Always consider yourself in the public eye. We are never "off the clock" when it comes to maintaining a professional public image. All it takes is one click of the mouse and you and your agency's reputation can plummet like the glide path of a tool box.

ENDNOTES

1. "What You Do Speaks So Loudly…" (2011) Quote Investigators. http://quoteinvestigator.com/2011/01/27/what-you-do-speaks/. Accessed August 18, 2012.
2. "Key Facts." (2012) Facebook Newsroom. http://newsroom.fb.com/content/default.aspx?NewsAreaId=22. Accessed August 18, 2012.

3. "Timeline – Wikileaks Founder Claims Political Asylum." Reuters. http://www.reuters.com/article/2012/06/20/uk-britain-ecuador-assange-wikileaks-idUKBRE85J0O820120620. Access August 19, 2012.
4. Bennett, Shea. (2012) "Twitter on Track for 500 Million Total Users By March, 250 Million Active Users By End of 2012." MediaBistro. http://www.mediabistro.com/alltwitter/twitter-active-total-users_b17655. August 19, 2012.
5. Fantz, Ashley. (2010) "On Wikileaks Scandal, Hacker Says He Didn't Want to be a Coward." CNN. http://articles.cnn.com/2010-07-29/us/lamo.profile.wikileaks_1_manning-adrian-lamo-documents?_s=PM:US. Accessed August 19, 2012.
6. Calman, KC. (2003) Evolutionary ethics: Can values change? *Journal of Medical Ethics*. http://jme.bmj.com/content/30/4/366.full. August 20, 2012.
7. Velasquez, Manuel, et al. (2010) "What is Ethics?" Santa Clara University – Markkula Center for Applied Ethics. http://www.scu.edu/ethics/practicing/decision/whatisethics.html. Accessed August 21, 2012.
8. "The Ethics of Disaster Relief." (2002). Santa Clara University – Markkula Center for Applied Ethics. http://www.scu.edu/ethics/publications/briefings/philanthropy.html. Accessed August 23, 2012.
9. "National Business Ethics Survey." (2012) Ethics Resource Center. http://www.ethics.org/resource/national-business-ethics-survey%C2%AE-fortune-500%C2%AE-employees. Accessed August 24, 2012.
10. Survey: Ethics violations at all levels of government. (2008) *USAToday*. http://www.usatoday.com/news/washington/2008-01-29-ethics-survey_N.htm. Accessed August 24, 2012.
11. "National Business Ethics Survey." (2007) Ethics Resource Center. http://www.ethics.org/files/u5/The_National_Government_Ethics_Survey.pdf. Accessed August 24, 2012.
12. Kerns, Charles D. (2003) Creating and sustaining an ethical workplace culture. *Graziadio Business Review*. http://gbr.pepperdine.edu/2010/08/Creating-and-Sustaining-an-Ethical-Workplace-Culture/. Accessed August 24, 2012.
13. Allison, Wes. (2007) "How Much Credit Does Guiliani Deserve for Crime Fighting?" Politifact. http://www.politifact.com/truth-o-meter/article/2007/sep/01/how-much-credit-giuliani-due-fighting-crime/. Accessed August 25, 2012.
14. Gladwell, Malcolm. (1996) Tipping point. Articles from the *New Yorker*. http://www.gladwell.com/1996/1996_06_03_a_tipping.htm. Accessed August 25, 2012.
15. Gladwell, Malcolm. (2002) *Tipping Point: How Little Things Make a Big Difference*. New York: Back Bay Books.
16. Dickerson, Brian. (2012) Broken windows theory of community policing will get major test in Detroit. *Detroit Free Press*. http://www.freep.com/article/20120524/COL04/205240458/Brian-Dickerson-Broken-windows-theory-of-community-policing-will-get-major-test-in-Detroit. Accessed August 26, 2012.

17. Kapucu, Naim and Ozerdem, Alpaslan. (2013) *Managing Emergencies and Crisis*. Burlington, MA: Jones and Bartlett.
18. "Cory Booker." (2012) Twitter. http://twitter.com/CoryBooker. Accessed August 27, 2012.
19. "Newark (city), New Jersey." (2012) U.S. Census QuickFacts. http://quickfacts.census.gov/qfd/states/34/3451000.html. Accessed August 27, 2012.
20. Gustin, Sam. (2010) "Mayor Hacks Snowmaggedon with Epic Tweets." *Wired*. http://www.wired.com/business/2010/12/hacking-snowmageddon/. Accessed August 27, 2012.
21. Crowe, Adam. (2012) *Disasters 2.0: The Impact of Social Media on Modern Emergency Management*. Boca Raton, FL: CRC Press.
22. Lee, Timothy B. (2012) "DC Police Chief Announces Shockingly Reasonable Cell Phone Policy." Ars Technica. http://arstechnica.com/tech-policy/2012/07/dc-police-chief-announces-shockingly-reasonable-cell-camera-policy/. Accessed August 28, 2012.
23. Wyler, Grace. (2012). Here's what you need to know about the gun running scandal that could destroy Obama's attorney general. *Business Insider*. http://www.businessinsider.com/what-is-fast-and-furious-2012-6. Accessed August 28, 2012.
24. "What Is a Whistleblower?" (n.d.) Government Accountability Project. http://www.whistleblower.org/about/what-is-a-whistleblower. Accessed August 29, 2012.
25. Harned, Patricia. (2012) "The Cost of 'Doing the Right Thing.'" Huffington Post. http://www.huffingtonpost.com/patricia-harned/the-cost-of-doing-the-rig_b_1215717.html. Accessed August 29, 2012.
26. Fachinger, Bettina. (2010) "Online Informers: Whistleblowing in the Information Age." Allianz. http://knowledge.allianz.com/demographics/current_affairs/?637/online-informers-whistleblowing-in-the-information-age. Accessed August 29, 2012.
27. Winter, Jana. (2012) Granpa, patriot who goes by "The Raptor" claims credit for taking down Al Qaeda website. *FoxNews*. http://www.foxnews.com/us/2012/04/10/grandpa-patriot-who-goes-by-raptor-claims-credit-for-taking-down-al-qaeda/. Accessed August 31, 2012.
28. Ousley, Jeff. (n.d) "Military Spouse Notified of Her Husband's Death on Facebook." Military Spouse Central. http://www.veteransunited.com/spouse/military-spouse-notified-of-her-husbands-death-on-facebook/. Accessed September 1, 2012.
29. HIPAA and social networking sites: A legal minefield for employers (2012) *American Academy of Ophthalmology*. http://www.aao.org/yo/newsletter/201201/article02.cfm. Accessed September 1, 2012.
30. Brafman, Ori and Brafman, Rom. (2009) *Sway: The Irresponsible Pull of Irrational Behavior*. New York: Broadway Books.
31. Zickuhr, Kathryn and Smith, Aaron. (2012) "Digital Differences." Pew Internet. http://pewinternet.org/Reports/2012/Digital-differences/Overview.aspx. Accessed September 3, 2012.

32. "A Different Kind of Internet." (2012) Google Fiber. https://fiber.google. com/about/. Accessed September 3, 2012.
33. Grohol, John M. (2012) "Sway: The Irresistible Pull of Irrational Behavior." PsychCentral. http://psychcentral.com/lib/2008/sway-the-irresistible-pull-of-irrational-behavior/. Accessed September 4, 2012.
34. "The Pygmalion Effect." (2012) Duquesne University – Center for Teaching Excellence. http://www.duq.edu/cte/teaching/pygmalion.cfm. Accessed September 4, 2012.
35. Shirky, Clay. (2009) *Here Comes Everybody: The Power of Organizing Without Organizations*. New York: Penguin Books.
36. Graham, Gordon. (2011) "Ignoring Problems Lying In Wait: The Ultimate High Stakes Gamble." Keynote Address at IAEM Annual Conference. Witnessed November 16, 2011.
37. Nhan, Doris. (2012) "How Can Yogurt Help Grow Your Company's Culture." SmartBlog on Leadership. http://smartblogs.com/leadership/2012/04/17/how-yogurt-can-help-you-grow-your-companys-culture/. Accessed September 7, 2012.

INDEX